First World War

and Army of Occupation

War Diary

France, Belgium and Germany

1 INDIAN CAVALRY DIVISION
Mhow Cavalry Brigade,
Brigade Signal Troop,
Brigade Machine Gun Squadron,
Mhow Pioneer Battalion, Royal Army Veterinary Corps
Mobile Veterinary Section,
Brigade Supply Officer and Brigade Transport Officer
19 December 1914 - 30 September 1916

WO95/1177

The Naval & Military Press Ltd
www.nmarchive.com
Published in association with The National Archives

Published by

The Naval & Military Press Ltd

Unit 10 Ridgewood Industrial Park,

Uckfield, East Sussex,

TN22 5QE England

Tel: +44 (0) 1825 749494

www.naval-military-press.com

www.nmarchive.com

This diary has been reprinted in facsimile from the original. Any imperfections are inevitably reproduced and the quality may fall short of modern type and cartographic standards.

Contents

Document type	Place/Title	Date From	Date To
Heading	##		
Heading	##		
Heading	B E F. 1 Ind. Cav. Div Mhow Bde Mhow Cav Bde Sig Troop 1915 to 1916 Dec Box 3310		
Heading	War Diary of Signal Troop, Mhow Cavalry Brigade From 1st March 1915 to 31st March 1915		
War Diary		15/03/1915	18/03/1915
War Diary	Clarques	19/03/1915	31/03/1915
Heading	War Diary of Signal Troop, Mhow Cavalry Brigade From 1st April 1915 To 30th April 1915		
War Diary	Clarques	01/04/1915	12/04/1915
War Diary	Mazinghem	13/04/1915	24/04/1915
War Diary	Zuytpeene	25/04/1915	28/04/1915
War Diary	Houtkerque	29/04/1915	30/04/1915
Heading	War Diary of Signal Troop, Mhow Cavalry Brigade. From 1st May 1915 To 31st May 1915		
War Diary	Houtkerque	01/05/1915	02/05/1915
War Diary	Zoutpeene	03/05/1915	06/05/1915
War Diary	Fontaine-Lez-Hermans	07/05/1915	17/05/1915
War Diary	Losinghem	18/05/1915	19/05/1915
War Diary	Fontaine-Lez-Hermans	20/05/1915	31/05/1915
Heading	War Diary of Signal Troop, Mhow Cavalry Brigade From 1st June 1915 To 30th June 1915		
War Diary	Funtaine-Lez-Hermans	01/06/1915	30/06/1915
Heading	War Diary of Signal Troop. Mhow Cavalry Brigade From 1st July 1915 To 31st July		
War Diary	Fontaine-Lez-Hermans	01/07/1915	31/07/1915
Heading	War Diary of Signal Troop, Mhow Cavalry Brigade From 1st August 1915 To 31st August 1915		
War Diary		01/08/1915	31/08/1915
Heading	War Diary of Signal Troop, Mhow Cavalry Brigade. From 1st September 1915 To 30th September		
War Diary		01/09/1915	30/09/1915
Heading	War Diary of Signal Troop, Mhow Cavalry Brigade From 1st October 1915 To 31st December 1915		
War Diary		01/10/1915	31/12/1915
Heading	War Diary of Signal Troop, Mhow Cavalry Brigade From 1st January 1916 To 31st January 1916		
War Diary		01/01/1916	31/01/1916
Heading	War Diary of Signal Troop, Mhow Cavalry Brigade From 1st February 1916 To 29 February 1916		
War Diary		01/02/1916	29/02/1916
Heading	War Diary of Signal Troop, Mhow Cavalry Brigade From 1st March 1916 To 31st March 1916		
War Diary	Field	01/03/1916	31/03/1916
Heading	War Diary of Signal Troop, Mhow Cavalry Brigade From 1st April 1916 To 30th April 1916		
War Diary	Field	01/04/1916	30/04/1916
Heading	War Diary of Signal Troop, Mhow Cavalry Division From 1st May 1916 To 31st May 1916		

War Diary	In the Field (Training Area)	01/05/1916	31/05/1916
Heading	War Diary of Signal Troop, Mhow Cavalry Brigade From 1st July 1916 To 31st July 1916		
War Diary	In the Field	01/07/1916	31/07/1916
Heading	War Diary of Signal Troop, Mhow Cavalry Brigade From 1st August 1916 To 31st August 1916		
War Diary	Rollecourt	01/08/1916	31/08/1916
Heading	War Diary of Signal Troop Mhow Cavalry Brigade From 1st September 1916 To 30th September 1916		
War Diary	Cambligneul	02/09/1916	02/09/1916
War Diary	St Michel	03/09/1916	03/09/1916
War Diary	Noyelle-en-Chaussee	04/09/1916	10/09/1916
War Diary	Remaisnil	11/09/1916	11/09/1916
War Diary	Anthisnes	12/09/1916	12/09/1916
War Diary	Annonville	13/09/1916	14/09/1916
War Diary	Morbaucourt	15/09/1916	25/09/1916
War Diary	Monteban	25/09/1916	25/09/1916
War Diary	Morbaucourt	26/09/1916	27/09/1916
War Diary	Bussy-Les-Daours.	28/09/1916	28/09/1916
War Diary	Ballon-Sun-Somme	29/09/1916	29/09/1916
War Diary	Douriez	30/09/1916	30/10/1916
War Diary	Douriez	01/10/1916	31/10/1916
Heading	War Diary of Signal Troop, Mhow Cavalry Brigade From 1st November 1916 To 30th November		
War Diary	Douriez	01/11/1916	30/11/1916
War Diary	Douriez	23/11/1916	23/11/1916
Heading	War Diary of Signal Troop, Mhow Cavalry Brigade From 1st December 1916 To 31 December 1916		
War Diary		01/12/1916	31/12/1916
Heading	B E F 1 Ind. Cav. Div. Mhow Bde Machine Gun Sqd 1916 July to 1916 Dec		
Heading	War Diary of Machine Gun Squadron, Mhow Cavalry Brigade From 1st July 1916 to 31st July 1916		
War Diary	Authieule	01/07/1916	01/07/1916
War Diary	Mont Louis Ferm	06/07/1916	06/07/1916
War Diary	Heirmont	19/07/1916	19/07/1916
War Diary	Roellecourt	22/07/1916	22/07/1916
Heading	War Diary of Machine Gun Squadron, Mhow Cavalry Brigade From 1st August 1916 To 31st August 1916		
War Diary	Roellecourt	01/08/1916	09/08/1916
War Diary	Cambligneul	09/08/1916	31/08/1916
Heading	War Diary of Machine Gun Squadron, Mhow Cavalry Brigade From 1st September 1916 To 30th September 1916		
War Diary	Cambligneul	01/09/1916	01/09/1916
War Diary	Rouellecourt	02/09/1916	02/09/1916
War Diary	Monchel	03/09/1916	03/09/1916
War Diary	Neuilly le Dien	04/09/1916	10/09/1916
War Diary	Mezerolles	11/09/1916	11/09/1916
War Diary	Authieule	12/09/1916	12/09/1916
War Diary	Querrieu	13/09/1916	13/09/1916
War Diary	Morlancourt	14/09/1916	24/09/1916
War Diary	Montauban	25/09/1916	25/09/1916
War Diary	Morlancourt	26/09/1916	26/09/1916
War Diary	Bussy Les Daours	27/09/1916	27/09/1916
War Diary	La Chaussee	28/09/1916	28/09/1916

War Diary	Vauchelles	29/09/1916	29/09/1916
War Diary	Ponches	30/09/1916	30/09/1916
Heading	War Diary of Machine Gun Squadron, Mhow Cavalry Brigade From 1st October 1916 To 30th November 1916		
War Diary	Hamel Les Ponches	01/10/1916	01/10/1916
War Diary	Labroye	02/10/1916	22/10/1916
War Diary	Coigneux	23/10/1916	26/10/1916
War Diary	Trenches	27/10/1916	30/10/1916
War Diary	Coigneux	31/10/1916	31/10/1916
Heading	War Diary of Mhow Brigade M.G. Squadron for November 1916		
War Diary	Coineux	01/11/1916	02/11/1916
War Diary	Serre Sector of Trenches	11/11/1916	15/11/1916
War Diary	Coineux	15/11/1916	20/11/1916
War Diary	Offeux	21/11/1916	21/11/1916
Heading	War Diary of Mhow Machine Gun Squadron From 1st December 1916 To 31st December 1916		
War Diary	Offeux	01/12/1916	31/12/1916
Heading	B E F 1 Indian Cav. Div. Mhow Bde Mhow Pioneer Bn 1916 Nov To 1916 Dec		
War Diary		20/11/1916	21/11/1916
War Diary	Fricourt Farm	22/11/1916	30/11/1916
Miscellaneous	To Staff Captain Mhow Cav Brde	31/12/1916	31/12/1916
War Diary	Fricourt Farm	01/12/1916	14/12/1916
Heading	B E F 1 Ind. Cav. Div Mhow Bde Mobile Vet Sect 1914 Dec 1916 Dec No Box		
Heading	War Diary of Mobile Veterinary Section. Mhow Brigade From 19th December 1914 To 28th February 1915		
War Diary	Marvilles	19/12/1914	20/12/1914
War Diary		21/12/1914	21/12/1914
War Diary	In Aruin	22/12/1914	23/12/1914
War Diary	Orleans	24/12/1914	03/01/1915
War Diary	Clarques	04/01/1915	07/01/1915
War Diary	Gemenghem	08/01/1915	12/02/1915
War Diary	Therouanne	13/02/1915	28/02/1915
Heading	War Diary of Mobile Veterinary Section, Mhow Brigade From 1st March 1915 To 31st March 1915		
War Diary	Therouanne	01/03/1915	10/03/1915
War Diary	Marles	11/03/1915	13/03/1915
War Diary	Estree Blanche	14/03/1915	16/03/1915
War Diary	Therouanne	01/03/1915	10/03/1915
War Diary	Marles	11/03/1915	13/03/1915
War Diary	Estree Blanche	14/03/1915	17/03/1915
War Diary	De Roms	18/03/1915	18/03/1915
War Diary	Le Rons	19/03/1915	31/03/1915
War Diary	Marles	12/03/1915	13/03/1915
War Diary	Estree Blanche	14/03/1915	17/03/1915
War Diary	De Roms	18/03/1915	18/03/1915
War Diary	Le Rons	18/03/1915	20/03/1915
War Diary	Estre Blanche	17/03/1915	17/03/1915
War Diary	De Roms	18/03/1915	18/03/1915
War Diary	Le Rons	18/03/1915	31/03/1915
War Diary	Le Rons	21/03/1915	05/04/1915
War Diary	Mazinghem	06/04/1915	11/04/1915

War Diary	Le Rons	12/04/1915	12/04/1915
War Diary	Mazinghem	13/04/1915	24/04/1915
War Diary	Zuytpeene	25/04/1915	29/04/1915
War Diary	Matou Belgium	30/04/1915	30/04/1915
War Diary	Watou	01/05/1915	01/05/1915
War Diary	Zuytpeene	02/05/1915	04/05/1915
War Diary	Nedonchelle	05/05/1915	31/05/1915
Heading	War Diary of Mobile Veterinary Section, Mhow Brigade From 1st April 1915 To 30th April 1915		
War Diary	Le Rons	01/04/1915	05/04/1915
War Diary	Mazinghem	06/04/1915	11/04/1915
War Diary	Le Rons	12/04/1915	12/04/1915
War Diary	Mazinghem	13/04/1915	24/04/1915
War Diary	Zuytpeene	23/04/1915	29/04/1915
War Diary	Watou Belgium	30/04/1915	30/04/1915
War Diary	War Diary of Mobile Veterinary Section, Mhow Brigade From 1st May 1915 To 31st May 1915.		
War Diary	Watou	01/05/1915	01/05/1915
War Diary	Zuytpeene	02/05/1915	04/05/1915
War Diary	Nedonchelle	05/05/1915	05/05/1915
War Diary	Watou	01/05/1915	01/05/1915
War Diary	Zuytpeene	02/05/1915	04/05/1915
War Diary	Nedonchelle	05/05/1915	21/05/1915
War Diary	Nedonchelle	06/05/1915	31/05/1915
War Diary	Nedonchelle	22/05/1915	31/05/1915
Heading	War Diary of Mobile Veterinary Section, Mhow Brigade From 1st June 1915 To 30th June 1915.		
War Diary	Nedonchelle	01/06/1915	30/06/1915
War Diary	Nedonchelle	01/06/1915	14/06/1915
War Diary	Nedonchelle	01/06/1915	30/06/1915
War Diary	Nedonchelle	15/06/1915	30/06/1915
Heading	War Diary of Veterinary Section Mhow Brigade From 1st July 1915 To 31st July 1915		
War Diary	Nedonchelle	01/07/1915	31/07/1915
Heading	War Diary of Mobile Veterinary Section. Mhow Cavalry Brigade From 1st September 1915 To 30th September 1915.		
War Diary	Picquigny	01/09/1915	23/09/1915
War Diary	Fieffes Picquigny	24/09/1915	24/09/1915
War Diary	Fieffes	25/09/1915	30/09/1915
Heading	War Diary of Mobile Veterinary Section, Mhow Cavalry Brigade From 1st October 1915 To 31st October 1915.		
War Diary	Fieffes	01/10/1915	01/10/1915
War Diary	Bouvain	02/10/1915	13/10/1915
War Diary	Berneuil	14/10/1915	17/10/1915
War Diary	Fienvillers	18/10/1915	22/10/1915
War Diary	Silencourt	23/10/1915	31/10/1915
Heading	War Diary of Mobile Veterinary Section; Mhow Brigade From 1st November 1915 To 30th November 1915		
Heading	War Diary of Mobile Veterinary Section; Mhow Brigade From 1st November, 1915. To 30th November, 1915.		
War Diary	Selincourt	01/11/1915	17/11/1915
War Diary		18/11/1915	21/11/1915

War Diary	Selincourt	22/11/1915	29/11/1915
War Diary		30/11/1915	30/11/1915
War Diary	Selincourt	01/11/1915	16/11/1915
War Diary		17/11/1915	21/11/1915
War Diary	Selincourt	22/11/1915	29/11/1915
War Diary		30/11/1915	30/11/1915
Heading	War Diary of Mobile Veterinary Section Mhow Cavalry Brigade From 1st December 1915 To 31st December 1915		
War Diary	Selincourt	01/12/1915	16/12/1915
War Diary	Valines	17/12/1915	31/12/1915
Heading	War Diary of Mobile Veterinary Section, Mhow Cavalry Brigade From 1st January 1916 To 31st January 1916.		
War Diary	Valines	01/01/1916	31/01/1916
Heading	War Diary of Mobile Veterinary Section, Mhow Cavalry Brigade From 1st February 1916 To 29 February 1916		
War Diary	Valines	01/02/1916	29/02/1916
Heading	War Diary of Mobile Veterinary Section, Mhow Cavalry Brigade From 1st March 1916 To 31st March 1916.		
War Diary	Valines	01/03/1916	31/03/1916
Heading	War Diary of Mobile Veterinary Section, Mhow Cavalry Brigade From 1st April 1916 To 30th April 1916		
War Diary	Maizicourt	01/04/1916	26/04/1916
War Diary	Noyelle	27/04/1916	27/04/1916
Heading	War Diary of Mobile Veterinary Section, Mhow Cavalry Brigade From 1st May 1916 To 31st May 1916.		
War Diary	Noyelle	06/05/1916	08/05/1916
War Diary	Mazicourt	09/05/1916	09/05/1916
War Diary	Ivergny	10/05/1916	31/05/1916
Heading	War Diary of Mobile Veterinary Section, Mhow Cavalry Brigade From 1st June 1916 To 30th June 1916.		
War Diary	Ivergny	13/06/1916	30/06/1916
Heading	War Diary of Mobile Veterinary Section, Mhow Cavalry Brigade From 1st July 1916 To 31st July 1916		
War Diary	Doullens	01/07/1916	02/07/1916
War Diary	Magicourt	03/07/1916	19/07/1916
War Diary	Roellecourt	20/07/1916	31/07/1916
Heading	War Diary of Mobile Veterinary Section, Mhow Cavalry Brigade From 1st August 1916 To 31st August 1916.		
War Diary	Roellecourt	01/08/1916	10/08/1916
War Diary	Combligueul	11/08/1916	31/08/1916
Heading	War Diary of Mobile Veterinary Section, Mhow Cavalry Brigade From 1st September 1916 To 30th September 1916		
War Diary	Cambligneul	01/09/1916	01/09/1916
War Diary	Graud Caugh	02/09/1916	02/09/1916
War Diary	Couchy Sus Cauche	03/09/1916	04/09/1916
War Diary	Noyelle-en-Chaussee	05/09/1916	10/09/1916
War Diary	Remaisnil	11/09/1916	11/09/1916

War Diary	Authieule	12/09/1916	12/09/1916
War Diary	Querrieu	13/09/1916	14/09/1916
War Diary	Morlancourt	15/09/1916	24/09/1916
War Diary	Mametz	25/09/1916	25/09/1916
War Diary	Morlancourt	26/09/1916	26/09/1916
War Diary	Bussy Les Daours	27/09/1916	27/09/1916
War Diary	Belloy Sur Somme	28/09/1916	28/09/1916
War Diary	Vauchelles Les Domart	29/09/1916	29/09/1916
War Diary	Douriez	30/09/1916	30/09/1916
Heading	War Diary of Mobile Veterinary Section, Mhow Cavalry Brigade From 1st October 1916 To 30th November 1916.		
War Diary	Douriez	01/10/1916	31/10/1916
Heading	War Diary of Mobile Veterinary Section, Mhow Cavalry Brigade For November 1916.		
War Diary	Douriez	01/11/1916	01/11/1916
War Diary	Belloy	02/11/1916	30/11/1916
Heading	War Diary of Mobile Veterinary Section, Mhow Cavalry Brigade From 1st December 1916 To 31st December 1916		
War Diary	Belloy	01/12/1916	31/12/1916
Heading	B E F 1 Ind Cav Div Mhow Bde Supply Officer 1915 Sept To 1916 Sept No Box		
War Diary	Villers-Sous-Ailly	15/09/1915	22/09/1915
War Diary	Bournaville	22/09/1915	22/09/1915
War Diary	Bernaville	23/09/1915	30/09/1915
War Diary	War Diary of Brigade Supply Officer; Mhow Cavalry Brigade From 1st October 1915 To 31st October 1915		
War Diary	Bernaville	01/10/1915	01/10/1915
War Diary	Ch De Beauvoir	02/10/1915	13/10/1915
War Diary	Berneuil	14/10/1915	16/10/1915
War Diary	Fienvillers	17/10/1915	21/10/1915
War Diary	Selincourt	22/10/1915	31/10/1915
War Diary	Bernaville	01/10/1915	01/10/1915
War Diary	Ch De Beauvoir	02/10/1915	13/10/1915
War Diary	Berneuil	14/10/1915	16/10/1915
War Diary	Fienvillers	17/10/1915	21/10/1915
War Diary	Selincourt	22/10/1915	31/10/1915
Heading	War Diary of Supply Officer, Mhow Cavalry Brigade From 1st November 1915 To 30th November 1915		
War Diary	Selincourt	01/11/1915	30/11/1915
Heading	War Diary of Supply Officer, Mhow Cavalry Brigade From 1st December 1915 To 31st December 1915		
War Diary	Selincourt	01/12/1915	15/12/1915
War Diary	Valines	16/12/1915	31/12/1915
Heading	War Diary of Supply Officer, Mhow Cavalry Brigade From 1st January 1916 To 31st January 1916		
War Diary	Valines	01/01/1916	31/01/1916
Heading	War Diary of Supply Officer, Mhow Cavalry Brigade From 1st February 1916 To 29th February 1916		
War Diary	Valines	01/02/1916	29/02/1916
Heading	War Diary of Supply Officer, Mhow Cavalry Brigade From 1st March 1916 To 31st March 1916.		
War Diary	Valines	01/03/1916	25/03/1916
War Diary	Maizicourt	26/03/1916	31/03/1916

Heading	War Diary of Supply Officer, Mhow Cavalry Brigade From 1st July 1916 To 31st July 1916		
War Diary	Doullens	01/07/1916	01/07/1916
War Diary	Maizicourt 3 Miles S. of Auxi Le Chateau	02/07/1916	18/07/1916
War Diary	Roellecourt	19/07/1916	31/07/1916
Heading	War Diary of Supply Officer, Mhow Cavalry Brigade From 1st August 1916 To 31st August 1916.		
War Diary	Roellecourt	01/08/1916	09/08/1916
War Diary	Cambligneul	10/08/1916	31/08/1916
Heading	War Diary of Supply Officer, Mhow Cavalry Brigade. From 1st September 1916 To 30th September 1916		
War Diary	Cambligneul	01/09/1916	01/09/1916
War Diary	Grand Camp (nr St Pol)	02/09/1916	02/09/1916
War Diary	Conchy Sur Canche	03/09/1916	03/09/1916
War Diary	Noyelles-en-Chaussee	04/09/1916	10/09/1916
War Diary	Remaisnil	11/09/1916	11/09/1916
War Diary	Authieule near Doullens	12/09/1916	12/09/1916
War Diary	Querrier	13/09/1916	14/09/1916
War Diary	Morlancourt	15/09/1916	24/09/1916
War Diary	Mametz	25/09/1916	25/09/1916
War Diary	Morlancourt	26/09/1916	26/09/1916
War Diary	Bussy-Les-Daours	27/09/1916	27/09/1916
War Diary	Belloy Sur Somme	28/09/1916	28/09/1916
War Diary	Vauchelles Les-Domart	29/09/1916	29/09/1916
War Diary	Douriez	30/09/1916	30/09/1916
Heading	B E F 1 Ind. Cav. Div. Mhow Bde. Bde Transport Officer 1916 July To 1916 Sep		
Heading	War Diary of Transport Officer, Mhow Cavalry Brigade. From 1st July 1916 To 31 July 1916		
War Diary	Doullens	01/07/1916	01/07/1916
War Diary	Doullens till 6.30 P.M. Now Maizicourt 10.45 P.M.	02/07/1916	02/07/1916
War Diary	Maigicourt	03/07/1916	13/07/1916
War Diary	Maigicourt till Line 8.30 A.M. Roellecourt and 4.45 P.M.	19/07/1916	19/07/1916
War Diary	Roellecourt	20/07/1916	31/07/1916
Heading	War Diary of Transport Officer, Mhow Cavalry Brigade From 1st August 1916 To 31st August 1916.		
War Diary	Roellecourt	01/08/1916	10/08/1916
War Diary	Cambligneul	10/08/1916	30/08/1916
Heading	War Diary of Transport Officer. Mhow Cavalry Brigade From 1st September 1916 To 30th September 1916		
War Diary	Cambligneul	01/09/1916	02/09/1916
War Diary	Grand Camp	03/09/1916	03/09/1916
War Diary	Cauchy-S-Canchi	04/09/1916	04/09/1916
War Diary	Noyelle-en-Chaussee	04/09/1916	11/09/1916
War Diary	Remaisnil	12/09/1916	12/09/1916
War Diary	Antende	13/09/1916	13/09/1916
War Diary	Allonville	15/09/1916	15/09/1916
War Diary	Querrieu	16/09/1916	27/09/1916
War Diary	Bussy-Les-Daours.	28/09/1916	28/09/1916
War Diary	Billoy	29/09/1916	29/09/1916
War Diary	Moufflers	30/09/1916	30/09/1916

B.E.F.FRANCE & FLANDERS.

1 INDIAN CAVALRY DIVISION

MHOW BDE. SIGNAL TROOP
1915 MAR TO 1916 DEC.

BDE MACHINE GUN SQUADRON.
1916 JULY TO 1916 DEC.

MHOW PIONEER BATTALION.
1916 NOV TO 1916 DEC.

MOBILE VETERINARY SECTION
1914 DEC TO 1916 DEC.

BRIGADE SUPPLY OFFICER.
1915 SEPT TO 1916 SEPT.

BDE TRANSPORT OFFICER.
1916 JULY TO 1916 DEC.

1177

B.E.F. FRANCE & FLANDERS.

1 INDIAN CAVALRY DIV

MHOW BDE. SIGNAL TROOP

1915 MAR TO 1916 DEC.

BDE MACHINE GUN SQUADRO

1916 JULY TO 1916 DEC.

MHOW PIONEER BATTALION.

1916 NOV TO 1916 DEC.

MOBILE VETERINARY SEC

1914 DEC TO 1916 DEC.

BRIGADE SUPPLY OFFICER.

1915 SEPT TO 1916 SEPT.

BDE TRANSPORT OFFICER.

1916 JULY TO 1916 SEP DEC

1177

BEF

1 IND. CAV. DIV

MHOW BDE

MHOW CAV Bde SIG TROOP

1915 MAR. TO 1916 DEC

Serial No. 205

121/5114

WAR DIARY

OF

Signal Troop, Mhow Cavalry Brigade.

From 1st March 1915 To 31st March 1915

Instructions regarding War Diaries and Intelligence Summaries are contained in F. S. Regs., Part II. and the Staff Manual respectively. Title pages will be prepared in manuscript.

WAR DIARY
or
INTELLIGENCE SUMMARY.
(Erase heading not required.)

Signal Troop
Mhow Cavalry Brigade.

Army Form C. 2118.

Hour, Date, Place	Summary of Events and Information	Remarks and references to Appendices
March. 15th	Usual routine. Brigade Training.	
" . 16th	Capt. A. F. Hartley, XI Lancers, took over duties of Brigade Signalling Officer from Lieut. Tottendale, 6th Dragoons. Usual routine.	
" 17th.	Received orders to change billets. Closed communication with C. I. H. + 2nd Lancers + collected their wire. Left 6th Dragoons wire standing for use of Lucknow Brigade	
" 18th	Brigade changed billets. Report centre at chateau in CLARQUES. Communication re-opened with Division + units by evening.	
CLARQUES. March 19th 20th. 21st. 22nd	Nothing to report. Usual routine + Bde. training.	
March 23rd	Brigade scheme. Regiments under bivouac at 7.15 p.m. 6th Dragoons + C. I. H. proceeded to entrench a first line. 2nd Lancers in support. Telephone communication opened with all units.	

Instructions regarding War Diaries and Intelligence Summaries are contained in F. S. Regs., Part II. and the Staff Manual respectively. Title pages will be prepared in manuscript.

WAR DIARY
or
INTELLIGENCE SUMMARY.
(Erase heading not required.)

Signal Troop
Mhow Cavalry Brigade.

Army Form C. 2118.

Hour, Date, Place	Summary of Events and Information	Remarks and references to Appendices
CLARQUES. March. 24th	Brigade filed past 7 foreign officers. Usual routine.	A new Douglas motor cycle was received on 31st to replace one cast as un-serviceable in February. The two others have been in continuous use for 5 months, + are showing signs of wear, requiring frequent renewals of spare parts.
March 25th – 29th	Usual routine + Brigade Training.	
March. 30th.	Brigade scheme. Rearguard + quick ~~detraining~~ billeting. Communication with units by Dispatch riders.	
March. 31st	Usual routine.	

A. Hartley. Lieut.
Mhow Bde. Sig. Officer.

(9 29 6) W4141—463 100,000 9/14 H W V Forms/C. 2118/10

WAR DIARY

OF

Signal Troop, Mhow Cavalry Brigade

From 1st April 1915 To 30th April 1915

Instructions regarding War Diaries and Intelligence Summaries are contained in F. S. Regs., Part II. and the Staff Manual respectively. Title pages will be prepared in manuscript.

WAR DIARY
or
INTELLIGENCE SUMMARY. Mhow Cavalry Bde.

(*Erase heading not required.*)

Signal Troop

Army Form C. 2118.

Hour, Date, Place	Summary of Events and Information	Remarks and references to Appendices
1st April 1915. CLARQUES.	Nothing to report. Usual Routine	
2nd April.	Brigade scheme. Mhow Bde. right flank guard to a division advancing. Helio Communication kept up with unit representing Division. Communication in Bde. by helio, flag, + dispatch riders. Returned to billets by 3 pm. Started to rain shortly after.	
3rd, 4th, 5th April	Nothing to report. Usual routine.	
6th April	Brigade changed billets temporarily to LAMBRES, NORREY-FONTES, + MOLINGHEM, as our area was required for troops passing through. Communication by Dispatch Riders.	
7th + 8th April.	Nothing to report.	
9th April.	Usual Routine. New Triumph motor cycle arrived.	
10th + 11th April	Usual routine. Nothing to report. ~~Regiments returned to original billets. Telephone communication re-established.~~	

(9 29 6) W4141—463 100,000 9/14 H W V Forms/C. 2118/10

Instructions regarding War Diaries and Intelligence Summaries are contained in F. S. Regs., Part II. and the Staff Manual respectively. Title pages will be prepared in manuscript.

WAR DIARY or INTELLIGENCE SUMMARY.

(*Erase heading not required.*)

Signal Troop
1st Cav. Bde.

Army Form C. 2118.

Hour, Date, Place	Summary of Events and Information	Remarks and references to Appendices
CLARQUES. April. 12th.	Regiments returned to original billets – Telephone communication re-established.	
MAZINGHEM " 13th	Bde. again changed billets to ~~Xxxx~~ LAMBRES. MAZINGHEM, MOLINGHEM, + NORREY-FONTES. Telephone communication established by 6 pm. Division transmitted through Corps Signals.	
" 14th + 15th	Collected our wire in late billeting area.	
" 16th	Tactical exercise + quick billeting scheme. Signal troop out, but practically no dispatch riders employed	
" 17th – 20th	~~XXX~~ Usual Routine. Sergt. Page detailed to attend an operators class at Corps Hd. Qrs. on 20th	
" 21st.	The Division marched past the United States attachés.	
" 22nd	Usual routine.	

(9 29 6) W4141—463 100,000 9/14 H W V Forms/C. 2118/10

Instructions regarding War Diaries and Intelligence Summaries are contained in F. S. Regs., Part II. and the Staff Manual respectively. Title pages will be prepared in manuscript.

WAR DIARY
or
~~INTELLIGENCE~~ SUMMARY. Signal Troop Mhow Cav. Bde.

(*Erase heading not required.*)

Army Form C. 2118.

Hour, Date, Place	Summary of Events and Information	Remarks and references to Appendices
MAZINGHEM. April. 23rd	Bde. day - in conjunction with Secunderabad Bde. Signal squadron represented Divn. Two regiments held line of observation. One in reserve. Helio communication obtained for about 5 minutes with Divn. at 11.15 + then sun disappeared for rest of day. Communication with Divn. + all units by dispatch - riders, as is almost universally the case in this country.	
April 24th	Marched at 5 p.m. to ZUYTPEENE, 1½ miles W. of CASSEL. arrived at 10 p.m. Units billeted in Farms round village. Communication by dispatch rider.	
ZUYTPEENE. 25th – 27th.	Ready to Move at ½ hours notice.	
28th.	Marched at 12.30 pm to HOUTKERQUE - arrived 4.20 p.m. Communication with units by dispatch rider,	

Instructions regarding War Diaries and Intelligence Summaries are contained in F. S. Regs., Part II. and the Staff Manual respectively. Title pages will be prepared in manuscript.

WAR DIARY
or
~~INTELLIGENCE~~ SUMMARY.
(Erase heading not required.)

Signal Troop
Mhow Cav. Bde.

Army Form C. 2118.

Hour, Date, Place	Summary of Events and Information	Remarks and references to Appendices
HOUTKERQUE – 29th – 30th April –	Ready to move at ½ hours notice A. Harter. Capt. Bde Sig. Offr.	

Serial No. 245.

121/5799

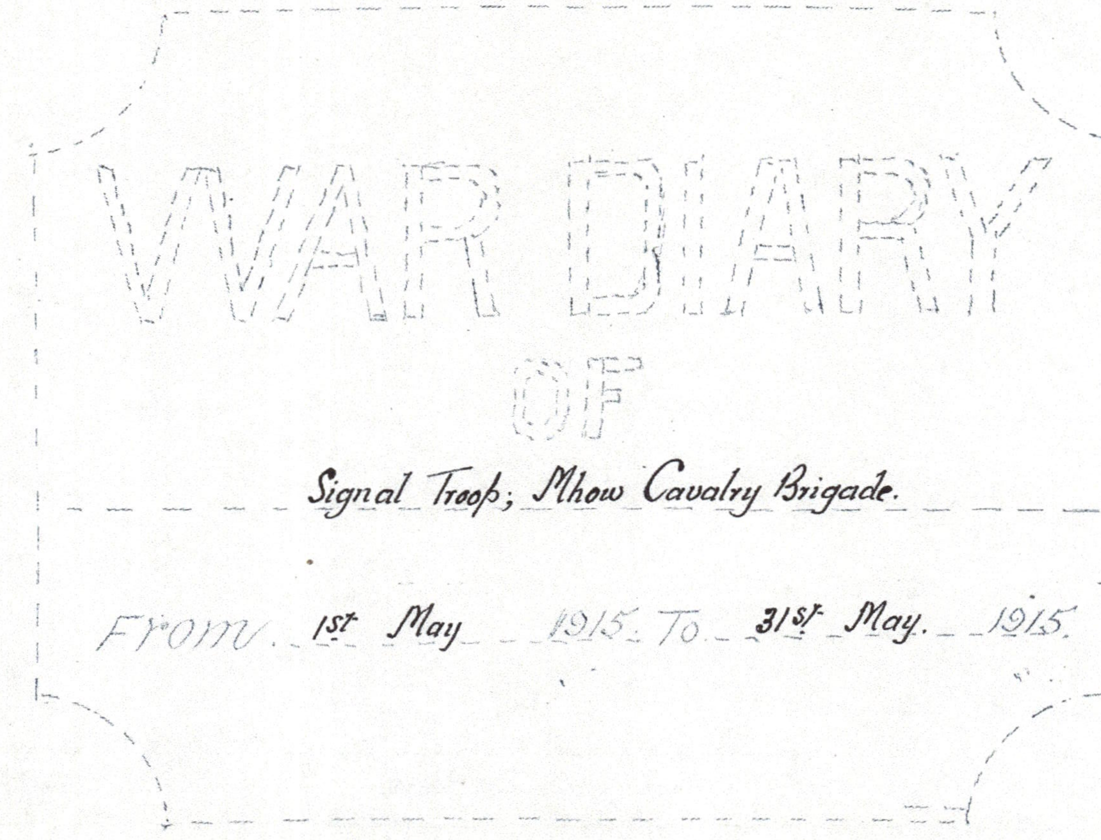

WAR DIARY

OF

Signal Troop; Mhow Cavalry Brigade.

From 1st May 1915 To 31st May. 1915.

Instructions regarding War Diaries and Intelligence Summaries are contained in F. S. Regs., Part II. and the Staff Manual respectively. Title pages will be prepared in manuscript.

WAR DIARY
or
~~INTELLIGENCE SUMMARY.~~
(*Erase heading not required.*)

Army Form C. 2118.

Signal Troop
Mhow Cav. Bde.

Hour, Date, Place	Summary of Events and Information	Remarks and references to Appendices
HOUTKERQUE. 1915 1st May –	Ready to move at ½ hours notice. Received orders at 11.45 p.m to move on following day.	
2nd May.	Marched at 6.15 am. to ZOUTPEENE.	
ZOUTPEENE. 3rd May.	Standing to	
" 4th May.	Marched South 8.30 p.m.	
5th May.	Arrived at FONTAINE-LEZ-HERMANS at 6 am. Dark + foggy night which combined with the badness of the maps (HAZEBROUCK 5A. 1/100,000) made night marching difficult. Marched about 24 miles.	
6th May	Put up line to C.I.H + 6th Dragoons. Ordered by Corps to take it down, owing to scarcity of wire. Communication by dispatch riders.	
FONTAINE-LEZ-HERMANS 7th — 16th May.	Ordered to be ready to move at short notice. Usual routine as far as possible. The Divisional H.Q. during this time were ~~at~~ billeted 10 miles away, + we had constant trouble on account of the length of the line.	

M Hatton [illegible]

(9 29 6) W4141—463 100,000 9/14 H W V Forms/C. 2118/10

Instructions regarding War Diaries and Intelligence Summaries are contained in F. S. Regs., Part II. and the Staff Manual respectively. Title pages will be prepared in manuscript.

Army Form C. 2118.

WAR DIARY
or
~~INTELLIGENCE SUMMARY.~~

(*Erase heading not required.*)

Signal Troop
Mhow Cav. Bde

Hour, Date, Place	Summary of Events and Information	Remarks and references to Appendices
17th May	Marched at 3 p.m. to LOSINGHEM - Bde. all in the village.	
LOSINGHEM 18th May.	Ready to move at very short notice.	
19th May.	Marched back to FONTAINE-LEZ-HERMANS at 2.45 p.m.	
FONTAINE-LEZ-HERMANS 20th - 31st May.	Bde at 3 hours notice. Divisional HQ are at Boisy [?], six miles away. Telephone communication has worked satisfactorily. Our AT cart has been changed for a limbered-waggon drawn by 4 mules, a great improvement. One British signaller has been trained in the care & flying of carrier-pigeons under Divisional arrangements.	

A Hatter [?] Capt.
Bde. Signalling Officer.

(9 29 6) W4141—463 100,000 9/14 H W V Forms/C. 2118/10

Serial No. 245

121/6128

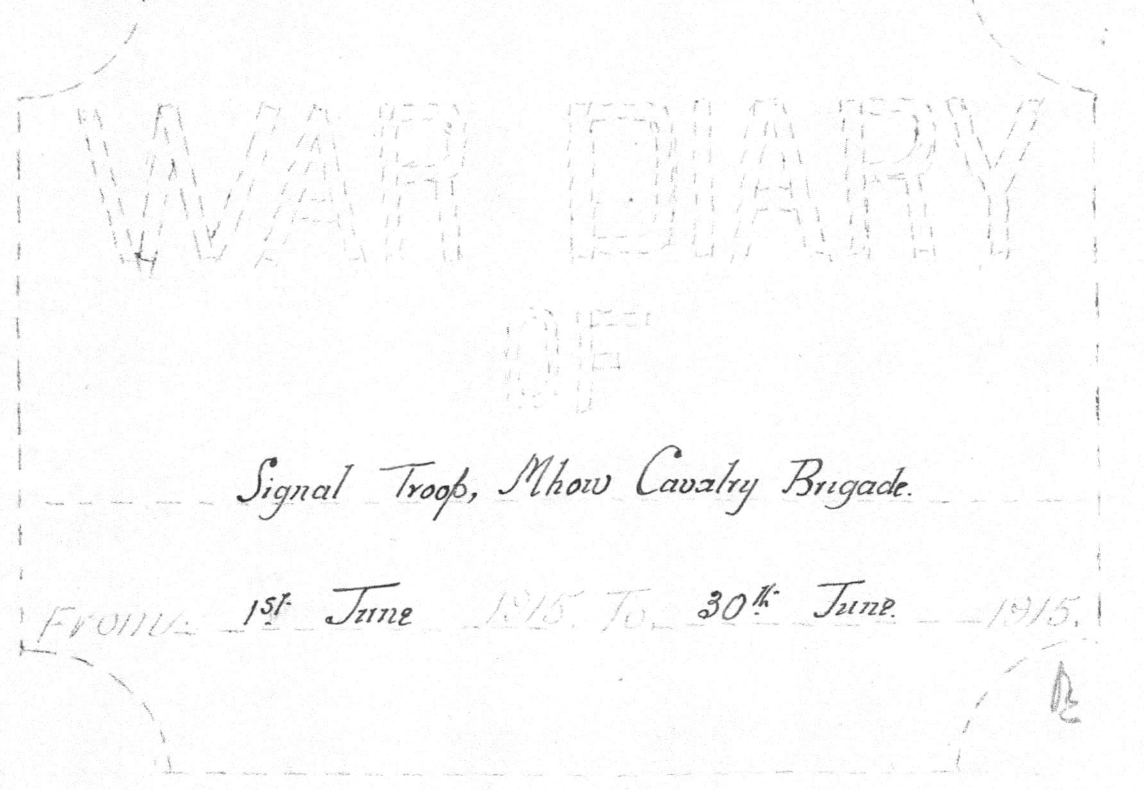

WAR DIARY OF

Signal Troop, Mhow Cavalry Brigade.

From 1st June 1915. To 30th June 1915.

Instructions regarding War Diaries and Intelligence Summaries are contained in F. S. Regs., Part II. and the Staff Manual respectively. Title pages will be prepared in manuscript.

WAR DIARY

~~or~~

~~INTELLIGENCE SUMMARY.~~

(*Erase heading not required.*)

Army Form C. 2118.

Signal Troop
Mhow Cav Bde

Hour, Date, Place	Summary of Events and Information	Remarks and references to Appendices
FONTAINE-LEZ-HERMANS		
June 1st – 4th	Usual Routine	
" 5th.	Bde. Signalling scheme with helio.	
" 6th – 20th	Usual routine. When the weather was suitable, all ranks were practiced in helio.	
" 21st	Bde day. Brigade held line of defence covering infantry entrenching. Helio communication was obtained with all units from hill 1 mile from report centre.	
" 22nd – 24th	Usual routine	
" 25th	Bde. scheme as on 21st. On account of rain & mist all communication was by dispatch rider	
" 26th – 30th.	Usual routine.	
	A telephone class was held for 15 days with advantage to the rate of sending of the signallers.	
	One man attended the signal squadron for a week's instruction in cable laying.	
	3 D III telephones have been received, filling us up to our full complement of 8 telephones (5 being D. 3)	
	A Hatten Capt.	
	Comdg Signal Troop. Mhow Cav. Bde.	

(9 29 6) W4141—463 100,000 9/14 H W V Forms/C. 2118/10

Serial No. 245

121/6502

WAR DIARY OF

Signal Troop Mhow Cavalry Brigade.

FROM 1st. July 1915. TO 31st. July 1915

Army Form C. 2118.

WAR DIARY
or
INTELLIGENCE SUMMARY.
(Erase heading not required.)

Instructions regarding War Diaries and Intelligence Summaries are contained in F. S. Regs., Part II. and the Staff Manual respectively. Title pages will be prepared in manuscript.

Signal Troop
Mhow Cavalry Bde

Hour, Date, Place	Summary of Events and Information	Remarks and references to Appendices
FONTAINE-LEZ-HERMANS July 1st – 7th	Usual routine. Helio practice whenever the weather was suitable.	
" 8th	Inspection of Ind. Cav. Corps by Lord Kitchener.	
" 9th – 11th	Instruction in cable laying.	
" 12th – 19th	Usual routine. Another 12 days telephone class was started on 12th.	
" 20th	Divisional with communication scheme. Dispatch riders almost invariably used. On one occasion flag was used by this Bde. to Divn. M.D.R's proved themselves to be quick & reliable.	
" 21st – 31st	Usual routine. We received 5 D III telephones on 26th making up our full complement. 7 more men have been taught how to handle carrier pigeons during the month	

A. Hartley Capt.
Comdg. Mhow Cav Bde Signal Troop

Serial No. 245

121/6948

WAR DIARY

OF

Signal Troop, Mhow Cavalry Brigade.

FROM 1st August 1915 TO 31st August 1915

Army Form O. 2118.

Instructions regarding War Diaries and Intelligence Summaries are contained in F. S. Regs., Part II, and the Staff Manual respectively. Title pages will be prepared in manuscript.

WAR DIARY
or
INTELLIGENCE SUMMARY. Signal Troop Mhow Cav Bde

(*Erase heading not required.*)

Hour, Date, Place.	Summary of Events and Information.	Remarks and references to Appendices.
7.45 am. Aug. 1st 1915	Marched to AUBIN St VAAST & route to III Army area. about 20 miles.	
8 am. Aug. 2nd	Marched to DOMART-EN-PONTHIEU. about 25 miles	
9.30 am Aug. 3rd	Marched to PICQUIGNY. about 11 miles. Permanent billets. 6th Dragoons in LA CHAUSSEE. Remainder of Bde in PICQUIGNY.	
Aug. 4th	Division laid cable to Brigade.	
Aug. 5th to Aug. 10th	Usual routine.	
Aug. 11th.	Signal Troop* (less a party left to work office at PICQUIGNY) embussed at 8 p.m. with 900 rifles of the Brigade en route to hold a section of the trenches. arrived FRANVILLERS at midnight.	* 5 British Signallers 5 Nat. " 2 Despatch riders

Army Form C. 2118.

Instructions regarding War Diaries and Intelligence Summaries are contained in F. S. Regs., Part II, and the Staff Manual respectively. Title pages will be prepared in manuscript.

WAR DIARY
or
INTELLIGENCE SUMMARY.

(*Erase heading not required.*)

Hour, Date, Place.	Summary of Events and Information.	Remarks and references to Appendices.
Aug. 12th	Brigade at FRANVILLARS.	
Aug. 13th.	Brigade marched to MARTINSART at 8 p.m. arriving there 1 a.m.	
Aug. 14th	Breakfast MARTINSART. Brigade went to trench line (fortified village of AUTHUILLE) at 4 p.m. Brigade was in support & to hold AUTHUILLE in case of attack.	
Aug. 15th	Reconnoitred AUTHUILLE with a view to laying cables to various parts of defences.	
Aug. 16th + 17th	Laid air lines to H.Q.s of each unit in front trenches of village defences.	
Aug 18th – 22nd	Laid alternative lines (partially buried + partially running in trenches) to H.Q.s of each unit in front trenches. Connected up the MOUND KEEP with a new air line	

Instructions regarding War Diaries and Intelligence Summaries are contained in F. S. Regs., Part II, and the Staff Manual respectively. Title pages will be prepared in manuscript.

WAR DIARY
or
INTELLIGENCE SUMMARY.

(Erase heading not required.)

Army Form C. 2118.

Hour, Date, Place.	Summary of Events and Information.	Remarks and references to Appendices.
Aug. 23rd	Relieved at night by LUCKNOW Bde. Brigade marched to BEAUCOURT.	
Aug 24th	Brigade at ~~Bea~~ BEAUCOURT, to be employed on digging under III Army.	
Aug. 25th	As there was no work for Signal Troop at BEAUCOURT, they returned to permanent billets at PICQUIGNY	
Aug. 26th – 30th	Usual routine	
Aug. 31st	Brigade being about to relieve 1st Ind. Cav. Divn in trenches. Signal Troop left at 6.45 p.m for BEAUCOURT.	

M Hatten, Lieut.
Cmdg. Mhow Cav. Bde. Signal Troop

Serial No. 245.

WAR DIARY

OF

Signal Troop Mhow Cavalry Brigade.

From 1st September 1915 To 30th September 1915

Army Form C. 2118.

Instructions regarding War Diaries and Intelligence Summaries are contained in F. S. Regs., Part II. and the Staff Manual respectively. Title pages will be prepared in manuscript.

WAR DIARY or INTELLIGENCE SUMMARY.

(*Erase heading not required.*)

Signal Troop Mhow Cav. Bde.

Hour, Date, Place	Summary of Events and Information	Remarks and references to Appendices
1 Sept.	Troop at BEAUCOURT, en route to trenches	
2 Sept.	Took over signalling arrangements from Ambala Signal Troop in 61 sub-sector.	
3 — 11 Sept.	In trenches. Nothing of unusual importance to note. We were pretty continuously annoyed by rifle-grenade + minenwerfer. ~~the latter~~ The latter cutting the cables entering the Signal office of the 6th Dragoons on two occasions. The damage done was very quickly repaired. In accordance with orders received from 51st Highland Division, we lowered the wires running at the sides of trenches to as near the bottom of the trench as ~~possible~~ practicable. A job which took a long time, but was almost finished when we were relieved.	

(9 29 6) W4141—463 100,000 9/14 H W V Forms/C. 2118/10

Army Form C. 2118.

Instructions regarding War Diaries and Intelligence Summaries are contained in F. S. Regs., Part II. and the Staff Manual respectively. Title pages will be prepared in manuscript.

WAR DIARY
or
INTELLIGENCE SUMMARY.
(Erase heading not required.)

Signal Troop Mhow Cav. Bde.

Hour, Date, Place	Summary of Events and Information	Remarks and references to Appendices
3 – 11 Sept.	A line was laid for the French mortar battery officer from the battery to his observing station. An alternative line from the left regt. to the centre regt. was also laid. The telephone system worked well throughout.	
12 Sept.	Relieved in the afternoon by Ambala Sig. Troop. Brigade relieved by 1 a.m. on 13th & marched to BEAUCOURT.	
13 Sept.	At BEAUCOURT. Marched that night back to permanent billets at PICQUIGNY.	
14 Sept.	At PICQUIGNY.	
15 Sept.	Brigade marched to new billets on transfer to 1st Divn. – Hd. Qrs. at VILLERS – SOUS – AILLY – Communication to units by Dispatch-rider.	
16 – 20 Sept.	Usual routine.	

(9 29 6) W 4141—463 100,000 9/14 H W V Forms/C. 2118/10

Army Form C. 2118.

Instructions regarding War Diaries and Intelligence Summaries are contained in F. S. Regs., Part II. and the Staff Manual respectively. Title pages will be prepared in manuscript.

WAR DIARY
or
INTELLIGENCE SUMMARY.
(Erase heading not required.)

Signal Troop
Mhow Cav. Bde.

Hour, Date, Place	Summary of Events and Information	Remarks and references to Appendices
21 Sept.	The Division was inspected by Lord Kitchener.	
22 Sept.	Marched to new billets at BERNAVILLE. All units in same place.	
23 – 30 Sept.	Usual routine. From 25th onwards Brigade was put on short notice to move, in consequence of operations of 1st Army.	

[illegible] Capt.
Cmdg. Sig. Troop
Mhow Cav. Bde

SERIAL NO 245.

Confidential

War Diary

of

Signal Troop, Mhow Cavalry Brigade.

FROM 1st October 1915 TO 31st December 1915.

Army Form C. 2118.

Instructions regarding War Diaries and Intelligence Summaries are contained in F. S. Regs., Part II. and the Staff Manual respectively. Title pages will be prepared in manuscript.

WAR DIARY
or
INTELLIGENCE SUMMARY.
(*Erase heading not required.*)

Signal Troop.
Mhow Cavalry Bde.

Hour, Date, Place	Summary of Events and Information	Remarks and references to Appendices
Oct 1st 1915	Divisional exercise. At conclusion Bde. changed billets. Hd. Qrs at BEAUVOIR. Communication to units by Dispatch riders.	
2nd – 4th	Usual routine.	
5th	Divisional exercise.	
6th – 7th	Usual routine.	
8th	Divisional exercise.	
9th — 10th	Usual routine.	
11th	Brigade exercise.	
12th	Usual routine.	
13th	Bde. changed billets. H.Q at BERNEUIL.	
14th	Usual routine.	

E. G. Atkinson Lieut
O. C. Signal Troop
Mhow Bde

(9 29 6) W4141—463 100,000 9/14 H W V Forms/C. 2118/10

Instructions regarding War Diaries and Intelligence Summaries are contained in F. S. Regs., Part II. and the Staff Manual respectively. Title pages will be prepared in manuscript.

WAR DIARY
or
INTELLIGENCE SUMMARY.
(Erase heading not required.)

Army Form C. 2118.

Signal Troop
MHOW Brigade

Hour, Date, Place	Summary of Events and Information	Remarks and references to Appendices
Oct. 15th	Divisional exercise	
16th	Usual routine. Division laid cable to Brigade.	
17th	Capt. Hartley left to join 1st York & Lancaster Regt. Bde. HQ changed billets to FIENVILLERS.	
18th – 21st	Usual routine. Lieut E. G. Atkinson 17th Cavalry from 1st I.C.D. Signal Squadron, took over command of Bde Signal Troop	
22nd	Bde. moves to new billeting area. Bde. HQ at SELINCOURT.	
23rd	Bde. settles in new billets.	
24th – 30th	Usual routine	
31st	~~Rout~~. Communications established with units.	E. G. Atkinson Lieut. O.C. Signal Troop Mhow Bde

(9 29 6) W4141—463 100,000 9/14 H W V Forms/C. 2118/10

Instructions regarding War Diaries and Intelligence Summaries are contained in F. S. Regs., Part II. and the Staff Manual respectively. Title pages will be prepared in manuscript.

WAR DIARY
or
INTELLIGENCE SUMMARY.
(*Erase heading not required.*)

Army Form C. 2118.

Signal Troop.
MHOW Brigade.

Hour, Date, Place	Summary of Events and Information	Remarks and references to Appendices
November.		
1st – 4th	Usual routine.	
5th	Inspection of transport by OC ASC.	
6th – 7th	Usual routine.	
8th	Divisional Parade for distribution of French decorations by Corps Commander. Detachment of Signal Troop in attendance.	
9th – 10th	Usual routine	
11th	Indian Cavalry Corps inspection by General Sir HH Allenby. K.C.B. Commanding 3rd Army.	
12th – 19th	Usual routine.	
20th	Bde. Staff ride.	
21st – 30th	Usual routine.	

E. G. ~~Atkinson~~ Lieut
O. C. Signal Troop
Mhow Bde

Instructions regarding War Diaries and Intelligence Summaries are contained in F. S. Regs., Part II. and the Staff Manual respectively. Title pages will be prepared in manuscript.

WAR DIARY
or
INTELLIGENCE SUMMARY.
(Erase heading not required.)

Army Form C. 2118.

Signal Troop.
MHOW Brigade.

Hour, Date, Place	Summary of Events and Information	Remarks and references to Appendices
December 1915		
1st – 2nd	Usual routine	
3rd	Postponement on account of heavy rain, of Bde. Staff Ride	
4th	Bde. Staff ride at LIOMER	
5th – 15th	Usual routine.	
16th	Change of billet. Bde. HQ at SAUCOURT.	
17th	Communications established with units.	
18th – 19th	Usual routine.	
20th – 24th	Usual routine. Signalling classes held.	
25th	XMAS DAY. Usual routine.	
26th – 30th	Usual routine. Signalling classes. Horses undergo MALLEIN test for Glanders.	
31st	Usual routine.	

E. G. Atkinson Lieut
O.C. Signal Troop
Mhow Bde

(9 29 6) W4141—463 100,000 9/14 H W V Forms/C. 2118/10

SERIAL NO. 245.

Confidential

War Diary

of

Signal Troop, Mhow Cavalry Brigade

FROM 1st January 1918 TO 31st January 1918

Instructions regarding War Diaries and Intelligence Summaries are contained in F. S. Regs., Part II. and the Staff Manual respectively. Title pages will be prepared in manuscript.

Army Form C. 2118.

WAR DIARY
or
INTELLIGENCE SUMMARY.
(Erase heading not required.)

Signal Troop
Mhow Cav Bde

Place	Date	Hour	Summary of Events and Information	Remarks and references to Appendices
Jan 1916	1st – 7th		Usual Routine Work. Signalling Classes daily.	
	8th – 16th		Usual Routine Signalling Classes daily	
	17 – 23rd		Usual Routine Signalling Classes daily.	
	24th		Brigade Route March.	
	25th		Usual Routine. Signalling Classes.	
	26th – 27th		" " New Div[isio]nl line laid	
	28 – 31st		Usual Routine. Signalling classes daily	

E. G. Atkinson Capt
O.C. Signal Troop
Mhow Cav Bde

2353 Wt. W2514/1454 700,000 5/15 D. D. & L. A.D.S.S./Forms/C. 2118.

SERIAL NO 245

Confidential

War Diary

of

Signal Troop, Mhow Cavalry Brigade

FROM 1st February 1916 TO 29th February 1916

Army Form C. 2118.

Instructions regarding War Diaries and Intelligence Summaries are contained in F. S. Regs., Part II. and the Staff Manual respectively. Title pages will be prepared in manuscript.

WAR DIARY
or
INTELLIGENCE SUMMARY.
(Erase heading not required.)

Signal Troop
Mhow Cav Bde
February 1916

Place	Date	Hour	Summary of Events and Information	Remarks and references to Appendices
Feb 1916	1st to 7th		Brigade Routine Work "Signalling Classes Daily"	
	8th to 16th		Brigade Routine Work "Signalling Classes Daily"	
	17th		Brigade Routine Work "Signalling Classes"	
	18th		Brigade Routine Work "Signalling Classes" Lecture for Officers	
	19th to 22nd		Brigade Routine Work "Signalling Classes Daily"	
	23rd		Brigade Routine Work "Signalling Classes Brigade Scheme (C.Os. and Squadron Commanders	
	24th to 28th		Brigade Routine Work "Signalling Classes Daily"	
	29th		Brigade Scheme "Signalling Classes"	

E. G. [illegible] Capt

SERIAL NO. 245.

Confidential

War Diary

of

Signal Troop, Mhow Cavalry Brigade

FROM 1st March 1916 TO 31st March 1916.

Army Form C. 2118.

Instructions regarding War Diaries and Intelligence Summaries are contained in F. S. Regs., Part II. and the Staff Manual respectively. Title pages will be prepared in manuscript.

WAR DIARY
or
INTELLIGENCE SUMMARY.
(Erase heading not required.)

March 1916

Signal Troop
Mhow Cav Bde.

Place	Date	Hour	Summary of Events and Information	Remarks and references to Appendices
FIELD	1st to 8th		Bde Routine Work. Signalling Classes daily.	
"	9th to 17th		Bde Routine Work. Signalling Classes daily.	
"	18th to 24th		Bde Routine Work. Signalling Classes daily.	All telephone lines taken in.
"	25th		First days march to new billeting area. Communication maintained by Motor DRs and Mounted DRs	
"	26th		Second march to new billeting area. Arrived new billets about 12 noon. Communication maintained by Motor DRs and Mounted DRs.	
"	27th		Commenced laying wire to units. Telephonic communication ~~communication~~ established with all units at 3 PM.	
"	28th to 30th		Brigade Routine Work. Signalling Classes daily.	
"	31st		Laying Air-line to complete divisional Air-line. E. G. Atkinson Capt Cmdg Signal Troop Mhow Cav Bde	

2353 Wt. W2514/1454 700,000 5/15 D. D. & L. A.D.S.S./Forms/C. 2118.

SERIAL NO 245.

Confidential

War Diary

of

Signal Troop, Mhow Cavalry Brigade

FROM 1st April 1916 TO 30th April 1916.

16/5/16

Instructions regarding War Diaries and Intelligence Summaries are contained in F. S. Regs., Part II. and the Staff Manual respectively. Title pages will be prepared in manuscript.

WAR DIARY
or
INTELLIGENCE SUMMARY.
(Erase heading not required.)

April 1916
Signal Troop
Mhow Cav: Bde.

Army Form C. 2118.

Hour, Date, Place	Summary of Events and Information	Remarks and references to Appendices
Field 1st – 8th	Brigade routine work. Signalling classes daily.	
Field 9th – 17th	Brigade routine work. Signalling classes daily.	
Field 18th	Brigade routine work. Signalling classes daily Airline replacing cable to units	
Field 19th	Brigade routine work. Signalling classes daily continuation of air line work.	
Field 20th	Brigade routine work. Signalling classes daily Air line completed to 2 units.	
Field 21st 22nd	Brigade routine work. Signalling classes daily Horse and saddle inspection. Marched for training area. Communication maintained by motor-cyclist despatch riders.	
Field 23rd	Telephonic communication with Division established.	E. B. Atkinson Capt Signal Troop Mhow Cav Bde
Field 24th	Telephonic communication with two units established, visual signalling work in vicinity training area.	

(9 29 6) W4141—463 100,000 9/14 H W V Forms/C. 2118/10

Instructions regarding War Diaries and Intelligence Summaries are contained in F. S. Regs., Part II. and the Staff Manual respectively. Title pages will be prepared in manuscript.

WAR DIARY
or
INTELLIGENCE SUMMARY.
(*Erase heading not required.*)

Army Form C. 2118.

April 1916
Signal Troop
Mhow Cav Bde.

Hour, Date, Place	Summary of Events and Information	Remarks and references to Appendices
Field 25th	Brigade field day — Visual Communication established with units — communication maintained on the move by mounted despatch rider.	
Field 26th — 27th	Staff ride by Reserve Corps Commander. Brigade routine work — Signalling class as usual.	
Field 28th — 30th	Brigade schemes carried out set by Division. Communication maintained on the move by Heliograph and flag.	
	E. G. Atkinson	Capt. Comdg. Signal Sqdn Mhow Cav. Bde

SERIAL NO 245.

Confidential

War Diary

of

Signal Troop, Mhow Cavalry Division.

FROM 1st May 1916 TO 31st May 1916.

Instructions regarding War Diaries and Intelligence Summaries are contained in F. S. Regs., Part II. and the Staff Manual respectively. Title pages will be prepared in manuscript.

WAR DIARY
or
INTELLIGENCE SUMMARY.
(Erase heading not required.)

Army Form C. 2118.

Hour, Date, Place	Summary of Events and Information	Remarks and references to Appendices
1st May In the field. (training area)	Brigade scheme – Communication maintained by mounted despatch rider Inspection of smoke helmets, Rifles, Ammunication, Equipment	
2nd May. In the field. (training area)	Divisional Scheme – Communication maintained on the march by visual and motor cyclists. When in training area by mounted despatch rider	
3rd May In the field (training area)	Divisional scheme – Communication maintained by means of motor cyclists and mounted despatch riders.	
4th May In the field. (training area)	Divisional scheme – Reserve Corps Commander out. Communication at times maintained by visual in training area.	
5th May In the field training area	Brigade routine work. Signalling classes continued.	
6th May In the field (training area)	Divisional scheme – Same scheme as carried out for Reserve Corps Commander.	
7th May In the field	Telephonic communication with units cut off, marched for permanent billeting area; brigade report centre at head of main body. Arrived permanent billets 11 am. telephone communication established with division and units 2 pm.	
8th May In the field.	Brigade routine work – Signalling classes continued.	
9th May "	"	
10th May "	Telephonic communication cut off. Marched for new billets. Report centre at head of main body. Arrived 12 noon. Telephonic communication established with division 1 pm.	

E. R. Alterns[?] Capt

(9 29 6) W4141—463 100,000 9/14 H W V Forms/C. 2118/10

Instructions regarding War Diaries and Intelligence Summaries are contained in F. S. Regs., Part II. and the Staff Manual respectively. Title pages will be prepared in manuscript.

Army Form C. 2118.

WAR DIARY
or
INTELLIGENCE SUMMARY.
(*Erase heading not required.*)

Hour, Date, Place	Summary of Events and Information	Remarks and references to Appendices
11th May. In the field.	Brigade routine work – Signalling classes daily. Dismounted brigade being re-organised.	
12th May. In the field.	Brigade routine work – Signalling classes daily.	
13th May. In the field.	Brigade routine work – Parade of dismounted Mhow Bde Section. Signallers of units paraded with Mhow Battalion for route march.	
14th May. In the field.	Erected air line – Signallers 2nd Lancers out for instruction in air line work. Communication established with all units.	
15th May. In the field.	Brigade routine work – Signalling classes daily. Inspection of smoke helmets. Iron rations. Rifle, bandolier ammunition.	
16th May. In the field.	Brigade routine work – Brigade routine work. Signalling classes daily.	
17th May. In the field.	Brigade routine work. 2nd Lancers instructed in telephone reading.	
18th May. In the field.	Brigade routine work – Signalling classes daily.	
19th May. In the field.	Brigade routine work – Signalling classes daily.	
20th May. In the field.	Brigade routine work. Signalling classes daily.	

E. G. Atkinson Capt

(9 29 6) W4141—463 100,000 9/14 H W V Forms/C. 2118/10

Army Form C. 2118.

Instructions regarding War Diaries and Intelligence Summaries are contained in F. S. Regs., Part II. and the Staff Manual respectively. Title pages will be prepared in manuscript.

WAR DIARY
or
INTELLIGENCE SUMMARY.
(Erase heading not required.)

Hour, Date, Place	Summary of Events and Information	Remarks and references to Appendices
21st — 23rd May. In the field.	Brigade routine work - Signalling classes daily.	
24th May. In the field.	Brigade routine work - Brigade inspected by Commander-in-Chief in billets in the afternoon.	
25th May — 30th May. In the field	Brigade routine work. Signalling classes daily	
31st May. In the field.	Divisional Day - Scheme set by the Reserve Corps Commander.	

E. G. Atkinson Capt
O.C. Signal Troop
Ambala Cav. Bde

(9 29 6) W4141—463 100,000 9/14 H W V Forms/C. 2118/10

SERIAL NO 245.

Confidential

War Diary

of

Signal Troop, Mhow Cavalry Brigade

FROM 1st July 1916 TO 31st July 1916.

Army Form C. 2118.

Instructions regarding War Diaries and Intelligence Summaries are contained in F. S. Regs., Part II. and the Staff Manual respectively. Title pages will be prepared in manuscript.

WAR DIARY

~~or~~

~~INTELLIGENCE SUMMARY.~~

(Erase heading not required.)

Signal Troop
[illegible] Cav Bde.

Place	Date	Hour	Summary of Events and Information	Remarks and references to Appendices
In the field	July 1st – 7th		Brigade routine work — Signalling classes daily	
"	8th – 18th		Brigade routine work — Signalling classes daily	
"	19th		Moved to new billeting area arriving same date. Communication established with Divn and two units by telephone.	
"	20th – 31st		Brigade routine work – Signalling classes daily. Visual Signalling ~~done~~ carried out on field days.	

[illegible] Capt.
Staff Capt.
for O.C. Signal Troop.

2353 Wt. W2544/1454 700,000 5/15 D. D. & L. A.D.S.S./Forms/C. 2118.

SERIAL NO 245.

Confidential War Diary

of

Signal Troop, Mhow Cavalry Brigade

FROM 1st August 1916 TO 31st August 1916.

Army Form C. 2118.

Signal Troop
Mhow Cav Bde

Instructions regarding War Diaries and Intelligence Summaries are contained in F. S. Regs., Part II. and the Staff Manual respectively. Title pages will be prepared in manuscript.

WAR DIARY
or
INTELLIGENCE SUMMARY.
(Erase heading not required.)

Hour, Date, Place	Summary of Events and Information	Remarks and references to Appendices
1st August 1916. Rollecourt	Telephonic communication established with Divn and units. Communication with working parties — trenches by motor cyclist	
10th August 1916 Cambligneul.	Moved to Cambligneul. Telephonic communication with division and one unit established. Telephonic communication also with working parties through 60th Division and 180th Brigade	
31st August 1916.	D.R.L.S. twice daily to all units and parties during the month.	

E. J. Altham Capt
O. C. Signal Troop
Mhow Cav Bde

(9 29 6) W4141—463 100,000 9/14 H W V Forms/C. 2118/10

SERIAL NO. 245

Confidential

War Diary

of

Signal Troop Mhow Cavalry Brigade

FROM 1st September 1916 TO 30th September 1916

Instructions regarding War Diaries and Intelligence Summaries are contained in F. S. Regs., Part II. and the Staff Manual respectively. Title pages will be prepared in manuscript.

WAR DIARY or INTELLIGENCE SUMMARY.

(*Erase heading not required.*)

Army Form C. 2118.

Signal Troop Mhow BDE

Place	Date	Hour	Summary of Events and Information	Remarks and references to Appendices
Camblignal	2nd/9		Marched to a new billeting area. Communication maintained by motor cyclist arrived in billets about 12 noon. Telephonic communication opened with division and two units	
St Michel	3rd/9		Marched to a new billeting area Communication maintained by motor cyclist Arrived in billets about 1 pm Telephonic communication to division.	
Noyelle-en-Chaussee	4th/9		Training area. Communication when in the field was carried out by visual Signalling and mounted despatch rider	
Noyelle-en-Chaussee	10th/9		Marched to a new billeting area. Communication maintained by motor cyclist arrived new billets telephonic communication established with division.	
Remaisnil	11th.		Marched to a new billeting area. Communication maintained by motor cyclist. Telephonic communication with division opened on arrival	
Authieule	12th.	-	Marched to a new billeting area Communication by motor cyclist Arrived new billeting area. Communication with division by push cyclist: by motor cyclist to units.	
Amonville	13.14 th		Marched to a new billeting area. Communication by motor cyclist On arrival telephonic communication opened with division. By runner to units	[illegible] Signal Troop Mhow Bde

2353 Wt. W2514/1454 700,000 5/15 D. D. & L. A.D.S.S./Forms/C. 2118.

Army Form C. 2118.

Instructions regarding War Diaries and Intelligence Summaries are contained in F. S. Regs., Part II. and the Staff Manual respectively. Title pages will be prepared in manuscript.

WAR DIARY
or
INTELLIGENCE SUMMARY.
(*Erase heading not required.*)

Signal Troop Mhow Bde

Place	Date	Hour	Summary of Events and Information	Remarks and references to Appendices
			push cyclist, by motor cyclist to units.	
Ammonville	13th/9 14th/9		Marched to a new billeting area. Communication by motor cyclist. On arrival telephonic communication opened with division. By runner to units.	
Morlancourt	15th/9 25th/9		Marched to a new billeting area. Communication by motor cyclist. Arrived billeting area.	
Montauban	25th		Communication with advanced Squadrons of two units by telephone, heliograph and mounted orderly. Advanced report centre Waterlot Farm. Transmitting visual signalling station thrown out ~~[illegible]~~ East of Delville Wood and ~~[illegible]~~ Waterlot Farm. Stations withdrawn evening 25th.	
			Marched to a new billeting area.	
Morlancourt	26th		Marched for a new billeting area but were recalled.	
"	27th		Marched to a new billeting area. Communication by motor cyclist. Communication opened ~~by~~ arrival by push cyclist	
Bussy-les-Daours	28th		Marched to a new billeting area.	
Belloy-sur-Somme	29th		Marched to a new billeting area. Communication by motor cyclist	
Dourig	30th		Communication by telephone.	R. G. Atkinson Capt. O.C. Signal Troop Mhow Bde

2353 Wt. W2544/1454 700,000 5/15 D. D. & L. A.D.S.S./Forms/C. 2118.

Instructions regarding War Diaries and Intelligence Summaries are contained in F. S. Regs., Part II. and the Staff Manual respectively. Title Pages will be prepared in manuscript.

WAR DIARY
or
INTELLIGENCE SUMMARY
(Erase heading not required.)

Army Form C. 2118.

1 DIV
Cav Brigade
[illegible] Bde

Place	Date	Hour	Summary of Events and Information	Remarks and references to Appendices
OCTOBER 1916				
DOURIEZ				
Sun	1st		Rest.	
Mon	2nd		The billets of the Brigade were altered and the Brigade disposed as follows:- Bde HQ, Supply, Mobile Vet. Sec } DOURIEZ; 6th Dgns DOMPIERRE and PONCHES; 2nd Drs RAYE-SUR-AUTHIE; M G Sqdn LABROYE; 'A' Batty RHA LE BOISLE and VERGEOLLAY	
Tues to Wed	3rd to 18th		Training.	
Thurs	19th		'A' Batty RHA left the Brigade to be attached to Reserve Army	
Frid.	20th		Training.	
Sat	21st		Advance party dismounted M G Squadron marched to OUTREBOIS en route for Reserve Army area for work in trenches.	
Sun	22nd		Lorry parties of D. M. Machine Gun Squadron left for Reserve Army area. A Batty RHA rejoined the Brigade & billetted in LE BOISLE	[illegible]

[signature]

2449 Wt. W14957/M90 750,000 1/16 J.B.C. & A. Forms/C.2118/12.

Army Form C. 2118.

Instructions regarding War Diaries and Intelligence Summaries are contained in F. S. Regs., Part II. and the Staff Manual respectively. Title Pages will be prepared in manuscript.

WAR DIARY
or
INTELLIGENCE SUMMARY
(Erase heading not required.)

Place	Date	Hour	Summary of Events and Information	Remarks and references to Appendices
OCTOBER 1916				
DOURIEZ				
Mon	23rd to		Training.	
Sat	28th			
Sat	28th		40 British OR + 60 Indian OR went up by Lorry to Reserve Army area as Brigade working party.	
Sun	29th		Training.	
Mon	30th			
Tues	31st		Orders received for move to new area on Nov 1st + 2nd	

Mhow Cavalry Brigade

[signature] Captain
Brigade Major

2449 Wt. W14957/M90 750,000 1/16 J.B.C. & A. Forms/C.2118/12.

Instructions regarding War Diaries and Intelligence Summaries are contained in F. S. Regs., Part II. and the Staff Manual respectively. Title Pages will be prepared in manuscript.

WAR DIARY
or
INTELLIGENCE SUMMARY

(Erase heading not required.)

Army Form C. 2118.

Mobile Vet^y Sect^n
Meerut Cavalry Bg^de
1st I. C. Division

Place	Date	Hour	Summary of Events and Information	Remarks and references to Appendices
Bouvig	1/10/16		Capt. Barton on leave took over charge of VI Dragoons + 2nd Lancers admitted 13 sick horses	
"	2/10/16		Admitted 7 sick horses inspected 2 sections of machine gun Sq^dn for contagious diseases	
"	3/10/16		Admitted 3 sick horses into Section; ordinary routine work —	
"	4/10/16		Evacuated 21 sick horses from Beaurainville to No 7 Vet^y H. Forges-le-Eau admitted one sick horse.	
"	5/10/16		Detailed one man to Division to take charge of float. Inspected 1 Sq^dn 38th C.I.H for contagious diseases —	
"	6/10/16		Collected one sick horse from Raye-sur-Authie left behind by 1st I. C. Divisional Ammunition Column R.H.A.	
"	7/10/16		Admitted one horse to Section —	
"	8/10/16		Admitted one sick horse to Section. Routine work as usual	
"	9/10/16		Admitted one horse, inspected one Sq^dn C.I.H. for contagious diseases	
"	10/10/16		Evacuated 7 horses by rail from Beaurainville to No 7 Vet^y H. Forges-le-Eau	
"	11/10/16		Admitted 5 sick + 1 cast horses from D.A.D.R	

2449 Wt. W14957/M90 750,000 1/16 J.B.C. & A. Forms/C.2118/12.

Army Form C. 2118.

Instructions regarding War Diaries and Intelligence Summaries are contained in F. S. Regs., Part II. and the Staff Manual respectively. Title Pages will be prepared in manuscript.

WAR DIARY
or
INTELLIGENCE SUMMARY

(Erase heading not required.)

Mobile Vetʸ Section
Mhow Cavalry Bgde
1st I.C. Division

Place	Date	Hour	Summary of Events and Information	Remarks and references to Appendices
Douriez	2/10	/16	Evacuated 21 horses by rail from Beaurainville to No 7 Vet H. Forges les Eaux	
"	13/10	/16	Admitted 2 sick horses. Had inspection of Section by D.D.V.S.	
"	14/10	/16	Admitted 2 sick horses inspected one Sqdn of 38th CIH for contagious diseases	
"	15/10	/16	General Routine work —	
"	16/10	/16	Inspected one section of Machine Gun Sqn for contagious diseases	
"	17/10	/16	Capt Bowling went Hospital Capt Barton in charge. admitted 2 sick horses	CMB
	18/10	/16	Inspection of section & general clean up.	
	19/10	/16.	Admitted 5 sick horses. General routine work.	CMB
	20/10	/16.	Evacuated 11 sick horses from Beaurainville.	CMB
	21/10	/16	Lieut Stevens in charge of Section	CMB
	22/10	/16	Inspection 1 Squad. CIH	CMB
	23/10	/16	Admitted 8 sick horses	CMB
	24/10	/16	Evacuated 11 sick horses. Capt Barton visited Section.	CMB
	25/10	/16.	Admitted 6 sick horses	CMB
	26/10	/16.	Admitted 4 sick horses Evacuated 5 by Road to Abbeville	CMB
	27/10	/16	Inspected 2 squad Lancers [illegible]	CMB

2449 Wt. W14957/M90 750,000 1/16 J.B.C. & A. Forms/C.2118/12.

Army Form C. 2118.

Instructions regarding War Diaries and Intelligence Summaries are contained in F. S. Regs., Part II. and the Staff Manual respectively. Title Pages will be prepared in manuscript.

WAR DIARY
or
INTELLIGENCE SUMMARY

(Erase heading not required.)

Mobile Vet[y] Sect[n]
Meerut Cav. Bg[de]
1st I. C. Div

Place	Date	Hour	Summary of Events and Information	Remarks and references to Appendices
28/10/16	Dommy.		Inspected Section & had general parade admitted 2 sick horses	GHB
29/10/16	"		D.D.V.S visited section & inspected equipment & mess quarters	GHB
30/10/16	"		Inspected Machine Gun Sq[dn] & admitted six sick horses to Section	GHB
31/10/16	"		Inspected 1 Sq[dn] C.I.H for contagious diseases. Evacuated 8 sick horses by road to Abbeville & was under orders to move.	
	"		admitted 6 horses from F.A.D.R for casting & 2 from 2nd Lancers	GHB

G H Bennet
Lt A V C

2449 Wt. W14957/M90 750,000 1/16 J.B.C. & A. Forms/C.2118/12.

Instructions regarding War Diaries and Intelligence Summaries are contained in F. S. Regs., Part II. and the Staff Manual respectively. Title Pages will be prepared in manuscript.

WAR DIARY
or
~~INTELLIGENCE SUMMARY~~

(Erase heading not required.)

Army Form C. 2118.

SIGNAL TROOP
MHOW CAV. BDE

Place	Date	Hour	Summary of Events and Information	Remarks and references to Appendices
October 1916				
DOURIEZ			Communication by D.R. to units + division, later telephone communication to D.W.: + 6th. Dragns.	
			Routine + training signallers of units	
			E. G. Atkinson Capt. O. C. Signal Troop Mhow Cav Bde	

2449 Wt. W14957/M90 750,000 1/16 J.B.C. & A. Forms/C.2118/12.

SERIAL NO. 245.

Confidential War Diary

of

Signal Troop, Mhow Cavalry Brigade

FROM 1st November 1916 TO 30th November 1916.

Army Form C. 2118.

WAR DIARY
or
~~INTELLIGENCE~~ SUMMARY.
(*Erase heading not required.*)

Headquarters
Mhow Cavalry Brigade.

Instructions regarding War Diaries and Intelligence Summaries are contained in F. S. Regs., Part II. and the Staff Manual respectively. Title pages will be prepared in manuscript.

Reference ABBEVILLE Sheet 1/100,000

Place	Date	Hour	Summary of Events and Information	Remarks and references to Appendices
NOVEMBER		1916		
DOURIEX				
	WED	1st	The Signal Troop marched to Billets at ESCARBOTIN (28 miles)	
	2nd –	5th	Brigade Routine Work.	
	5th	30th	Signal Class of young Signallers –	
	(23rd)		Reorganization of the Signal Troop to British Personnel	

A. Varenbey? 2Lt
O.C. Signal Troop
Mhow Bde

2353 Wt. W2544/1454 700,000 5/15 D. D. & L. A.D.S.S./Forms/C. 2118.

SERIAL No 245

Confidential

War Diary

of

Signal Troop, Mhow Cavalry Brigade

FROM 1st December 1916 TO 31st December 1916

Instructions regarding War Diaries and Intelligence Summaries are contained in F. S. Regs., Part II. and the Staff Manual respectively. Title pages will be prepared in manuscript.

Army Form C. 2118.

WAR DIARY ~~or INTELLIGENCE SUMMARY.~~

(Erase heading not required.)

Signal Troop
Mhow Cav Bde
December 1916

Hour, Date, Place	Summary of Events and Information	Remarks and references to Appendices
Dec 1st 1916 to 22nd Dec	Brigade Routine Work Signalling Classes daily	
Dec 23rd	Brigade Routine Work & Signalling Classes daily 2nd Lt Day relieved by 2nd Lt. Longworth Dames	
Dec 24th to 31st Dec	Brigade Routine Work Signalling Classes daily	
		M. Birch Reynardson Lt O.C. Signal Troop Mhow Bde.

(9 29 6) W4141—463 100,000 9/14 H W V Forms/C. 2118/10

Army Form C. 2118.

Instructions regarding War Diaries and Intelligence Summaries are contained in F. S. Regs., Part II. and the Staff Manual respectively. Title pages will be prepared in manuscript.

WAR DIARY
or
~~INTELLIGENCE SUMMARY.~~
(Erase heading not required.)

Signal Troop
Mhow Cav Bde
December 1916

Hour, Date, Place	Summary of Events and Information	Remarks and references to Appendices
Dec 1st 1916 to 22nd Dec	Brigade Routine Work Signalling Classes daily	
Dec 23rd	Brigade Routine Work & Signalling Classes daily 2nd Lt Day relieved by 2nd Lt Longworth Dames	
Dec 24th to 31st Dec	Brigade Routine Work Signalling Classes daily	

M. Birch Reynardson Lt
O.C. Signal Troop
Mhow Bde

(9 29 6) W4141—463 100,000 9/14 H W V Forms/C. 2118/10

BEF

1 IND. CAV. DIV.

MHOW BDE

MACHINE GUN SQD

1916 JULY to 1916 DEC

SERIAL NO 321.

Confidential

War Diary

of

Machine Gun Squadron, Mhow Cavalry Brigade

FROM 1st July 1916 TO 31st July 1916.

Instructions regarding War Diaries and Intelligence Summaries are contained in F. S. Regs., Part II. and the Staff Manual respectively. Title pages will be prepared in manuscript.

WAR DIARY

or

~~INTELLIGENCE SUMMARY~~. J.C.H.

(Erase heading not required.)

M.G. Squadron Mhow Cav Bde

Army Form C. 2118.

Place	Date	Hour	Summary of Events and Information	Remarks and references to Appendices
	1916			
AUTHIEULE	July 5th	6 p.m.	The Machine Gun Squadron moved out of billets, and marched via BERNAVILLE — PROUVILLE to the MAZICOURT Area and billeted in MONT LOUIS FERM	Ref. Map LENS No 11 1/100,000
MONT LOUIS FERM	July 6	11 a.m.	The Machine Gun Squadron changed billets and moved to HEIRMONT	
HEIRMONT	July 19th	8 a.m.	The Machine Gun Squadron moved via AUXI-LE-CHATEAU — LIGNY-SUR-CANCHE to ROELLECOURT	
ROELLECOURT	July 22nd	9 P.M.	1 Sec. of machine guns were sent to protect the Ammunition Depot at LA BELLE ~~Et~~ EPINE against Aeroplanes should they attempt to bomb it. This duty has been carried out by a section every night up to the present date	

J.C. Humfrey Capt
Comdg. Mhow M.G. Sqdn.

2353 Wt. W2544/1454 700,000 5/15 D. D. & L. A.D.S.S./Forms/C. 2118.

SERIAL NO 321.

Confidential War Diary

of

Machine Gun Squadron, Mhow Cavalry Brigade

FROM 1st August 1916 TO 31st August 1916.

Instructions regarding War Diaries and Intelligence Summaries are contained in F. S. Regs., Part II. and the Staff Manual respectively. Title Pages will be prepared in manuscript.

WAR DIARY
or
~~INTELLIGENCE SUMMARY~~ JCH
(Erase heading not required.)

Army Form C. 2118.

M.G. Squadron
Mhow Bde

Place	Date	Hour	Summary of Events and Information	Remarks and references to Appendices
ROELLECOURT	Aug 1st–9th		1 Sec of Machine guns were on duty nightly at ammunition dump at LA BELLE EPINE	
ROELLECOURT	Aug 9th	9 am	The Squadron marched via SAVY to new billets at CAMBLIGNEUL	
CAMBLIGNEUL	Aug 9th to 31st		1 Sec. of Machine Guns were on duty nightly at Ammunition dump at LA BELLE EPINE	

J.C. Humfrey Capt
Cmdg Mhow M.G. Squadron

2449 Wt. W14957/M90 750,000 1/16 J.B.C. & A. Forms/C.2118/12.

SERIAL NO. 321.

Confidential War Diary

of

Machine Gun Squadron, Mhow Cavalry Brigade

FROM 1st September 1916 TO 30th September 1916

Army Form C. 2118.

Instructions regarding War Diaries and Intelligence Summaries are contained in F. S. Regs., Part II. and the Staff Manual respectively. Title Pages will be prepared in manuscript.

WAR DIARY
or
~~INTELLIGENCE SUMMARY~~

(Erase heading not required.)

MHOW M.G. SQDN.

Place	Date	Hour	Summary of Events and Information	Remarks and references to Appendices
CAMBLIGNEUL	1st Sep	–	In billets – training	
ROUELLECOURT	2	–	Marched to ROUELLECOURT.	
MONCHEL	3	–	Marched to MONCHEL	
NEUILLY LE DIEN	4	–	Marched to NEUILLY LE DIEN.	
"	5	–	Manoeuvres in St RIQUIER Training Area.	
"	6	–	" " "	
"	7	–	" " "	
"	8	–	" " "	
"	9	–	" " "	
"	10	–	" " "	
MEZEROLLES	11	–	Marched to MEZEROLLES.	
AUTHIEULE	12	–	" " AUTHIEULE	
QUERRIEU	13	–	" " Camp ½ mile N.E. of QUERRIEU	
MORLANCOURT	14	–	" at 4 a.m. to valley between MORLANCOURT and VILLE SOUS CORBIE.	
"	15	–	In readiness to move from above camp	
"	16	–	" " "	
"	17	–	" " "	
	18			
	19			
	20			
	21			
	22			
	23			
	24			

[illegible] Capt
for O.C. Mhow M.G. [illegible]
27.9.16

2449 Wt. W14957/M90 750,000 1/16 J.B.C. & A. Forms/C.2118/12.

Instructions regarding War Diaries and Intelligence Summaries are contained in F. S. Regs., Part II. and the Staff Manual respectively. Title Pages will be prepared in manuscript.

WAR DIARY
or
INTELLIGENCE SUMMARY

(Erase heading not required.)

Army Form C. 2118.

MHOW M.G. SQDN.

Place	Date	Hour	Summary of Events and Information	Remarks and references to Appendices
MONTAUBAN	25 Sep	–	4 guns to each Regt. Regts in various positions of readiness. Returned MORLANCOURT evening.	
MORLANCOURT	26	–	Marched towards BUSSY LES DAOURS, and back.	
BUSSY LES DAOURS	27	–	Marched to " " "	
LA CHAUSSEE	28	–	" " LA CHAUSSEE.	
VAUCHELLES	29	–	" " VAUCHELLES LES DOMART.	
PONCHES	30	–	" " PONCHES	

K. E. Whitworth Capt.
for O.C. Mhow M.G. Sqdn.
29.9.16

2449 Wt. W14957/M90 750,000 1/16 J.B.C. & A. Forms/C.2118/12.

SERIAL NO 321

Confidential

War Diary

of

Machine Gun Squadron, Mhow Cavalry Brigade

FROM 1st October 1916 TO ~~31st October~~ 30th November 1916.

Instructions regarding War Diaries and Intelligence Summaries are contained in F. S. Regs., Part II. and the Staff Manual respectively. Title Pages will be prepared in manuscript.

WAR DIARY
or
~~INTELLIGENCE SUMMARY~~
(Erase heading not required.)

Army Form C. 2118.

Place	Date	Hour	Summary of Events and Information	Remarks and references to Appendices
HAMEL LES PONCHES	1st Oct	—	Billet routine.	
LABROYE	2nd Oct	—	Marched to LABROYE	
"	3rd to 20th	—	Billet routine & Training.	
"	21st	—	The following transport left for COIGNEUX (XIII Corps Area) — 6 limbers, 1 Water cart, & 2 bicycles.	
"	22nd	—	M.G. Sqdn — strength, 4 B.Os., 2 I.Os., 58 B.O.R., 92 I.O.R. — left for COIGNEUX in lorries.	
COIGNEUX	23rd	—	M.G. Sqdn at COIGNEUX. Details at LABROYE.	
"	24	—	— " — — " —	
"	25	—	— " — — " —	
"	26	—	M.G. Sqdn relieved 76th Bde M.Gs in the SERRE sector. Details at LABROYE.	
TRENCHES	27	—	In trenches opposite SERRE. — " —	
"	28	—	— " — — " —	
"	29	—	— " — 1 B.O.R. wounded	
"	30	—	— " — 2 — " — 2 horses killed & 4 wounded by premature burst. Relieved during night 30/31 by 8th M.G. Coy. Returned to billets COIGNEUX.	
COIGNEUX	31	—	In billets COIGNEUX	

[illegible] Capt
for O.C. [illegible] M.G. Sqdn

14th Nov '16

2449 Wt. W14957/M90 750,000 1/16 J.B.C. & A. Forms/C.2118/12.

Confidential

WAR DIARY
of
MHOW Brigade M.G. Squadron
for
November 1916

Instructions regarding War Diaries and Intelligence Summaries are contained in F. S. Regs., Part II. and the Staff Manual respectively. Title Pages will be prepared in manuscript.

WAR DIARY
or
~~INTELLIGENCE~~ SUMMARY JCH
(Erase heading not required.)

Mhow M.G. Sqdn

Army Form C. 2118.

Place	Date	Hour	Summary of Events and Information	Remarks and references to Appendices
COINEUX	Nov 1st		Squadron remained in billets. Six Light Draught were received from Squadron detail under Corp Millar. Details marched from LABROYE to CAHON	
	Nov 2nd		Details marched to OFFREUX	
SERRE SECTOR OF TRENCHES	Nov 11th		The Squadron moved up to the trenches in SERRE Sector to their battle positions. The night 11/12th was spent in firing on enemy wire and communication trenches. Two guns were left in Reserve in COURCELLES under JEMADAR JAUMA KHAN	
	Nov 12th		The guns in the line took bearings & ranges on to their targets which they were to fire at during the attack on SERRE. During the night fire was kept up on the enemy's third & fourth lines and wire	
	Nov 13th		The Squadron took part in the attack on SERRE. Two guns under Sergt G?king were sent forward to JOHN COPSE with orders to cover the attack from the left flank and to engage any enemy machine or Lewis guns and riflemen who might appear in the front row of trench to oppose our infantry. The artillery preparation had been so thorough that there were no enemy in the front row trench & consequently this Section did not do much firing during the attack. They were unable to fire at the second row trench owing to the contours of the ground	

2449 Wt. W14957/M90 750,000 1/16 J.B.C. & A. Forms/C.2118/12.

Instructions regarding War Diaries and Intelligence Summaries are contained in F. S. Regs., Part II. and the Staff Manual respectively. Title Pages will be prepared in manuscript.

WAR DIARY
or
~~INTELLIGENCE SUMMARY~~ JCH
(Erase heading not required.)

Army Form C. 2118.

Mhow M.G. Sqdn

Place	Date	Hour	Summary of Events and Information	Remarks and references to Appendices
	Nov 13		The remaining 5 guns kept up a "barrage" to the left of the attack. This 'barrage' so prisoners stated had seriously interfered with the movement of troops which were unable to move across the open & had to keep to the trenches, thereby preventing an organised counter attack from the left flank. The attack failed owing to the state of the ground which was waterlogged. During the afternoon the Germans shelled all the trenches heavily but no casualties received from it. The night 13/14 was quiet and fire was [illegible] Lieuts. WINDHAM & WALTER were wounded and 3 other ranks	
	Nov 14		The enemy aircraft were active and flew over the trenches observing. Those that came within range were engaged by machine guns but none were brought down	
COINEUX	Nov 15		Was quiet no firing taking place. The Squadron was relieved in the afternoon ~~and~~ by 76th M.G. Coy & returned to billets at COINEX. The road by which the limbers had to go was shelled heavily but they all passed down it without loss. The men were sent down a further communication trench & were not shelled.	
	Nov 20		The Squadron marched to LA BELLE ~~E~~ JCH EGLISE station and entrained for OFFEUX at 10.30 Am. The train left at 2.30 pm	

2449 Wt. W14957/M90 750,000 1/16 J.B.C. & A. Forms/C.2118/12.

Instructions regarding War Diaries and Intelligence Summaries are contained in F. S. Regs., Part II. and the Staff Manual respectively. Title Pages will be prepared in manuscript.

WAR DIARY
or
~~INTELLIGENCE SUMMARY~~ J.C.H. Mhow M.G. Sqdn.

(Erase heading not required.)

Army Form C. 2118.

Place	Date	Hour	Summary of Events and Information	Remarks and references to Appendices
OFFEUX	Nov 21st		The squadron arrived at WOINCOURT at 1 AM. and detrained. They were met by led horses and marched to billets arriving there at 4.30 AM.	

J C Humphrey Capt.
Cmdg M.G. Sqdn.

2449 Wt. W14957/M90 750,000 1/16 J.B.C. & A. Forms/C.2118/12.

SERIAL NO. 321

Confidential War Diary

of

Mhow Machine Gun Squadron.

FROM 1st December 1916 TO 31st December 1916.

Army Form C. 2118.

Instructions regarding War Diaries and Intelligence Summaries are contained in F. S. Regs., Part II. and the Staff Manual respectively. Title Pages will be prepared in manuscript.

WAR DIARY
or
~~INTELLIGENCE SUMMARY~~

(Erase heading not required.)

Mhow Machine Gun Squadron

Place	Date	Hour	Summary of Events and Information	Remarks and references to Appendices
DEFEED X	Dec 1st to Dec 31st		Ordinary billet routine & training	

J C Humfrey Capt
Cmdg M G Sqn

2449 Wt. W14957/M90 750,000 1/16 J.B.C. & A. Forms/C.2118/12.

BEF

1 INDIAN CAV. DIV.

MHOW BDE

MHOW PIONEER ~~BDE~~ BN

1916 NOV to 1916 DEC

MHOW PIONEER BATTALION

WAR DIARY

~~or~~

~~INTELLIGENCE SUMMARY.~~

(*Erase heading not required.*)

Army Form C. 2118.

Instructions regarding War Diaries and Intelligence Summaries are contained in F. S. Regs., Part II. and the Staff Manual respectively. Title pages will be prepared in manuscript.

Place	Date	Hour	Summary of Events and Information	Remarks and references to Appendices
	20.11.16		Battalion Transport left billets and proceeded to MOYENNEVILLE.	
	21.11.16		Battalion Transport proceeded to PONT-REMY.	
			Battalion left billets, entrained with transport at PONT-REMY and detrained at ALBERT. In billets at ALBERT during night of 21/22-11-16	
FRICOURT FARM	22.11.16		Battalion and transport marched from ALBERT and encamped at FRICOURT FARM.	
"	23.11.16		Inniskilling Company proceeded to BAZENTIN-LE-PETIT.	
			2nd Lancers and 38th C.I. Horse companies working at hutting & draining at FRICOURT FARM.	
"	24.11.16		PARTY of 300, 2nd Lancers and 38th C.I. Horse, working on railway cutting near BAZENTIN-LE-GRAND. Other working parties as before.	
"	25.11.16		Working parties as on 24.11.16.	
"	26.11.16		Working parties as on 23.11.16.	
"	27.11.16		Party of 250, 2nd Lancers and 38th C.I. Horse, working on railway cutting near BAZENTIN-LE-GRANG. Other working parties as before.	
			CASUALTY:- 1 B.O. Rank, 6th Inniskilling Dragoons. Superficial shrapnel wound.	
"	28.11.16		Working parties as on 27.11.16.	
"	29.11.16		Working parties as on 28.11.16.	
"	30.11.16		Working parties as on 29.11.16.	

[signature] Lt. Col.
Mhow Pioneer Battn.

38th C.I. Horse.
D. Sqd.
31-12-16.

To
Staff Captain,
Mhow Cav. Bde.

Memo,

Encloses War Diary for December 1916 of MHOW PIONEER BATT: and 5 copies of Secret publication No. S.S. 111.C. forwarded with Bde Major's memo 4(b)16 B.M. dated 25-11-16.

W.W. Page Lt.
(Adjutant, Mhow Pioneer Batt.)

6 encl.

Army Form C. 2118.

Instructions regarding War Diaries and Intelligence Summaries are contained in F. S. Regs., Part II. and the Staff Manual respectively. Title pages will be prepared in manuscript.

WAR DIARY
or
~~INTELLIGENCE SUMMARY.~~

(*Erase heading not required.*)

Hour, Date, Place	Summary of Events and Information	Remarks and references to Appendices
FRICOURT FARM 1. 12. 16	Working parties as on 30. 11. 16, viz 250, 2nd Lancers and 38th C.I. Horse, on railway cutting near BAZENTIN-LE-GRAND, remainder of these Companies on hutting and draining at FRICOURT FARM. Inniskilling Company at BAZENTIN-LE-PETIT. Casualties: 2 B.O.R. (Inniskilling Dragoons), wounded by shrapnel.	
2. 12. 16.	Working parties as above, with exception of 1 Platoon from Inniskilling Coy. which returned from BAZENTIN-LE-PETIT to Camp at FRICOURT FARM on short relief.	
3. 12. 16.	No railway working party. Working party as usual at FRICOURT Camp. Casualties: 1 B.O.R. (Inniskilling Dns) slightly wounded by H.E shell.	
4. 12. 16	Working parties on railway and at Camp as usual. Fatigue party loading stores at G. Dump, near ALBERT. B. Platoon of Inniskilling Coy. returned to BAZENTIN-LE-PETIT. C Platoon of the same Coy. march to FRICOURT Camp on short relief. R.E. details at BAZENTIN relieved by details from Camp.	
5. 12. 16	Working parties as usual on Railway and at Camp as usual. G.O.C. 4th Cav. Div. visited the Camp. Casualties. 2 other ranks, R.E. wounded, one seriously, by H.E. shell.	

Instructions regarding War Diaries and Intelligence Summaries are contained in F. S. Regs., Part II. and the Staff Manual respectively. Title pages will be prepared in manuscript.

WAR DIARY
or
INTELLIGENCE SUMMARY.
(Erase heading not required.)

Army Form C. 2118.

Hour, Date, Place	Summary of Events and Information	Remarks and references to Appendices
FRICOURT FARM 6. 12. 16.	Working parties as usual on Railway and at Fricourt Camp. 'C' Platoon of Tunnelling Coy. returned to BAZENTIN. 'A' Platoon of the same Coy. marched to Camp on short relief. Lieut. G. S. C. Hearsey reported his arrival.	
7. 12. 16.	Working parties as usual on Railway and at Camp. Major R. G. M. PRICHARD, 38th C.I.H. Coy, Capt. O. A. DUKE and Lieut N. B. WILSON, 2nd Lancers Coy. proceeded to rejoin their units. MAJOR H. Y. SALKELD, 2nd Lancers, took over command of 2nd Lancers Coy.	
8. 12. 16	Working parties as usual on Railway and at FRICOURT Camp.	
9. 12. 16	Working parties as usual on Railway and at FRICOURT Camp. 'A' Platoon of Tunnelling Coy. returned to BAZENTIN. 'D' Platoon of the same Coy. marched to FRICOURT CAMP on short relief.	
10. 12. 16	No work on railway or at Camp.	

(73989) W4141—463. 400,000. 9/14. H.&J.Ltd. Forms/C. 2118/10.

Instructions regarding War Diaries and Intelligence Summaries are contained in F. S. Regs., Part II. and the Staff Manual respectively. Title pages will be prepared in manuscript.

WAR DIARY
or
INTELLIGENCE SUMMARY.
(Erase heading not required.)

Army Form C. 2118.

Hour, Date, Place	Summary of Events and Information	Remarks and references to Appendices
FRICOURT FARM.		
11. 12. 16	Advance party of SIALKOT PIONEER Battn. arrived at Fricourt Camp. Working parties as usual on Railway and at Fricourt Camp.	
12. 12. 16	No working parties employed, owing to weather conditions.	
13. 12. 16	Inniskilling Company moved back to FRICOURT Camp from BAZENTIN-LE-PETIT.	
	Working parties as usual at FRICOURT CAMP and on Railway. Advance party of Battn. proceeded to ALBERT.	
14. 12. 16.	Battalion proceeded to and entrained at ALBERT. Detrained at PONTREMY and returned to billets.	
	[illegible] Mhow Pioneer Battn.	

(73989) W4141—463. 400,000. 9/14. H.&J.Ltd. Forms/C. 2118/10.

B.E.F.

1 IND. CAV DIV

MHOW Bde

MHOW Bde MOBILE
VET SECT

1914 DEC ~~to~~
~~1916 MAY~~ 1916 DEC

NO Box

Serial No. 201.

121/4719

WAR DIARY

OF

Mobile Veterinary Section; Mhow Brigade.

From 19th December 1914 to 28th February 1915

DB
10/3.

Army Form C. 2118.

Instructions regarding War Diaries and Intelligence Summaries are contained in F. S. Regs., Part II, and the Staff Manual respectively. Title pages will be prepared in manuscript.

Mobile Veterinary Section [illegible] or Mhow Brigade

INTELLIGENCE SUMMARY.

(Erase heading not required.)

Hour, Date, Place.	Summary of Events and Information.	Remarks and references to Appendices.
7 p.m. Marseilles 19.12.14	Received orders to report at 9 a.m. next day at 55 Chartes Street	
20.12.14 Marseilles	Orders to mobilise & entrain at 3 p.m. next day. Deficient one man one deficient	The mobilization was very much hurried
21.12.14	Drew horses from remount depot & entrained	
22.12.14 In train	In train till midnight. Arrived Orleans	
23.12.14	Marched to La Corcotte camp	
24.12.14 Orleans	Nil	
25.12.14 –	Nil	
26.12.14 –	One man admitted hospital	
27.12.14 –	—	
28.12.14 –	Handed one section over to Capt Dudgeon AVC & marched to La Secke camp	
29.12.14 –	—	
30.12.14 –	—	
31.12.14 –	—	
1.1.15 –	Received orders to entrain for Blendecques the next day	
2.1.15 –	Entrained at Orleans	
3.1.15	In train one mule driver missed train	
4.1.15 Blarques	Detrained at Blendecques & marched to Blarques	
5.1.15 –	Reported to S.V.O. 21 C.D.	
6.1.15	Billets not satisfactory arranged to move.	

Army Form C. 2118.

Instructions regarding War Diaries and Intelligence Summaries are contained in F. S. Regs., Part II, and the Staff Manual respectively. Title pages will be prepared in manuscript.

WAR DIARY ~~or~~ INTELLIGENCE SUMMARY.

Mobile Veterinary Section Mhow Brigade

(*Erase heading not required.*)

Hour. Date. Place.		Summary of Events and Information.	Remarks and references to Appendices.
7.1.15	Clarques	Destroyed a charger belonging to Capt Fox R.E. Mule driver reported for duty. One horse admitted	
8.1.15	Guemonghem	Moved billets. Destroyed one horse	
9.1.15	—	Fetched veterinary stores from Aire	
10.1.15	—	Admitted five horses	
11.1.15	—	—	
12.1.15	—	—	
13.1.15	—	Attended meeting of V.Os of 2nd I.C.D.	
14.1.15	—	—	
15.1.15	—	Admitted three horses	
16.1.15	—	—	
17.1.15	—	Admitted one, destroyed one	
18.1.15	—	— four	
19.1.15	—	Inspected at Clarques with ADVS	
20.1.15	—	Conference of OCs Mobile Vety Sections	
21.1.15	—	Road march	
22.1.15	—	Admitted two	
23.1.15	—	— 3 Evacuated three	
24.1.15	—	— three — sixteen	
27.1.15	—	— one	
28.1.15	—	— three	
29.1.15	—	— two. An outbreak of mange in RE horses at Clarques.	

Instructions regarding War Diaries and Intelligence Summaries are contained in F. S. Regs., Part II, and the Staff Manual respectively. Title pages will be prepared in manuscript.

WAR DIARY

Mobile Veterinary Section *or* [illegible] Brigade

INTELLIGENCE SUMMARY.

(Erase heading not required.)

Army Form C. 2118.

Hour, Date, Place.		Summary of Events and Information.	Remarks and references to Appendices.
30.1.15	Glomenghem	Admitted ten horses & one mule. This has caused rather a crush in the stables. Some picketed in the open. One more case of mange in R.E. at Blaringhem	
31.1.15	—	Admitted two horses.	
1.2.15	—	Got 250 francs from Field ~~Cas~~ Cashier & opened an impress account. Admitted five horses & evacuated seventeen horses & one mule.	
2.2.15	—	Admitted three horses & destroyed one.	
3.2.15	—	Evacuated twenty four horses. Received 80 francs for pay of establishment.	
4.2.15	—	Admitted thirty two horses.	
5.2.15	—	Admitted eleven horses & evacuated three cases mange.	
6.2.15	—	Admitted five. Evacuated ~~4~~ nineteen horses.	
7.2.15	—	Admitted fifteen horses.	
8.2.15	—	Admitted twenty one horses.	
9.2.15	—	Nil.	
10.2.15	—	Evacuated forty four horses.	
11.2.15	—	Received six hundred francs from Field Cashier for impress account & paid for cart & harness. Also bought head collars & ropes.	
12.2.15	—	Went to Aire to try & buy nose bags. Could not get any.	

Army Form C. 2118.

Instructions regarding War Diaries and Intelligence Summaries are contained in F. S. Regs., Part II, and the Staff Manual respectively. Title pages will be prepared in manuscript.

WAR DIARY
Mobile Veterinary Section or Meerut Brigade
INTELLIGENCE SUMMARY.
(Erase heading not required.)

Hour, Date, Place.	Summary of Events and Information.	Remarks and references to Appendices.
13.2.15 Theroanne	Changed billets to Theroanne. Horses in sheds & men in cellars. Not so good as previous billets but the men are more alone, no houses near & this is better than having them in a village. One cart horse transferred for use in new cart	
14.2.15 —	Two batmen arrived	
15.2.15 —	Nil	
16.2.15 —	Nil	
17.2.15 —	Inspection of transport. One sowar went to hospital. ~~Evacuated~~ Eleven horses admitted.	
18.2.15 —	Evacuated ~~eleven horses &~~ thirteen horses & gave the NCO i/c of evacuating party strict orders to bring back all line gear unless he got a written order from an officer to leave it with the horses. This was necessary as all head collars had been retained in veterinary hospital & cannot be replaced. This causes great discontent with units sending horses for evacuation. Two sowars joined for duty.	
19.2.15	Nil	

Army Form C. 2118.

Instructions regarding War Diaries and Intelligence Summaries are contained in F. S. Regs., Part II, and the Staff Manual respectively. Title pages will be prepared in manuscript.

WAR DIARY

Mobile Veterinary Section or Mhow Brigade

INTELLIGENCE SUMMARY.

(Erase heading not required.)

Hour, Date, Place.	Summary of Events and Information.	Remarks and references to Appendices.
20.2.15 Thérouanne	Went on leave & left Capt Leeming AVC in charge	
21.2.15 –	Nil	
22.2.15 –	Nil	
23.2.15 –	Nil	
24.2.15 –	Four horses admitted	
25.2.15 –	Nil	
26.2.15 –	Returned to duty & took over from Capt Leeming AVC	
27.2.15 –	Route march to practice men & animals. Found that	
28.2.15 –	NCO of conducting party despatched on 18 instant had been ordered to leave head collars & ropes with horses.	

R C Matthews Capt AVC
Mobile Veterinary Section
Mhow Brigade

Serial No. 201.

WAR DIARY

OF

Mobile Veterinary Section, Mhow Brigade.

From 1st March 1915 to 31st March 1915.

Instructions regarding War Diaries and Intelligence Summaries are contained in F. S. Regs., Part II, and the Staff Manual respectively. Title pages will be prepared in manuscript.

WAR DIARY
or
INTELLIGENCE SUMMARY.

(*Erase heading not required.*)

Army Form C. 2118.

Mobile Vet Section
MHOW Brigade

Hour, Date, Place.	Summary of Events and Information.	Remarks and references to Appendices.
1.3.15 Therouanne	Went to Aire to get head collars. None to be got anywhere	
2.3.15 —	Went to Aire for Ordnance stores	
3.3.15 —	Admitted nine horses & evacuated eleven.	
4.3.15 —	Nil	
5.3.15 —	Inspected sick at Erecques & Mametz Admitted two horses	
6.3.15 —	~~Nil~~ N.C.O. & 4 of conducting party sent with evacuated horses on 3rd inst returned without headcollars or ropes	
7.3.15 —	Nil	
8.3.15 —	Admitted one Remount horse for damage to stable in Glominghem.	
9.3.15 —	Went to Aire & arranged to evacuate fourteen horses tomorrow. Came back & found that I will probably have to evacuate double this number. This may cause confusion. Two new [illegible] arrived for duty	
10.3.15 —	Evacuated twenty ~~[illegible]~~ + horses & one mule. four horses & three mules returned by Col [illegible] AVC. One horse & three mules returned to their units. This left four on hand. One mule & three horses sent to section to take for evacuation. Thus six horses & one mule remain with section. This was most inconvenient	+ twenty three horses & one mule evacuated

Instructions regarding War Diaries and Intelligence Summaries are contained in F. S. Regs., Part II, and the Staff Manual respectively. Title pages will be prepared in manuscript.

WAR DIARY
or
INTELLIGENCE SUMMARY.
(Erase heading not required.)

Army Form C. 2118.

Mobile Vet. Section
MHOW Brigade

Hour. Date. Place.	Summary of Events and Information.	Remarks and references to Appendices.
1.3.15 Thiennes	Went to Aire to get head collars. None to be got anywhere	
2.3.15 "	Went to Aire for Ordnance stores	
3.3.15 "	Admitted nine horses & evacuated eleven	
4.3.15 "	Nil	
5.3.15 "	Inspected sick at Enquin & Mametz Admitted two horses	
6.3.15 "	NCO. of conducting party sent with evacuated horses on 3rd instant returned without head collars or ropes	
7.3.15 "	Nil	
8.3.15 "	Admitted one. Received claim for damage to stable at Glomenghem	
9.3.15 "	Went to AIRE & arranged to evacuate further horses tomorrow came back & found that I will probably have to evacuate double this number. This may cause confusion. Two new shoers arrived for duty	
10.3.15 "	Evacuated twenty three horses & one mule four horses & three mules returned by Col Essex AVC. One horse & three mules returned to their units this left four horses on hand. One mule & three horses sent to section too late for evacuation. Thus six horses & one mule remain with section. This was most inconvenient.	

Army Form C. 2118.

Mobile Vet Section
MHOW Brigade

Instructions regarding War Diaries and Intelligence Summaries are contained in F. S. Regs., Part II, and the Staff Manual respectively. Title pages will be prepared in manuscript.

WAR DIARY
or
INTELLIGENCE SUMMARY.

(*Erase heading not required.*)

Hour. Date, Place.	Summary of Events and Information.	Remarks and references to Appendices.
11.3.15 ~~[illegible]~~ ~~[illegible]~~ MARLES	[illegible] to ~~[illegible]~~ MARLES march about 15 miles. [illegible] came along [illegible] Evacuated [illegible] Admitted [illegible] 2nd Lancers	
12.3.15 MARLES	Admitted one horse 2 Lancers. Remained all day at MARLES	
13.3.15 MARLES	One sergeant one corporal one shoeing smith & eight men arrived for duty. Billeted them in a colliery house.	
14.3.15 ESTREE BLANCHE	Orders arrived at 3 p.m. & marched at six p.m. to ~~FLA~~ ~~FLÉCHINELT~~ FLÉCHINELLE main at ~~Es~~ ESTREE BLANCHE about 15 miles arrived at midnight. Had great difficulty in finding billets	
15.3.15 ESTREE BLANCHE	Remained all day at FLÉCHINELLE [illegible] [illegible] [illegible] [illegible] Some of the sick horses show signs of fatigue after the march of last night.	
16.3.15 ESTRE Blanche	Arranged to evacuate horses tomorrow ~~[illegible]~~ Checked all hospital stores. Duffadar [illegible] Singh admitted to hospital	

Instructions regarding War Diaries and Intelligence Summaries are contained in F. S. Regs., Part II, and the Staff Manual respectively. Title pages will be prepared in manuscript.

WAR DIARY

or

INTELLIGENCE SUMMARY.

(Erase heading not required.)

Army Form C. 2118.

Hour, Date, Place.	Summary of Events and Information.	Remarks and references to Appendices.
1.3.15 Therouanne	Went to Aire to get head collars. None to be got anywhere	
2.3.15 —	Went to Aire for dressing stores	
3.3.15 —	Admitted nine horses & evacuated eleven.	
4.3.15 —	Nil	
5.3.15 —	Inspected sick at Brecques & Mametz Admitted two horses	
6.3.15 —	~~Nil~~ N.C.O. & 4 of Conducting Party sent with evacuated horses on 3rd inst returned without headcollars or ropes	
7.3.15 —	Nil	
8.3.15 —	Admitted one. Received claim for damage to stable in Glomenghem.	
9.3.15 —	Went to Aire & arranged to evacuate fourteen horses tomorrow. Came back & found that I will probably have to evacuate double this number. This may cause confusion. Two new sowars arrived for duty	
10.3.15 —	Evacuated twenty ~~eight~~+ horses & one mule. Four horses & three mules returned by Col Essex AVC. One horse & three mules returned to their units. This left four on hand. One mule & three horses sent to section too late for evacuation. Thus six horses & one mule remain with section. This was most inconvenient	+ twenty three horses & one mule evacuated

Army Form C. 2118.

WAR DIARY

or

INTELLIGENCE SUMMARY.

(*Erase heading not required.*)

Instructions regarding War Diaries and Intelligence Summaries are contained in F. S. Regs., Part II, and the Staff Manual respectively. Title pages will be prepared in manuscript.

Hour, Date, Place.	Summary of Events and Information.	Remarks and references to Appendices.
11.3.15 ~~Lozinghem~~ ~~Lozinghem~~ MARLES	Turned out at 12.15 a.m. & marched at half past three to ~~MARLES~~ MARLES. March about 15 miles. Lame horses came along fairly well. Evacuated one to its unit. Admitted two 2nd Lancers	
12.3.15 MARLES	Admitted one horse 2 Lancers. Remained all day at MARLES.	
13.3.15 MARLES	One sergeant one corporal one shoeing smith & eight men arrived for duty. Billeted them in a colliery house.	
14.3.15 ESTREE BLANCHE	Orders arrived at 3 p.m. & marched at six p.m. to ~~FLA FLECHINELL~~ FLECHINELLE mine at ~~E~~ ESTREE BLANCHE about 15 miles arrived at midnight. Had great difficulty in finding billets	
15.3.15 ESTREE BLANCHE	Remained all day at FLECHINELLE mine. Received orders to be ready to move at two hours notice. Some of the sick horses show signs of fatigue after the march of last night.	
16.3.15 ESTRE Blanche	Arranged to evacuate horses tomorrow. ~~Chegg~~ Checked all hospital stores. Duffadar Channa Singh admitted to hospital	

Instructions regarding War Diaries and Intelligence Summaries are contained in F. S. Regs., Part II, and the Staff Manual respectively. Title pages will be prepared in manuscript.

WAR DIARY

or

INTELLIGENCE SUMMARY.

(*Erase heading not required.*)

Army Form C. 2118.

Hour. Date. Place.	Summary of Events and Information.	Remarks and references to Appendices.
17.3.15 ESTRE BLANCHE	Evacuated 15 horses & 2 mules to Hazebrouck & one horse to lame to entrain to Mobile Vet Section Secunderabad Brigade. Received a notice that Brigade move at 8 a.m. tomorrow morning	
18.3.15 LE ROMS	Marched at 8 a.m to ~~LE ROM~~ LE RONS about 9 miles. Got into good billets. Horses in sheds. Admitted one case from 6th Dragoons. One mule driver kicked by a mule & sent to hospital	
19.3.15 LE RONS	Bought three hundred kilos of coal from Mr TARTAR at BLENDECQUES & seventy six kilos of bedding straw from Mr BEAUVOIS, ROND. This latter is another name for LE RONS. Map is said by the local inhabitants to be spelt wrong. Admitted two horses. Was absent all the morning attending to RE 2nd Division.	
20.3.15 LE RONS	The following is a list of billets section has occupied CLARQUES Arrived 2.1.15 & left 8.1.15 1 officer ~~in~~ Mr VANBREMERSCH's house 1 Interpreter Mdm Vve LORIDAN 13 Natives in a shed Mr M LORIDAN GLOMENGHEM arrived 8.1.15 left 13.2.15 1 officer Mr DEBOMY 1 Interpreter Mr MASSE-GOZET 6 Natives Mr ~~M~~ LEGRAND-DARCY 7 Natives Mr MASSE-DELAIRE	

Army Form C. 2118.

Instructions regarding War Diaries and Intelligence Summaries are contained in F. S. Regs., Part II, and the Staff Manual respectively. Title pages will be prepared in manuscript.

WAR DIARY

or

INTELLIGENCE SUMMARY.

(Erase heading not required.)

Hour. Date, Place.	Summary of Events and Information.	Remarks and references to Appendices.
20.3.15 LE RONS	S^T AUGUSTINE arrived 13.2.15 left 11.3.15	
	1 Officer & 1 Interpreter Mr E CANLER	
	15 Natives Mr DE GOURNAY	
	2 Europeans 14.2.15 to 11.3.15 Mr DELAYEN-DUBOIS	
	MARLES-LES-MINES arrived 11.3.15 left 14.3.15	
	{1 Officer Mr GOURDIN	
	{1 Interpreter EPICERIE du NORD	
	11 British from 13.3.15 to 14.3.15 residing in an empty house belonging to the colliery company	
	FLECHINELLE arrived 14.3.15 left 18.3.15	
	1 Officer Mr MERCIER	
	1 Interpreter Mr DENIS	
	1 Sergeant Mr LAVERSIN	
	17 Natives Colliery office	
	10 British In an outhouse near camp	
	LE RONS arrived 19.3.15	
	1 Officer Mr BEAUVOIS	
	1 Interpreter Mr BEAUVOIS	
	1 Sergeant Mme THOMAS	
	15 Natives & 10 British } Mr GREBERT	
	Admitted three cases Central India Horse. Gave full instructions to dressers.	

Army Form C. 2118.

Instructions regarding War Diaries and Intelligence Summaries are contained in F. S. Regs., Part II, and the Staff Manual respectively. Title pages will be prepared in manuscript.

WAR DIARY
or
INTELLIGENCE SUMMARY.

(Erase heading not required.)

Hour. Date, Place.	Summary of Events and Information.	Remarks and references to Appendices.
21.3.15 LE RONS	Admitted two cases.	
22.3.15 LE RONS	Handed over veterinary charge of 2 Divisional RE to Capt PORTEOUS AVC. Admitted five cases.	
23.3.15 LE RONS	Returned one horse cured to 2nd Lancers. Admitted one. Drew four hundred francs for imprest account & four hundred for pay of men. Paid establishment British only. Indians did not want money. One sick shock driver returned to duty	
24.3.15 LE RONS	Nil	
25.3.15 LE RONS	Admitted one case	
26.3.15 LE RONS	Admitted one case	
27.3.15 LE RONS	Admitted one case Inspection by ADVS, 2nd Indian Cavalry Division	
28.3.15 LE RONS	Nil	
29.3.15 LE RONS	Admitted one case. Inspection transport.	
30.3.15 LE RONS	Inspection by Col Essex AVC	
31.3.15 LE RONS	Evacuated six cases Admitted one.	

Instructions regarding War Diaries and Intelligence Summaries are contained in F. S. Regs., Part II, and the Staff Manual respectively. Title pages will be prepared in manuscript.

WAR DIARY

or

INTELLIGENCE SUMMARY.

(Erase heading not required.)

Army Form C. 2118.

Mobile Vet. Section
[illegible] Brigade

Hour. Date. Place.	Summary of Events and Information.	Remarks and references to Appendices.
3	MARLES	
MARLES		
12 3 15 MARLES	[illegible] MARLES	
13 3 15 MARLES	[illegible]	
14 3 15 ESTREE BLANCHE	[illegible] ~~LA FLÉCHINELLE~~ FLÉCHINELLE [illegible] ESTREE BLANCHE [illegible]	
15 3 15 ESTREE BLANCHE	[illegible] FLÉCHINELLE [illegible]	
16 3 15 ESTREE Blanche	[illegible]	

Instructions regarding War Diaries and Intelligence Summaries are contained in F. S. Regs., Part II, and the Staff Manual respectively. Title pages will be prepared in manuscript.

WAR DIARY
or
INTELLIGENCE SUMMARY.
(*Erase heading not required.*)

Army Form C. 2118.

Mobile Vet Section
MHOW Brigade

Hour, Date, Place.	Summary of Events and Information.	Remarks and references to Appendices.
17.3.15 ESTRE BLANCHE	Evacuated 15 horses & 2 mules to Boulogne & one horse to lame to entrain to Mobile Vet Section Secunderabad Brigade. Received a notice that Brigade move at 8 a.m. tomorrow morning	
18.3.15 LE RONS	Marched at 8 a.m. to ~~LE RONS~~ LE RONS about 9 miles got into good billets. Horses in sheds. Admitted one case from 6th Dragoons. [illegible]	
19.3.15 LE RONS	Bought three hundred kilos of coal from Mr TARTAR at BLENDECQUES & seventy six kilos of bedding straw from Mr BEAUVOIS, ROND. The latter is another name for LE RONS. Map is said by the local inhabitants to be spelt wrong. Admitted two horses. Was absent all the morning attending to RE 2nd Division.	
20.3.15 LE RONS	The following is a list of billets section has occupied CLARQUES Arrived 4.1.15 & left 8.1.15 1 Officer in Mr VANBREMERSCH'S house 1 Interpreter Mdm Vve LORIDAN 13 Natives in a shed Mr M LORIDAN GLOMENGHEM arrived 8.1.15 left 13.2.15 1 Officer Mr DEBOMY 1 Interpreter Mr MASSE-GOZET 5 Natives Mr ~~M~~ LEGRAND-DARCY 7 Natives Mr MASSE-DELAIRE	

Instructions regarding War Diaries and Intelligence Summaries are contained in F. S. Regs., Part II, and the Staff Manual respectively. Title pages will be prepared in manuscript.

WAR DIARY

or

INTELLIGENCE SUMMARY.

(Erase heading not required.)

Army Form C. 2118.

Mobile Vet Section
MHOW Brigade

Hour. Date. Place.	Summary of Events and Information.	Remarks and references to Appendices.
17.3.15 ESTRE BLANCHE	Evacuated 15 horses & 2 mules [illegible] & one horse [illegible] Mobile Vet Station [illegible] Brigade. [illegible] Brigade [illegible] 8 a.m. tomorrow morning	
18.3.15 LE RONS	[illegible] LE RONS [illegible] One mule [illegible] broken leg & mule & sent to hospital	
19.3.15 LE RONS	[illegible] TARTAR [illegible] BLENDECQUES [illegible] RONQ [illegible] LE RONS [illegible]	
20.3.15 LE RONS	[illegible] following is a list of billets [illegible]	
	CLARQUES arrived 8.1.15 – left 8.1.15	
	1 Officer Mr VANBREMERSCH'S [illegible]	
	1 Interpreter Mdm Vve LORIDAN	
	13 [illegible] Mr M LORIDAN	
	GLOMENGHEM arrived 8.1.15 left 13.2.15	
	1 Officer Mr DE BOMY	
	1 Interpreter Mr MASSE-GOZET	
	6 [illegible] Mr M LEGRAND-DARCY	
	7 [illegible] Mr MASSE-DELAIRE	

Instructions regarding War Diaries and Intelligence Summaries are contained in F. S. Regs., Part II, and the Staff Manual respectively. Title pages will be prepared in manuscript.

WAR DIARY
or
INTELLIGENCE SUMMARY.
(Erase heading not required.)

Army Form C. 2118.

Mobile Vet. Section
MHOW Brigade

Hour, Date, Place.	Summary of Events and Information.	Remarks and references to Appendices.
20.3.15 LE RONS	St AUGUSTINE arrived 13.2.15 left 11.3.15 1 Officer & 1 Interpreter Mme E CANLER 15 Natives Mr DE GOURNAY 2 Europeans 14.2.15 to 11.3.15 Mme DELAYEN-DUBOIS MARLES-LES-MINES arrived 11.3.15 left 14.3.15 1 Officer Mr GOURDIN 1 Interpreter EPICERIE du NORD 11 British from 13.3.15 to 14.3.15 on duty in an empty house belonging to the colliery company FLECHINELLE arrived 14.3.15 left 18.3.15 1 Officer Mr MERCIER 1 Interpreter Mr DENIS 1 Sergeant Mr LAVERSIN 17 Natives Colliery office 10 British In an outhouse near camp LE RONS arrived 19.3.15 1 Officer Mr BEAUVOIS 1 Interpreter Mr BEAUVOIS 1 Sergeant Mdm THOMAS 15 Natives & 10 British Mr GREBERT Admitted three cases Central India Horse. Gave full instructions to dressers.	

Instructions regarding War Diaries and Intelligence Summaries are contained in F. S. Regs., Part II, and the Staff Manual respectively. Title pages will be prepared in manuscript.

WAR DIARY
or
INTELLIGENCE SUMMARY.

(*Erase heading not required.*)

Army Form C. 2118.

Mobile Vet Section
MHOW Brigade

Hour. Date, Place.	Summary of Events and Information.	Remarks and references to Appendices.
10 3 15 LE RONS	St AUGUSTINE arrived 13 2 15 left 11 3 15	
	1 Officer 1 Interpreter Mme E CANLER	
	15 British Mr DE GOURNAY	
	2 Europeans 14 2 15 to 11 3 15 Mme DELAYEN-DUBOIS	
	MARLES-LES-MINES arrived 11 3 15 left 14 3 15	
	1 Officer Mr GOURDIN	
	{ 1 Interpreter EPICERIE AU NORD	
	11 British from 13 3 15 – 14 3 15 [illegible]	
	[illegible]	
	FLECHINELLE arrived 14 3 15 left 17 3 15	
	1 Officer Mr MERCIER	
	1 Interpreter Mme DENIS	
	1 Sergeant Mr LAVERSIN	
	1 [illegible] [illegible]	
	10 British [illegible]	
	LE RONS arrived 17 3 15	
	1 Officer Mr BEAUVOIS	
	1 Interpreter Mr BEAUVOIS	
	1 Sergeant Mme THOMAS	
	15 Natives } Mr GREBERT	
	10 British }	
	[illegible]	
	[illegible].	

Army Form C. 2118.

WAR DIARY
or
INTELLIGENCE SUMMARY.
(Erase heading not required.)

Instructions regarding War Diaries and Intelligence Summaries are contained in F. S. Regs., Part II, and the Staff Manual respectively. Title pages will be prepared in manuscript.

Mobile Vet Section
MHOW Brigade

Hour, Date, Place.	Summary of Events and Information.	Remarks and references to Appendices.
21.3.15 LE RONS	Admitted two cases.	
22.3.15 LE RONS	Handed over veterinary charge of 2 Divisional RE to Capt PORTEOUS AVC. Admitted five cases.	
23.3.15 LE RONS	Returned one horse cured to 2nd Lancers. Admitted one. Drew four remount forms for compass account & four remounts for pay of men. Paid establishment British only. Indians had not received money. One sick whole drawn returned to unity	
24.3.15 LE RONS	Nil	
25.3.15 LE RONS	Admitted one case	
26.3.15 LE RONS	Admitted one case	
27.3.15 LE RONS	Admitted one case. Inspection by ADVS, 2nd Indian Cavalry Division	
28.3.15 LE RONS	Nil	
29.3.15 LE RONS	Admitted one case. Inspection Brigadier.	
30.3.15 LE RONS	Inspection by Lt Essex AVC	
31.3.15 LE RONS	Evacuated six cases. Admitted one.	

Instructions regarding War Diaries and Intelligence Summaries are contained in F. S. Regs., Part II, and the Staff Manual respectively. Title pages will be prepared in manuscript.

WAR DIARY

or

INTELLIGENCE SUMMARY.

(Erase heading not required.)

Army Form C. 2118.

Mobile Vet Section
[illegible] Bryade

Hour, Date, Place.	Summary of Events and Information.	Remarks and references to Appendices.
21.3.15 LE RONS	Admitted ten cases.	
22.3.15 LE RONS	Handed over veterinary charge of 2 Divisional RE to Capt PORTEOUS AVC. Admitted five cases.	
23.3.15 LE RONS	[illegible]	
24.3.15 LE RONS	Nil	
25.3.15 LE RONS	Admitted one case.	
26.3.15 LE RONS	Admitted one case.	
27.3.15 LE RONS	Admitted one case [illegible] ADVS [illegible]	
[illegible] RONS	[illegible]	
[illegible] RONS	[illegible]	
[illegible]	[illegible]	

Army Form C. 2118.

Instructions regarding War Diaries and Intelligence Summaries are contained in F. S. Regs., Part II, and the Staff Manual respectively. Title pages will be prepared in manuscript.

WAR DIARY
or
INTELLIGENCE SUMMARY.

Mobile Veterinary Section

(Erase heading not required.) MHOW Brigade

Hour, Date, Place.	Summary of Events and Information.	Remarks and references to Appendices.
1.4.15 LE RONS	Admitted one case	
2.4.15 — —	Ordered to move billets but order cancelled. This is much better. Constant change of billets disheartens the men. Pt Carpenter admitted hospital	
3.4.15 — —	~~Muleteer~~ Muleteer No 1954 Kashim admitted hospital. Admitted two cases.	
4.4.15 — —	Admitted one case. Remaining under treatment nineteen.	Pt Simmonds ~~[illegible]~~ returned to duty
5.4.15 — —	Received orders in evening to change billets next day moving independently by 10.30 a.m. Discharged one charger (Major Fox)	
6.4.15 MAZINGHEM	Marched to MAZINGHEM at 10 a m & arrived about 3 pm. Evacuated eight sick at AIRE on the road. All the sick came along well. Ten remaining under treatment	
7.4.15 MAZINGHEM	Admitted two cases, discharged one. Eleven remain under treatment. Pt Simmonds sent sick.	
8.4.15 —	Admitted one case. Remaining under treatment twelve	
9.4.15 —	Admitted nine cases. Evacuated twelve. Five sick & seven cast. Remaining under treatment nine. Pt Simmonds returned to duty	
10.4.15 —	Admitted six. Under treatment fifteen	
11.4.15 —	Admitted thirteen. Discharged one. Remaining under treatment twenty seven. Of the cases admitted eleven were cases of fever. One line horse has fever also	

Army Form C. 2118.

Instructions regarding War Diaries and Intelligence Summaries are contained in F. S. Regs., Part II, and the Staff Manual respectively. Title pages will be prepared in manuscript.

WAR DIARY

or

INTELLIGENCE SUMMARY.

(Erase heading not required.) Mobile Vet Section MHOW Bde

Hour. Date, Place.	Summary of Events and Information.	Remarks and references to Appendices.
12.4.15 LE Rons	Marched to LE RONS ten miles. Admitted two, evacuated eight, left sick at MAZINGHEM twelve remaining nine. Received orders to march back to Mazinghem on 13 instant	
13.4.15 MAZINGHEM	Returned to Mazinghem horses in out houses. Readmitted the twelve sick left here ~~the~~ yesterday Remaining twenty one	
14.4.15 —	Admitted two. Discharged to units two. Remaining twenty one	
15.4.15 —	Admitted three. Discharged one cast horse to Capt Alcock S&T Corps Secunderabad Brigade to be Aired. Remaining twenty three	
16.4.15 —	~~Admitted four~~. One case pneumonia died Remaining ~~twenty one~~ twenty two	
17.4.15 —	Evacuated to Vet Ostruher Hoolignent eight Admitted four remaining eighteen	
18.4.15 —	Returned seven cases of fever cured Remaining eleven	
19.4.15 —	Admitted five cases. Pte Simmonds sent to hospital Remaining sixteen	
20.4.15 —	Admitted seven cases. Remaining twenty three.	
21.4.15 —	Admitted four case Evacuated eighteen	
22.4.15 —	Went to Ecques to bring in a case of fever left left behind by 6 Dragoons Admitted one case	
23.4.15 —	Admitted one case. Destroyed one	
24.4.15 —	Received orders to be ready to march at two hours notice, got this order at 11 a.m. Ordered at 4.15 p.m. to march to ~~Cas~~ CASSELL at 5 p.m. Distance 14 miles. Great confusion on road. Transport took wrong road. Arrived at Cassell about 4 a.m. No signs of brigade. Fed animals & took a motor to find Head Quarters Found them to be at ~~ZUYT~~ ZUYTPEENE. Marched there. Left four horses with Maxi at MAZINGHEM Admitted six	

Instructions regarding War Diaries and Intelligence Summaries are contained in F. S. Regs., Part II, and the Staff Manual respectively. Title pages will be prepared in manuscript.

WAR DIARY

or

INTELLIGENCE SUMMARY.

(Erase heading not required.)

Army Form C. 2118.

Hour. Date, Place.	Summary of Events and Information.	Remarks and references to Appendices.
25-4-15 ZUYTPEENE	Arrived about half past seven in the morning. Reported to ADVS 2nd Dvn that four horses had been left at MAZINGHEM. Also saw railway authorities & found that there is no R.T.O. nearer than HAZELBROUCK. Arranged to evacuate sick as soon as possible. Ordered to be in readiness to move at one hour's notice	
26-4-15 —	Remained at ZUYTPEENE. Evacuated nine horses to Aire. These left at 8 a m & the sergeant & party returned at 6 p m. Arranged with O.C. MVS, Secunderabad Brigade to receive any sick cases. Admitted seven remaining eleven.	
27-4-15 —	Arranged that horses can be evacuated from CAESTRE.	
28-4-15 —	Evacuated seven horses & one mule. Ordered to be ready to move at once. Arranged to leave ten horses at ZUYTPEENE & one at WAEMERS-CAPPEL which is too lame to be brought to Zuytpeene. No movement order was given. Remained ready to start.	
29-4-15 —	Received orders at 5 p m to march at 5 a m which was later altered to 6 a m. Arranged to evacuate five cases on 30th inst & to leave four behind.	
30-4-15 Watou. Belgium	Marched at 6 a m about 12 miles. Evacuated five sick under Cpl Carter at CAESTRE. Left four cases with maire. On march took over one lame mule. Arrived about noon	

Army Form C. 2118.

WAR DIARY

or

INTELLIGENCE SUMMARY.

(Erase heading not required.)

Mobile Veterinary Section
MHOW Brigade

Instructions regarding War Diaries and Intelligence Summaries are contained in F. S. Regs., Part II, and the Staff Manual respectively. Title pages will be prepared in manuscript.

Hour, Date, Place.	Summary of Events and Information.	Remarks and references to Appendices.
1.5.15 WATOU	Was sent by A.D.V.S. to see sick cases at last billets. Saw one case wound cornet at Waemers Cappel & destroyed it. Two cases pneumonia & one wound at OEHTEZEELE. One case lame NORDPEENE + One lame case N Bde RHA & one pneumonia three fever at ZUYTPEENE. Received orders at midnight to march at 7 a m to old billets at ZUYTPEENE. + care of Mr BOGAERT GASTON	
2.5.15 ZUYTPEENE	Marched at 7 a m & arrived about 11 a m. Sent a corporal to CAESTRE to arrange evacuation. This can be done tomorrow. Took over the case the N Bde RHA left at ZUYTPEENE. One pony 2nd Dr Signal Squadron left at Mr CLAYS HAUTKERQUE with pneumonia. One case Fever left by Lt Forrest AVC with Mr RENE VANLICHTEWELDE at HAUTKERQUE tail ticket number MW 161. Capt Leaning AVC left at farm VERSCHAVE in HAUTEKIRQUE two horses 6 Dragoons (one transport & one troop horse) & his own charger. Transport horse under-run frog, troop horse kick, charger fever.	
3.5.15 —	Evacuated 20 horses & one mule at CAESTRE. Muleteer Nº 1885 HASHMAT ALI sent to quarter guard of 6th Dragoons. Admitted three cases. Remaining eight.	
4.5.15 —	Received orders at 6.30 to march at 8.30 to new billeting area. Marched all night.	
5.5.15 NEDONCHELLE	Evacuated seven horses Mobile Vet Section Secunderabad en route. Arrived at NEDONCHELLE at about 10 a m. March about 26 miles. Horses fatigued but all fed well. New billets satisfactory.	

Army Form C. 2118.

WAR DIARY
or
INTELLIGENCE SUMMARY.
(Erase heading not required.)

Mobile Veterinary Section
III HOW Brigade

Instructions regarding War Diaries and Intelligence Summaries are contained in F. S. Regs., Part II, and the Staff Manual respectively. Title pages will be prepared in manuscript.

Hour. Date, Place.	Summary of Events and Information.	Remarks and references to Appendices.
6.5.15 NEDONCHELLE	Nil	
7.5.15 —	Court martial held on Muleteer Hashmat Ali	
8.5.15 —	No 1544 Driver Sardara sent to replace Hashmat Ali who is transferred.	
9.5.15 —	Evacuated five horses to MVS Secunderabad Div. Took over duties of Brigade Vet Officer to relieve Capt Leaning AVC	
10.5.15 —	Visited 6th Dragoons.	
11.5.15 —	4 suspicious cases of mange reported to be in contact with 6th Dragoon horses. Visited the place. Does not appear to be mange. In contact horses could not be seen. Isolated necessary cases	
12.5.15 —	Saw in contact horses all healthy. Not mange. Lieut Maynard AVC took over duties of Brigade Vet Officer.	
13.5.15 —	Nil	
14.5.15 —	Ptes Mooney & Murry awarded 14 days F.P. No 2 for drunkenness.	
15.5.15 —	Capt Leaning AVC returned from leave	
16.5.15 —	Lt Maynard returned to Divisional Troops. Brigade ordered to be ready to move at one & a half hours notice.	
17.5.15 —	A Echelon moved at 3-40 p.m. MV Section remained to collect the sick	
18.5.15 —	Arranged to move to LOZENGHEM tomorrow to join brigade.	
19.5.15 —	Marched eight miles to LOZENGHEM & was ordered back to NEDONCHELLE with brigade. One sick horse left at LOZENGHEM	
20.5.15 —	Nil	
21.5.15 —	Limbered wagon arrived to replace 2 mule carts, then & the two drivers & four mules returned to Brigade Transport Officer	

Instructions regarding War Diaries and Intelligence Summaries are contained in F. S. Regs., Part II, and the Staff Manual respectively. Title pages will be prepared in manuscript.

WAR DIARY
or
INTELLIGENCE SUMMARY.

(*Erase heading not required.*)

Army Form C. 2118.

Mobile Veterinary Section
MHOW Bgde

Hour, Date, Place.	Summary of Events and Information.	Remarks and references to Appendices.
	No 127 Pte SHEEN joined from Mobile Vety Section Meerut Bgde	
	No 1525 Driver HASTY, J & No 14720 Driver TURNER. C.W [illegible] of ASC Corps joined	
22.5.15 NEDONCHELLE	Nil	
23.5.15 —	Nil	
24.5.15 —	Nil	
25.5.15 —	Inspection by G.O.C. of transport. Arranged to have sides of wagon raised.	
26.5.15 —	Nil	
27.5.15 —	Wagon sent to AIRE for repair	
28.5.15 —	No 127 Pte Sheen AVC transferred to No 10 Vety Hospital Neufchatel	
29.5.15 —	Visited LIERES to see a sick horse left behind by N Bty RHA. Handed case over to Capt Taylor AVC No 3 Vety Section 2nd Division as his section is much nearer than this one	
30.5.15 —	Nil	
31.5.15 —	Nil	

121/5504

Serial No. 201

WAR DIARY

OF

Mobile Veternary Section; Mhow Brigade.

From 1st April 1915 To 30th April 1915

WAR DIARY
or
INTELLIGENCE SUMMARY.

MHOW Brigade

(Erase heading not required.)

Army Form C. 2118.

Instructions regarding War Diaries and Intelligence Summaries are contained in F. S. Regs., Part II, and the Staff Manual respectively. Title pages will be prepared in manuscript.

Hour, Date, Place.	Summary of Events and Information.	Remarks and references to Appendices.
1.4.15 LE BONS	Admitted one case	
2.4.15 — —	Ordered to move billets [illegible] excellent. This is much better. Constant change of billets disheartens the men. Pte Carpenter admitted hospital	
3.4.15 — —	~~Muleteer~~ Muleteer No 1954 Kashim admitted hospital. Admitted two cases.	
4.4.15 — —	Admitted one case. Remaining under treatment nineteen.	Pte Simmonds returned to duty
5.4.15 — —	Received orders in evening to change billets next day moving independently by 10.30 a.m. Discharged one charger (Major Fox)	
6.4.15 MAZINGHEM	Marched to MAZINGHEM at 10 a.m. & arrived about 3 p.m. Evacuated eight sick at AIRE on the road. All the sick came along well. Ten remaining under treatment	
7.4.15 MAZINGHEM	Admitted two cases, discharged one. Eleven remain under treatment. Pte Simmonds went sick.	
8.4.15 —	Admitted one case. Remaining under treatment twelve	
9.4.15 —	Admitted nine cases. Evacuated twelve. Five sick & seven cast. Remaining under treatment nine. Pte Simmonds returned to duty	
10.4.15 —	Admitted six. Under treatment fifteen	
11.4.15 —	Admitted thirteen. Destroyed one. Remaining under treatment twenty seven. Of the cases admitted eleven were cases of fever. One line horse has fever also	

Army Form C. 2118.

Instructions regarding War Diaries and Intelligence Summaries are contained in F. S. Regs., Part II, and the Staff Manual respectively. Title pages will be prepared in manuscript.

WAR DIARY
or
INTELLIGENCE SUMMARY.
(Erase heading not required.) Mobile Vet. Section MHOW Bde.

Hour, Date, Place.	Summary of Events and Information.	Remarks and references to Appendices.
12.4.15 LE RONS	Marched to LE RONS six miles. Admitted two, evacuated eight, left sick at MAZINGHEM twelve remaining nine. Received orders to march back to Mazinghem on 13th inst.	
13.4.15 MAZINGHEM	Returned to Mazinghem. Horses in out houses. Readmitted the twelve sick left here yesterday. Remaining twenty one	
14.4.15 —	Admitted two. Discharged to units two. Remaining twenty one	
15.4.15 —	Admitted three. Discharged one cast horse to Capt Hewitt S&T Corps Secunderabad Brigade to be tried. Remaining twenty three	
16.4.15 —	~~Admitted four~~ One case pneumonia died. Remaining ~~twenty six~~ twenty two	
17.4.15 —	Evacuated to Vet Hospital Abbeville eight. Admitted four remaining eighteen	
18.4.15 —	Returned seven cases of fever cured. Remaining eleven	
19.4.15 —	Admitted five cases. Pte Simmonds sent to hospital. Remaining sixteen	
20.4.15 —	Admitted seven cases. Remaining twenty three.	
21.4.15 —	Admitted four case. Evacuated eighteen	
22.4.15 —	Went to Ecques to bring in a case of fever left behind by 6 Dragoons. Admitted one case	
23.4.15 —	Admitted one case. Destroyed one	
24.4.15 —	Received orders to be ready to march at two hours notice, got this order at 11 a.m. Ordered at 4.15 p.m to march to ~~Cas~~ CASSELL at 5 p.m. Distance 14 miles. Great confusion on road. Transport both sides of road. Arrived at Cassell about 4 a.m. No signs of brigade. Fed animals & took a motor to find Head Quarters. Found them to be at ~~ZUY~~ ZUYTPEENE. Marched there. Left four horses with Maori at MAZINGHEM. Admitted six	

Army Form C. 2118.

Instructions regarding War Diaries and Intelligence Summaries are contained in F. S. Regs., Part II, and the Staff Manual respectively. Title pages will be prepared in manuscript.

WAR DIARY
or
INTELLIGENCE SUMMARY.

(Erase heading not required.)

Hour, Date, Place.	Summary of Events and Information.	Remarks and references to Appendices.
23-4-15 ZUYTPEENE	Arrived about half past seven in the morning. Reported to ADVS 2nd Div that four horses had been left at MAZINGHEM. Also saw railway authorities & found that there is no R.T.O. nearer than HAZELBROUCK. Arranged to evacuate sick as soon as possible. Ordered to be in readiness to move at one hour's notice	
26-4-15 —	Remained at ZUYTPEENE. Evacuated nine horses to Aire. Train left at 8 a.m. & the sergeant & party returned at 6 p.m. Arranged with O.C. MVS, Secunderabad Brigade to receive any sick cases. Admitted seven remaining eleven	
27-4-15 —	Arranged that horses can be evacuated from CAESTRE.	
28-4-15 —	Evacuated seven horses & one mule. Ordered to be ready to move at once. Arranged to leave ten horses at ZUYTPEENE & one at WAEMERS-CAPPEL which is too lame to be brought to Zuytpeene. No movement order was given. Remained ready to start.	
29-4-15 —	Received orders at 5 p.m. to march at 5 a.m. which was later altered to 6 a.m. Arranged to evacuate five cases on 30th inst & to leave four behind.	
30-4-15 Watou Belgium	Marched at 6 a.m. about 12 miles. Evacuated five sick under Cpl Carter at CAESTRE. Left four cases with Maire. On march took over one lame mule. Arrived about noon	

Serial No. 201

121/5799

WAR DIARY

OF

Mobile Veternary Section, Mhow Brigade.

From 1st May 1915 To 31st May 1915.

WAR DIARY
or
INTELLIGENCE SUMMARY.
(*Erase heading not required.*)

Army Form C. 2118.

Instructions regarding War Diaries and Intelligence Summaries are contained in F. S. Regs., Part II, and the Staff Manual respectively. Title pages will be prepared in manuscript.

Mobile Veterinary Section
MHOW Brigade

Hour. Date, Place.	Summary of Events and Information	Remarks and references to Appendices.
1.5.15 WATOU	Was sent by ADVS to see sick cases at their billets. Saw six cases [illegible] at Waemers Cappel & destroyed it. Two cases pneumonia & one [illegible] at OCHTEZEELE. One case lame NORDPEENE + One lame case NB[n] RHA & one pneumonia three fever at ZUYTPEENE. Received orders at midnight to march at 7 a m to old billets at ZUYTPEENE + care of Mr BOGAERT GASTON	
2.5.15 ZUYTPEENE	Marched at 7 a m & arrived about 11 a m. Sent a corporal to CAESTRE to arrange evacuation. This can be done tomorrow. Took over the case the NB[n] RHA left at ZUYTPEENE. One pony 2nd Dr Signal Squadron after Mr CLAYS HAUTKERQUE with pneumonia. One case Fever left by Lt Forrest AVC [illegible] Mr RENE VANLICHTEWELDE at HAUTKERQUE. Took ticket number MW 161. Capt Canning AVC left at farm VERSCHAVE in HAUTEKIRQUE two horses 6 Dragoons (one transport & one sick horse) & his own charger. Transport horse under-run frog, sick horse kick, charger fever.	
3.5.15 —	Evacuated 20 horses & one mule at CAESTRE. Muleteer No 1885 HASHMAT ALI sent to quarter guard of 6th Dragoons. Admitted three cases. Remaining eight.	
4.5.15 —	Received orders at 6-30 to march at 8-30 to new billeting area. Marched all night	
5.5.15 NEDONCHELLE	Evacuated seven horses Mobile Vet Section Secunderabad on route. Arrived at NEDONCHELLE at about 10 a m. March about 26 miles. Horses fatigued but all fed well. New billets satisfactory	

Instructions regarding War Diaries and Intelligence Summaries are contained in F. S. Regs., Part II, and the Staff Manual respectively. Title pages will be prepared in manuscript.

WAR DIARY
or
INTELLIGENCE SUMMARY.

(*Erase heading not required.*)

Army Form C. 2118.

[illegible] Veterinary Section [illegible] Brigade

Hour, Date, Place.	Summary of Events and Information.	Remarks and references to Appendices.
1.5.15 WATOU	Was sent to ADVS [illegible] at [illegible] [illegible] pneumonia [illegible] at CAESTRE [illegible] [illegible] N B[illegible] RHA [illegible] pneumonia [illegible] at ZUYTPEENE [illegible] at 7 a.m. [illegible] ZUYTPEENE [illegible] M. BOGAERT GASTON	[illegible] HARDIFEENE[+]
2.5.15 ZUYTPEENE	[illegible] at 7 a.m. [illegible] 11 a.m. [illegible] to CAESTRE [illegible] [illegible] N B[illegible] RHA at ZUYTPEENE [illegible] Signal Squadron [illegible] M. CLAYS HAUTKERQUE with pneumonia [illegible] [illegible] M. RENE VANLICHTEVELDE at HOUTKERQUE [illegible] VERSCHAVE [illegible] HAUTEKIRQUE [illegible] Transport horse [illegible] charger fever.	
3.5.15 —	Evacuated 20 horses [illegible] at CAESTRE [illegible] [illegible] [illegible]	
4.5.15 —	Received orders at 6.30 [illegible] marched at 7.30 to new billeting area [illegible]	
5.5.15 NEDONCHELLE	[illegible] at NEDONCHELLE at about 10 a.m. [illegible] 26 miles [illegible]	

WAR DIARY
or
INTELLIGENCE SUMMARY.

(Erase heading not required.)

Army Form C. 2118.

Mobile Veterinary Section
MHOW Brigade

Instructions regarding War Diaries and Intelligence Summaries are contained in F. S. Regs., Part II, and the Staff Manual respectively. Title pages will be prepared in manuscript.

Hour, Date, Place.	Summary of Events and Information.	Remarks and references to Appendices.
6.5.15 NEDONCHELLE	Nil	
7.5.15 —	Court martial held on Mule-leader Hashmat Ali	
8.5.15 —	No 1544 Driver Sardara sent to replace Hashmat Ali who is transferred.	
9.5.15 —	Evacuated five horses to MVS Secunderabad Div. Took over duties of Brigade Vet Officer to relieve Capt Leaning AVC	
10.5.15 —	Visited 6th Dragoons	
11.5.15 —	2 suspicious cases of mange reported to be in contact with 6 Dragoon horses. Visited the place. Does not appear to be mange. In contact horses could not be seen. Isolated necessary cases	
12.5.15 —	Saw in contact horses all healthy. Not mange. Lieut Maynard AVC took over duties of Brigade Vet Officer.	
13.5.15 —	Nil	
14.5.15 —	Ptes Morony & Murry awarded 14 days F.P. No 2 for drunkenness	
15.5.15 —	Capt Leaning AVC returned from leave	
16.5.15 —	Lt Maynard returned to Divisional Troops Brigade. Ordered to be ready to move at one & a half hours notice.	
17.5.15 —	A Echelon moved at 3.40 p.m. MV Section remained to collect the sick	
18.5.15 —	Arranged to move to LOZENGHEM tomorrow to join brigade.	
19.5.15 —	Marched eight miles to LOZENGHEM & was ordered back to NEDONCHELLE with brigade. One sick horse left at LOZENGHEM	
20.5.15 —	Nil	
21.5.15 —	Limbered wagon arrived to replace 2 mule carts, these & the two drivers & four mules returned to Brigade Transport Officer	

Instructions regarding War Diaries and Intelligence Summaries are contained in F. S. Regs., Part II, and the Staff Manual respectively. Title pages will be prepared in manuscript.

WAR DIARY
or
INTELLIGENCE SUMMARY.

(Erase heading not required.)

Army Form C. 2118.

[illegible] Mobile Veterinary Section [illegible] Brigade

Hour, Date, Place.	Summary of Events and Information.	Remarks and references to Appendices.
6 5 15 NEDONCHELLE	Nil	
	Court martial held on [illegible] Dost Mahomed Ali	
7 5 15 —	No 1544 Driver Sardara sent to replace Dost Mahomed Ali who is in [illegible]	
8 5 15 —	Evacuated five horses to MVS [illegible] took over duties of Brigade	
9 5 15 —	Vet Officer [illegible] Staff Learning AVC	
10 5 15 —	Visited 6th Dragoons	
11 5 15 —	Suspicious case of mange reported to be in contact with 6 Dragoon horses [illegible] [illegible] mange [illegible]	
	[illegible]	
12 5 15 —	[illegible] healthy [illegible] mange [illegible] Maynard AVC	
	took over duties of Brigade Vet Officer.	
13 5 15 —	Nil	
14 5 15 —	[illegible]	
15 5 15 —	[illegible] Learning AVC [illegible]	
16 5 15 —	[illegible] Maynard [illegible]	
	[illegible]	
17 5 15 —	[illegible]	
18 5 15 —	[illegible] to move to LOZENGHEM [illegible] Brigade.	
19 5 15 —	[illegible] LOZENGHEM [illegible] back to NEDONCHELLE	
20 5 15 —	with Brigade [illegible] LOZENGHEM	
	Nil	
21 5 15 —	[illegible]	
	[illegible]	

Instructions regarding War Diaries and Intelligence Summaries are contained in F. S. Regs., Part II, and the Staff Manual respectively. Title pages will be prepared in manuscript.

WAR DIARY
or
INTELLIGENCE SUMMARY.
(*Erase heading not required.*)

Army Form C. 2118.

Mobile Veterinary Section
MHOW Bde

Hour. Date, Place.	Summary of Events and Information.	Remarks and references to Appendices.
	No 127 Pte SHEEN joined from Mobile Vet Section Meerut Bde	
	No 1525 Driver HASTY. J & No 14720 Driver TURNER. C. W.	ASC of A S Corps
	joined	
22.5.15 MERVILLE	Nil	
23.5.15 —	Nil	
24.5.15 —	Nil	
25.5.15 —	Inspection by GOC of Transport. Arranged to have sides of wagon raised.	
26.5.15 —	Nil	
27.5.15 —	Wagon sent to AIRE for repair	
28.5.15 —	No 127 Pte Sheen AVC transferred to No 10 Vet Hospital Neufchatel	
29.5.15 —	Visited LIERES to see a sick horse left behind by III Bde RHA Handed case over to Capt Taylor AVC No 3 Vet Section 2nd Division as his section is much nearer than this one	
30.5.15 —	Nil	
31.5.15 —	Nil	

Instructions regarding War Diaries and Intelligence Summaries are contained in F. S. Regs., Part II, and the Staff Manual respectively. Title pages will be prepared in manuscript.

WAR DIARY
or
INTELLIGENCE SUMMARY.

(Erase heading not required.)

Army Form C. 2118.

Mobile Veterinary Section
MHCM Bde

Hour, Date, Place.	Summary of Events and Information.	Remarks and references to Appendices.
	No 127 Pte SHEEN joined from Mobile Vet Section Meerut Bde	
	No 1525 Driver HASTY. J. S No 14726 Driver TURNER. C. W.	[illegible] ASC attd
	joined	
22 5 15 [illegible]	Nil	
23 5 15 —	Nil	
24 5 15 —	Nil [illegible] of GOC [illegible] arranged to have [illegible] wagon [illegible];	
26 5 15 —	Nil	
27 5 15 —	[illegible]	
28 5 15 —	No 127 Pte Sheen AVC transferred to No 10 Vet [illegible] [illegible]	
29 5 15 —	Went to LIERES to see a sick horse left behind by III Bde RHA [illegible]	
	[illegible] over to Capt Taylor AVC No 3 Vet Section 2nd Division as this section	
	is much nearer than this one	
30 5 15 —	Nil	
31 5 15 —	Nil	

Serial No. 201.

121/6128

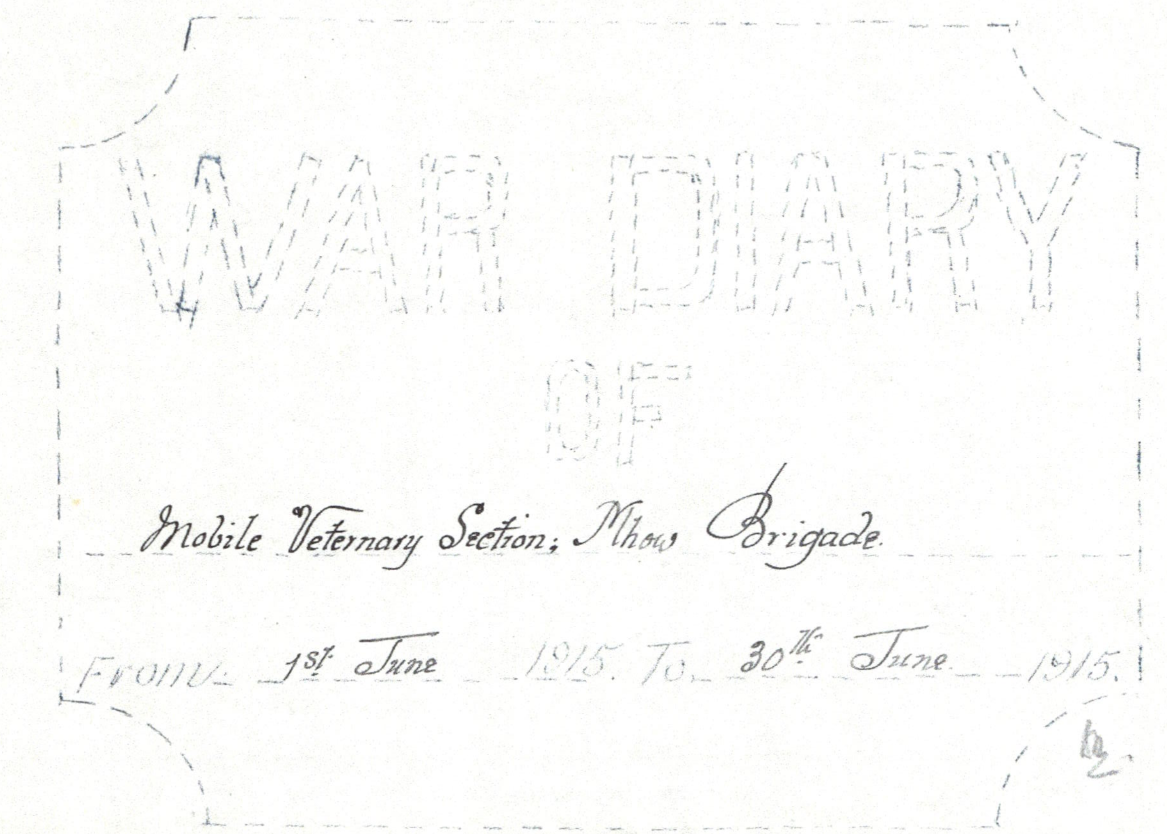

WAR DIARY

OF

Mobile Veternary Section; Mhow Brigade.

From 1st June 1915. To 30th June 1915.

Army Form C. 2118.

WAR DIARY
or
INTELLIGENCE SUMMARY.
(Erase heading not required.)

Mobile Veterinary Section
MHOW Brigade

Instructions regarding War Diaries and Intelligence Summaries are contained in F. S. Regs., Part II, and the Staff Manual respectively. Title pages will be prepared in manuscript.

Hour. Date, Place.	Summary of Events and Information.	Remarks and references to Appendices.
1.6.15 NEDONCHELLE	Suspected case of mange in 6th Dragoons. Consultation held with DVS. & A.D.V.S.	
2.6.15 —	Evacuated fifteen horses to Railhead Vet. Section at AIRE. Diagnosis of mange (sarcoptic) in 6th Dragoons confirmed. Arranged to evacuate sick from AIRE tomorrow.	
3.6.15 —	No. 1525 Pte Hasty ASC thrown from his mule & admitted sick to hospital. Evacuated 13 cases of mange at AIRE base came from 6 Dragoons & sent to Vet. Hospital ABBEVILLE	
4.6.15 —	Nil.	
5.6.15 —	Visited X Bn RHA & 38th Central India Horse	
6.6.15 —	Visited 2nd Lancers	
7.6.15 —	Nil	
8.6.15 —	Visited 38th Central India Horse	
9.6.15 —	Visited 2nd Lancers. One case suspicious of mange	
10.6.15 —	Examined 2 Lancers mange case but did not find parasite	
11.6.15 —	One case among sick suspicious of mange could not find parasite	
12.6.15 —	Nil	
13.6.15 —	Nil	
14.6.15 —	Inspected 2 Lancers & 38th Central India Horse with A.D.V.S., 2nd Division	

Army Form C. 2118.

Instructions regarding War Diaries and Intelligence Summaries are contained in F. S. Regs., Part II, and the Staff Manual respectively. Title pages will be prepared in manuscript.

WAR DIARY
or
INTELLIGENCE SUMMARY.
(Erase heading not required.)

Mobile Veterinary Section
MHOW Brigade

Hour, Date, Place.	Summary of Events and Information.	Remarks and references to Appendices.
15.6.15 NEDONCHELLE	Evacuated to LILLERS & one to railhead section at AIRE.	
	Inspection of remounts by OC Indian Cavalry Corps	
16.6.15 —	Nil	
17.6.15 —	Proceeded to LILLERS to arrange evacuation of horses	& to buy head collars
18.6.15 —	Visited 38 C.I.H. & evacuated from LILLERS. No T2/601	Dr W T COURTNEY A.S.C. joined for duty
19.6.15 —	Visited 2 Lancers	
20.6.15 —	No 2855 Corporal Barton AVC transferred to MV Section	Meerut Brigade
	Visited ADVS 2nd I.C.D. Handed over duties of Brigade	Vety Officer to
	Lieut Barton AVC. Arranged to evacuate 21 mange cases	6 Dragoons at LILLERS
	tomorrow.	
21.6.15 —	Evacuated 21 horses, mange cases, from LILLERS. No 216	Pte Carpenter sent on
	7 days leave.	
22.6.15 —	Routine work	
23.6.15 —	Evacuated one case mange MHOW Brigade Staff	from LILLERS
24.6.15 —	Nil	
25.6.15 —	Nil	
26.6.15 —	Arranged to evacuate mange cases from LILLERS	
27.6.15	Evacuation countermanded.	
28.6.15 —	Nil	
29.6.15 —	Evacuated six horses & one mule from LILLERS	
30.6.15 —	Nil	

Instructions regarding War Diaries and Intelligence Summaries are contained in F. S. Regs., Part II, and the Staff Manual respectively. Title pages will be prepared in manuscript.

WAR DIARY
or
INTELLIGENCE SUMMARY.
(Erase heading not required.)

Army Form C. 2118.

Mobile Veterinary Section
MHOW Brigade

Hour, Date, Place.		Summary of Events and Information.	Remarks and references to Appendices.
1.6.15	MEDONCHELLE	Suspected case of mange in 6th Dragoons. Consultation held with DVS & ADVS	
2.6.15	—	Evacuated sicken horses to Railhead Vet[y] Section at AIRE. Diagnosis of mange (sarcoptic) in 6th Dragoons confirmed. Arranged to evacuate sick from AIRE tomorrow.	
3.6.15	—	No 1525 Pte Hussey A S C thrown from his mule & admitted sick to hospital. Evacuated 13 cases of mange at AIRE. Cases came from 6 Dragoons & sent to Vet[y] Hospital ABBEVILLE	
4.6.15	—	Nil	
5.6.15	—	Visited X B[y] RHA & 38th Central India Horse	
6.6.15	—	Visited 2nd Lancers	
7.6.15	—	Nil	
8.6.15	—	Visited 38th Central India Horse	
9.6.15	—	Visited 2nd Lancers. One case suspicious of mange	
10.6.15	—	Examined 2 Lancers mange case but did not find parasite	
11.6.15	—	One case among horses sick suspicious of mange. Could not find parasite	
12.6.15	—	Nil	
13.6.15	—	Nil	
14.6.15	—	Inspected 2 Lancers & 38th Central India Horse with A.D.V.S., 2nd Division	

Instructions regarding War Diaries and Intelligence Summaries are contained in F. S. Regs., Part II, and the Staff Manual respectively. Title pages will be prepared in manuscript.

WAR DIARY
or
INTELLIGENCE SUMMARY.

(Erase heading not required.)

Army Form C. 2118.

[illegible] Veterinary Section
[illegible]

Hour, Date, Place.	Summary of Events and Information.	Remarks and references to Appendices.
1.6.15 [illegible]	[illegible] of mange in [illegible]	
2	DVS — ADVS	
2.6.15 —	Evacuated [illegible] to [illegible] Vet Section at AIRE	
	[illegible] of mange [illegible]	
	Evacuated [illegible] from AIRE [illegible]	
3.6.15 —	No 1525 [illegible] ASC [illegible] from [illegible]	
	[illegible] Evacuated 13 cases of mange at AIRE [illegible] came from	
	[illegible] & sent to Vet Hospital ABBEVILLE	
4.6.15 —	Nil	
5.6.15 —	Visited X Bty RHA & 38th Central India Horse	
6.6.15 —	Visited 2nd Lancers	
7.6.15 —	Nil	
8.6.15 —	Visited 38th Central India Horse	
9.6.15 —	Visited 2nd Lancers. One case suspicious of mange	
10.6.15 —	Examined 2 Lancers mange case but did not find parasite	
11.6.15 —	[illegible] case among [illegible] suspicious of mange [illegible]	
	[illegible]	
12.6.15 —	Nil	
13.6.15 —	Nil	
14.6.15 —	Inspected 2 Lancers & 38th Central India Horse with ADVS, 2nd Division	

Army Form C. 2118.

Instructions regarding War Diaries and Intelligence Summaries are contained in F. S. Regs., Part II, and the Staff Manual respectively. Title pages will be prepared in manuscript.

WAR DIARY
or
INTELLIGENCE SUMMARY.
(*Erase heading not required.*)

Mobile Veterinary Section
MHOW Brigade

Hour, Date, Place.	Summary of Events and Information.	Remarks and references to Appendices.
15.6.15 NEDONCHELLE	Evacuated to LILLERS & one to railhead [illegible] at AIRE. Inspection of remounts by O.C. Indian Cavalry Corps.	
16.6.15 —	Nil	
17.6.15 —	Proceeded to LILLERS to arrange evacuation of horses	& to buy head collars
18.6.15 —	Visited 38 C.I.H. — evacuated from LILLERS. No. I.2/601 [illegible]	Dr W T COURTNEY A.S.C. for duty
19.6.15 —	Visited 2 Lancers	
20.6.15 —	No. 2655 Corporal Barton A.V.C. transferred to M.V. Section. Visited A.D.V.S. 2 I.C.D. Handed over duties of Brigade Vet Officer to Lieut Barton A.V.C. Arranged to evacuate 21 mange cases 6 Dragoons at LILLERS tomorrow.	Meerut Brigade
21.6.15 —	Evacuated 21 horses, mange cases, from LILLERS. [illegible] McCarthy sent on 7 days leave.	
22.6.15 —	Routine work	
23.6.15 —	Evacuated one case mange MHOW Brigade Staff	from LILLERS
24.6.15 —	Nil	
25.6.15 —	Nil	
26.6.15 —	Arranged to evacuate mange cases from LILLERS	
27.6.15	Evacuation countermanded.	
28.6.15 —	Nil	
29.6.15 —	Evacuated six horses & one mule from LILLERS	
30.6.15 —	Nil	

Instructions regarding War Diaries and Intelligence Summaries are contained in F. S. Regs., Part II, and the Staff Manual respectively. Title pages will be prepared in manuscript.

WAR DIARY or INTELLIGENCE SUMMARY.

Mobile Veterinary Section MHOW Brigade

(Erase heading not required.)

Army Form C. 2118.

Hour, Date, Place.	Summary of Events and Information.	Remarks and references to Appendices.
15.6.15 MEDONCHELLE	Evacuated to LILLERS & one to railhead section at AIRE. Inspection of remounts by OC Indian Cavalry Corps.	
16.6.15 —	Nil	
17.6.15 —	Proceeded to LILLERS to arrange evacuation of horses	& to buy head collars
18.6.15 —	Visited 38 CIH & evacuated from LILLERS. No T2/601	Dr W T COURTNEY A.S.C. joined for duty
19.6.15 —	Visited 2 Lancers	
20.6.15 —	No 2855 Corporal Carlin AVC transferred to MV Section Meerut Brigade. Visited ADVS 2 ICD. Handed over duties of Brigade Vet Officer to Lieut Barton AVC. Arranged to evacuate 21 mange cases 6 Dragoons at LILLERS tomorrow.	
21.6.15 —	Evacuated 21 horses, mange cases, from LILLERS. No 216	Pte Carpenter went on 7 days leave.
22.6.15 —	Routine work	
23.6.15 —	Evacuated one case mange MHOW Brigade Staff	from LILLERS
24.6.15 —	Nil	
25.6.15 —	Nil	
26.6.15 —	Arranged to evacuate mange cases from LILLERS	
27.6.15	Evacuation countermanded.	
28.6.15 —	Nil	
29.6.15 —	Evacuated six horses & one mule from LILLERS	
30.6.15 —	Nil	

Serial No. 201

121/6502

WAR DIARY

OF

Veterinary Section Mhow Brigade.

FROM 1st July 1915 To 31st July 1915

Instructions regarding War Diaries and Intelligence Summaries are contained in F. S. Regs., Part II. and the Staff Manual respectively. Title pages will be prepared in manuscript.

WAR DIARY
or
INTELLIGENCE SUMMARY.
(Erase heading not required.)

Army Form C. 2118.

Veterinary Section
MHOW Brigade

Hour, Date, Place	Summary of Events and Information	Remarks and references to Appendices
1.7.15 NEDONCHELLE	Nil	
2.7.15 —	Nil	
3.7.15 —	Nil	
4.7.15 —	Went on leave & handed over to Lieut Barton AVC	
10.7.15 —	Returned from leave & ~~took over charge~~	
11.7.15 —	Took over charge	
12.7.15 —	Pte Lewis awarded 14 days field punishment No 2 for drunkenness	
13.7.15 —	Evacuated sick horses from LILLERS	
14.7.15 —	Nil	
15.7.15 —	Nil	
16.7.15 —	Made P.M. Examn of a cow the property of Mr LAURENT-CREPIN NEDONCHELLE that died. Death due to irritation of stomach.	
17.7.15 —	Nil	
18.7.15 —	Nil	
19.7.15 —	Evacuated from LILLERS	
20.7.15 —	Nil	
21.7.15 —	Nil	
22.7.15 —	Evacuated from LILLERS	
23.7.15 —	Nil	
24.7.15 —	Evacuated 28 horses & 2 mules from LILLERS	

(73989) W4141—463. 400,000. 9/14. H.&J.Ltd. Forms/C. 2118/10.

Instructions regarding War Diaries and Intelligence Summaries are contained in F. S. Regs., Part II. and the Staff Manual respectively. Title pages will be prepared in manuscript.

WAR DIARY
or
INTELLIGENCE SUMMARY.
(*Erase heading not required.*)

Army Form C. 2118.

Hour, Date, Place	Summary of Events and Information	Remarks and references to Appendices
25.7.15 NEDONCHELLE	Nil	
26.7.15 —	Nil	
27.7.15 —	Received orders late in afternoon to proceed to England	
28.7.15 —	Evacuated nineteen horses from LILLERS	
29.7.15 —	Proceeded to England.	
30.7.15 —	Report to Headquarters "Mhow Cavalry Brigade" & take over Mobile Veterinary Section. ~~&c.~~ Report to D.D.V.S. 1st Army & A.D.V.S. of Division	
31.7.15 —	Receive orders to move from NEDONCHELLE to neighbourhood of St. VAAST. Issue necessary instructions.	

R.G. Davis
Lieut. AVC

(73989) W4141—463. 400,000. 9/14. H.&J.Ltd. Forms/C. 2118/10.

Serial No. 201

Confidential

121/7286

War Diary

of

Mobile Veternary Section; Mhow Cavalry Brigade.

FROM 1st September 1915 TO 30th September 1915.

M.V.S. Lahore Cav. Bde.

Army Form C. 2118.

Instructions regarding War Diaries and Intelligence Summaries are contained in F. S. Regs., Part II. and the Staff Manual respectively. Title pages will be prepared in manuscript.

WAR DIARY
or
INTELLIGENCE SUMMARY.
(Erase heading not required.)

Hour, Date, Place	Summary of Events and Information	Remarks and references to Appendices
1/9/15 PICQUIGNY	Evacuate 7 horses Pte Murray	
2/9/15 "	Nothing to report	
3/9/15 "	— do	
4/9/15 "	— do — except one horse destroyed fracture of outer trochlea of femur	
5/9/15 "	— do	
6/9/15 "	— do —. L/c Duffadar Sudagar Khan, promoted to Duffadar.	
7/9/15 "	Evacuated 8 horses at Ailly, asked R.T.O. ABBEVILLE by letter to let men return by passenger. Visit from A.D.V.S.	
8/9/15 "	Pay establishment European. Receive 3 horses for evacuation	
9/9/15 "	Nothing to report	
10/9/15	— do —	
11/9/15	Evacuate 8 horses from AILLY sur SOMME.	
12/9/15	Receive instructions to move into 1st Divisional Area.	
13/9/15	Write A.D.V.S. with regard to smoke helmets (horses). Wire O/c Meerut M.V.S. to take 4 horses for evacuation. " B.V.O. that I cannot receive any more horses for evacuation. Orders countermanded. M.V.S. not to move with Brigade	
14/9/15	Receive 3 horses & 1 mule for evacuation. Sgt Ledwich & Pte Evcs gone on leave	
15/9/15	Evacuate 4 horses to Meerut M.V.S. at Longpré. A.D.V.S. calls for report re 3 horses of 2nd Lancers left at NEDONCHEL. Sowar Shib Singh admitted to Hospital, S. Bani Singh, 2nd Lancers detailed to take his place, though I did not ask for anyone R.L.Dawn	

(73989) W4141—463. 400,000. 9/14. H.&J.Ltd. Forms/C. 2118/10.

Instructions regarding War Diaries and Intelligence Summaries are contained in F. S. Regs., Part II. and the Staff Manual respectively. Title pages will be prepared in manuscript.

WAR DIARY
or
INTELLIGENCE SUMMARY.
(Erase heading not required.)

Army Form C. 2118.

Hour, Date, Place	Summary of Events and Information	Remarks and references to Appendices
15/9/15 (contd) PICQUIGNY	Visit from ADVS re shoeing & mats	
	Sixteen horses handed to me by O.C. Mob Vet Sect Lucknow Brigade again I am unable to get forage for them from Supplies.	
16/9/15 —do—	ADVS comes over to inspect the 16 horses 2 only are fit to be returned this I do, they are sent to 36th Lancers the rest have to be evacuated still short of forage.	
	Go to SIRANCOURT to see mare belonging to Mme Vignon, suffering from Pneumonia, consider it likely to die as they have it in much too confined a stable.	
	Visit 8th Hussars & bring away their A, 2000. go on to Headquarters at St PIERRE A GOUY to inform the Staff Captain that I may be made use of till Lieut Barton returns.	
	Receive 1 mule that fell down a cellar the day before, no one however claims it.	
17/9/15 —do—	Evacuate 7 horses & one mule to ABBEVILLE & ask for another truck. Supplies have now to be drawn at 10 a.m.	
	Visited by ADVS & new D.V.O. to arrange details of work	
18/9/15 —do—	Evacuate 6 horses to ABBEVILLE. Interpreter arrives from MHOW late AMBALA. M.V.S. & reports to me as permanently attached to M.V.S.	
	R J Daws	

(73989) W4141—463. 400,000. 9/14. H.&J.Ltd. Forms/C. 2118/10.

Instructions regarding War Diaries and Intelligence Summaries are contained in F. S. Regs., Part II. and the Staff Manual respectively. Title pages will be prepared in manuscript.

WAR DIARY
or
INTELLIGENCE SUMMARY.
(Erase heading not required.)

Army Form C. 2118.

Hour, Date, Place		Summary of Events and Information	Remarks and references to Appendices
19/9/15	PICQUIGNY	Proceed to MONTIGNY as instructed by ADVS. discover 2 horses instead of one both unfit to move at present.	
20/9/15	— do —	Nothing to report	
21/9/15	— do —	ADVS. instructions re evacuation of horses at LONGPRE, send + fetch the 2 horses from MONTIGNY, leave instructions as to settlement of claim.	
22/9/15	— do —	Evacuate 26 horses from LONGPRE, 2nd Cav Division moves except AMBALA Brigade, receive 23 more horses for evacuation, receive instructions to change billets + be prepared to move at 5.30pm on 23/9/15.	
23/9/15	— do —	Evacuate 31 horses from AILLY Sur SOMME, whilst away the B.V.O. sends in 8 more horses for evacuation, I consider this is not quite necessary & that they should have been sent in before, it is in my opinion exceeding his duty, as he must know it is impossible to evacuate & move at the same time	
~~24/9/15~~	~~— do —~~	Move off at 6 pm according to instructions pick up the Brigade at La Chausse with sick horses of 8th Hussars + 30th Lancers in my wake March via VIGNACOURT, CANAPLES to FIEFFES arriving about 9.30 pm	
24/9/15	FIEFFES — do —	Arrange & evacuate 16 horses from CANAPLES, detail Pte LEWIS to fetch a horse from BOURDON left by Field Troop. R.E. unable to travel all the way, instructions to be ready to move at once	

R.J. Davis

(73989) W4141—463. 400,000. 9/14. H.&J.Ltd. Forms/C. 2118/10.

Instructions regarding War Diaries and Intelligence Summaries are contained in F. S. Regs., Part II. and the Staff Manual respectively. Title pages will be prepared in manuscript.

Army Form C. 2118.

WAR DIARY
or
INTELLIGENCE SUMMARY.
(*Erase heading not required.*)

Hour, Date, Place	Summary of Events and Information	Remarks and references to Appendices
25/9/15 FIEFFES	Fetch horse from BOURDON & evacuate him from railhead at DOULLENS it is reported to me that 2 horses have been left at CANAPLES by Auxiliary Horse Transport, also wire received from D.D.V.S. to collect 1 horse from BOURDON 2 mules from HANGEST & one horse from WARLUS Detail Sergt Ledwith for latter duty and instruct him to proceed direct to ABBEVILLE. Further wire to say one horse at MONTIGNY this I expect to be a mistake as it is one of the 2 I have already collected & notified	
26/9/15 — do —	Detail Cpl Brown to proceed to MONTIGNY to discover if there is a horse there, none as I thought, I have already collected.	
27/9/15 — do —	Arrange truck & evacuate 3 horses from CANAPLES, & instruct Pte Murray to bring back Veterinary Stores. Draw 600 francs from Field Cashier for payment of Section	
28/9/15 — do —	Wire D.D.V.S. re horses collected & also write to him & A.D.V.S. Pay men. Harris charged with being drunk Pte Murray returns with information that Stores will be sent on	
29/9/15 — do —	Apply to Staff Capt. for severe punishment for Harris, he advise F.G.C.M. Make summary of evidence, it is returned with information that I have been attached to 8th Hussars for discipline, & that M.G.C. directs that Harris is to be brought before O.C. 8th Hussars & case dealt with summarily	

R.R.

Instructions regarding War Diaries and Intelligence Summaries are contained in F. S. Regs., Part II. and the Staff Manual respectively. Title pages will be prepared in manuscript.

WAR DIARY
or
INTELLIGENCE SUMMARY.
(Erase heading not required.)

Army Form C. 2118.

Hour, Date, Place	Summary of Events and Information	Remarks and references to Appendices
30/9/15 FIEFFES.	I go to Adjutant 8th Hussars and point out that this disciplinary attachment is most unusual, if not impossible, she advises me to see Staff Capt again I do and receive the explanation that it has been done for my benefit in those cases, in which I am unable to give a very severe punishment. I therefore return & punish Harris myself. Visit Lieut Ward at BERNAVILLE & tell him that I have requested ~~the~~ Staff Capt to make enquiries re changing the natives of the Section. Weather fine after a weeks rain. R. L. Davis Lieut AVC Comdg [illegible] Sec: Lahore Cav Bde	

(73989) W4141—463. 400,000. 9/14. H.&J.Ltd. Forms/C. 2118/10.

Serial No. 201

Confidential

121/7601

War Diary

of

Mobile Veterinary Section; Mhow Cavalry Brigade

FROM 1st October 1915 TO 31st October 1915.

Instructions regarding War Diaries and Intelligence Summaries are contained in F. S. Regs., Part II. and the Staff Manual respectively. Title pages will be prepared in manuscript.

WAR DIARY
or
INTELLIGENCE SUMMARY.
(*Erase heading not required.*)

Army Form C. 2118.

Hour, Date, Place	Summary of Events and Information	Remarks and references to Appendices
1/10/15 BIEFFES	Receive orders to rejoin Mhow Brigade at FROHEN LE GRAND. Move away at 2 reach FROHEN LE GRAND at 6pm Have to wait till about 8 p.m. when I then receive instructions to move on to BOUVAIN, the men & horses I put into a field as it is too dark to see or find any place	
2/10/15 BOUVAIN	Pick out a billet, put lines down fix up horses & men, visited by A.D.V.S. who points out several things to me, regret that I have not had time to fix everything perfectly as I only got into billet the same morning.	
3/10/15 "	Evacuate 8 horses at railhead DOULLENS, orders to get there before 2, well before 2 kept waiting as usual get back 3.30 pm	
4/10/15 "	Take over the Central India Horse 38th from Lieut Barton, inspect the sick thereof horses all hacked up, suggest to Brig Major they're getting over fatigued & not hard & fit as desirable A.D.V.S visits me again, One horse shot & buried	
5/10/15 "	Everything cleaned up, men included, for inspection by Col. Essell, who inspects addresses the men & is extremely complimentary about the Section.	
6/10/15 "	Inspect C.I.H. send away 11 horses for evacuation	
7/10/15 "	Evacuate 25 horses from DOULLENS 3/or Casting Inspect. C.I.H.	

O.C. Mobile (R.I.D.) Veterinary Section
Mhow Cavalry Brigade
1st Indian Cav. Division

(73989) W4141—463. 400,000. 9/14. H.&J.Ltd. Forms/C. 2118/10.

Instructions regarding War Diaries and Intelligence Summaries are contained in F. S. Regs., Part II. and the Staff Manual respectively. Title pages will be prepared in manuscript.

WAR DIARY
or
INTELLIGENCE SUMMARY.
(*Erase heading not required.*)

Army Form C. 2118.

Hour, Date, Place		Summary of Events and Information	Remarks and references to Appendices
8/10/15	BOUVAIN	Inspect. 38th C.I.H. nothing to report	
9/10/15	— do —	— do — — do — ADVS. visits me again	
10/10/15	— do —	Evacuate 8 horses from DOULLENS	
11/10/15	— do —	Nothing to report	
12/10/15	— do —	Pte Harris put back on the lines & applies for transfer, Pte Rippin also applies, Pte Monteith made cook, receive orders to march tomorrow to new billet at BERNEUIL	
13/10/15	— do —	Evacuate 10 horses from DOULLENS Ready to march at 10 am, kept waiting til 12.15 official time 11-15 reach BERNEUIL at 3 pm, bad billets all round & bad water for horses	
14/10/15	BERNEUIL	Get settled in billets	
15/10/15	— do —	Inspect. A. B. & D. squadrons C.I.H. (sick) unable to locate Machine Gun Sect or C squadron, a squadron is billeted in each of five villages. GORGES, VACQUERIE, EPECAMPS, DOMESMONT, LANCHES. Report to Supply Officer that Section is short of Emergency Rations for 11 men & 26 horses. R J Davis	

(73989) W4141—463. 400,000. 9/14. H.&J.Ltd. Forms/C. 2118/10.

Instructions regarding War Diaries and Intelligence Summaries are contained in F. S. Regs., Part II. and the Staff Manual respectively. Title pages will be prepared in manuscript.

WAR DIARY
or
INTELLIGENCE SUMMARY.
(Erase heading not required.)

Army Form C. 2118.

Hour, Date, Place	Summary of Events and Information	Remarks and references to Appendices
16/10/15 BERNEUIL	Inspect sick horses of B.I.H. Evacuate 11 horses from CANAPLES	
17/10/15 – do –	Evacuate 15 horses from CANAPLES on receiving order to move to FIENVILLERS Move at 12.30 from BERNEUIL arrive at 2 p.m. Billet horses & men myself.	
18/10/15 FIENVILLERS.	Inspect B.I.H. and fix lines etc. etc.	
19/10/15 – do –	Inspect B.I.H. Start at 10 am back at 3 p.m. A.D.V.S. brings small anvils for turning up toes of horse shoes.	
20/10/15 – do –	Draw money & pay whole establishment. Evacuate 24 horses from DOULLENS	
21/10/15 – do –	Evacuate 8 horses from CANAPLES receive orders to move to SILENCOURT.	
22/10/15 – do –	Move to SILENCOURT start 9.30 am via BERNEUIL. DOMART SURCAMPS. L'ETOILE. LE QUESNOY. WARLUS. MERICOURT. AUMONT. to SILENCOURT. Bad billets for both horses & men.	
23/10/15 SILENCOURT	Arrange & change billets, getting horses under cover & men more satisfactorily arranged	
24/10/15 – do –	Endeavour to find B.I.H. No sick to be seen in A squadron or headquarters. Evacuate 2 from C Squadron, unable to find B.H.Q.	
25/10/15	Deal with correspondence all the morning & apply for leave also apply for transfer with view to promotion of Sergt J. H. Ledwith.	R. L. Davis O.C. M.V.S. Mhow Cav. Bdge.

(73989) W4141—463. 400,000. 9/14. H.&J.Ltd. Forms/C. 2118/10.

Instructions regarding War Diaries and Intelligence Summaries are contained in F. S. Regs., Part II. and the Staff Manual respectively. Title pages will be prepared in manuscript.

WAR DIARY
or
INTELLIGENCE SUMMARY.
(Erase heading not required.)

Army Form C. 2118.

Hour, Date, Place		Summary of Events and Information	Remarks and references to Appendices
26/10/15	SILENCOURT	Inspect the sick horses C.I.H. BROCOURT & VILLERS.	
27/10/15	—do—	Evacuate 8 horses from LONGPRE, this place is in my opinion much too far away for evacuating purposes under present conditions. R.T.O requires to be notified before 10. AM in future	
28/10/15	—do—	Inspect C.I.H. We have quite bad weather just now, and mud is becoming very prevalent	
29/10/15	—do—	Inspect C.I.H. VILLERS. BROCOURT. CAMPSART	
30/10/15	—do—	Evacuate 8 horses from LONGPRÉ.	
31/10/15	—do—	Inspect C.I.H. VILLERS, FRESNEVILLE. Bad weather continues and several pairs of boots give way. Claims put in for damage to orchard & buildings, but on investigation they are abandoned	

R.H.Davis Capt. AVC
OC. M.V.S
Mhow Cavalry Brigade

CR/114.

(73989) W4141—463. 400,000. 9/14. H.&J.Ltd. Forms/C. 2118/10.

Serial No. 201.

121
7780

Confidential

War Diary

of

Mobile Veterinary Section; Mhow Brigade.

FROM 1st November 1915 TO 30th November 1915

Serial No. 201.

121/7780.

C O N F I D E N T I A L

W A R D I A R Y

OF

Mobile Veterinary Section; Mhow Brigade.

FROM 1st November, 1915. TO 30th November, 1915.

C.R./417/6/12/15. Army Form C.2118.

Date and Place.		Summary of Events and Information.	Remarks and references to Appendices
1/11/15.	SELINCOURT.	Inspect sick horses Headquarters and Machine Gun Section 38th C.I.H.	
2/11/15.	-do-	Inspect sick horses A & C. squadrons 38th C.I.H. Evacuate 8 horses.	
3/11/15.	-do-	Draw pay from Field Cashier (270 francs) and pay Establishment office work.	
4/11/15.	-do-	Inspect A & B & D. squadrons 38th C.I.H. (sick).	
5/11/15.	-do-	" A & C -do- -do-	
6/11/15	-do-	Inspect Mob. Vet. Section, saddlery and rifles, harness etc. and make arrangements for painting limber.	
7/11/15.	-do-	Nothing to report.	
8/11/15.	-do-	Inspect C.I.H. B & D squadrons at BROCOURT & A at VILLIERS. Evacuate 8 horses.	
9/11/15.	-do-	-do- C " " FRESNEVILLE & A Machine Gun Section.	
10/11/15.	-do-	Pvte. H. Harris goes on leave, all men in this Section have now had one lot of leave. Evacuate 8 horses from LONGPRE. Limbered waggon painted, but no divisional marks.	
11/11/15.	-do-	Attend Corps Parade by 3rd Army Commander at L'Arbre a MOUCHES. Bad day, very cold and rainy.	

Date and Place.		Summary of Events and Information.	Remarks and references to Appendices
12/11/15.	SELINCOURT.	Inspect C.I.H. A & Machine Gun Section, sick.	
13/11/15.	-do-	C.I.H. at BROCOURT. Issue of 10% mud-proof footwear, which I give out to the British, do not understand why issue cannot be made to whole Section, as all are in need of this, as it is Transport drivers have with the Indians to do without, am informed it is not possible to get more.	
14/11/15.	-do-	Nothing to report.	
15/11/15.	-do-	Inspect sick at BROCOURT & VILLERS. Evacuate 8 horses from LONGPRE. Weather turns very cold and snow falls to a depth of 3 inches.	
16/11/15.	-do-	Roads very hard and slippery, so stop exercise, no frost nails or cogs are to be obtained.	
17/11/15.	-do-	Inspect C.I.H. at FESNEVILLE, CAMPSART & VILLERS but roads are not safe. Men are instructed in rifle and use thereof, by instructor from 6th Inniskilling Dragoons, twice a week. I have arranged for this. Captain Barton goes on leave and I take over his work.	
18/11/15.		Mess cart to be painted, Pvte. Turner A.S.C. late for stables fined 4 days pay, he applies for transfer which is forwarded and refused. Roads too bad to go out so I arrange programme of work and clear up correspondence.	
19/11/15.		Inspect sick of 6th Inniskilling Dragoons at HORNOY. Accident case admitted.	

Date and Place.		Summary of Events and Information.	Remarks and references to Appendices
20/11/15.		Inspect sick of 2nd Lancers. AUMONT, DROMESNIL, HALLIVILLERS. Evacuate 8 horses from LONGPRE.	
21/11/15.		Accident case dies. P.M. reveals nothing but fractured navicular, local farmer takes the carcase for dogs.	
22/11/15.	SELINCOURT.	Inspect whole Regimental sick. C.I.H. Still very cold, misty and hoar frost, ABDUL SHAKUR 2nd Lancers dislocates his shoulder and is sent to hospital.	
23/11/15.	-do-	Inspect sick Inniskillings and attend to correspondence.	
24/11/15.	-do-	Draw 520 francs from Field Cashier and pay men. Inspect 2nd Lancers sick. Orders arrive to transfer Segt. J.F. Ledwith to No.5 Vety. Hospital.	
25/11/15.	-do-	Inspect sick horses C.I.H. Sgt. Harrison arrives from No. 26 M.V.S.	
26/11/15.	-do-	Sgt. Ledwith goes. Inspect sick of Inniskillings.	
27/11/15.	-do-	Inspect sick of 2nd Lancers.	
28/11/15.	-do-	Evacuate 7 horses from LONGPRE. Capt. Barton returns from leave and resumes his duties.	
29/11/15.	-do-	Inspect sick of Central India Horse, Saddlery & Rifle inspection of Section.	
30/11/15.		Inspect C.I.H. VILLERS & FRESNEVILLE. Apply for leave.	

(Sd.) R.T. Davis.
Capt. A.V.C.

O.C., M.V.S.

Mhow Cav: Bdge.

Instructions regarding War Diaries and Intelligence Summaries are contained in F. S. Regs., Part II. and the Staff Manual respectively. Title pages will be prepared in manuscript.

WAR DIARY
or
INTELLIGENCE SUMMARY.
(*Erase heading not required.*)

Army Form C. 2118.

C.R.
417
6/12/15

Hour, Date, Place		Summary of Events and Information	Remarks and references to Appendices
1/11/15	SELINCOURT.	Inspect Sick horses Headquarters & Machine Gun Section 38th C.I.H	
2/11/15	-do-	" " " A & C squadrons 38th C.I.H. Evacuate 8 horses	
3/11/15	-do-	Draw pay from Field Cashier (270 francs) & pay Establishment. ~~and~~ office work	
4/11/15	-do-	Inspect A & B & D squadrons 38th C.I.H. (sick)	
5/11/15	-do-	" A & C -do ——do——	
6/11/15	-do-	Inspect Mob. Vet. Section, saddlery & rifles harness etc & make arrangements for painting limber.	
7/11/15	-do-	Nothing to report.	
8/11/15	-do-	Inspect C.I.H. B & D squadrons at BROCOURT & A at VILLERS Evacuate 8 horses	
9/11/15	-do-	—— do —— C " " FRESNEVILLE & A & Machine Gun Section.	
10/11/15	-do-	Pte H. Harris goes on leave all men in this Section have now had one lot of leave. Evacuate 8 horses from LONGPRE Limbered waggon painted, but no divisional marks.	
11/11/15	-do-	Attend Corps Parade by 3rd Army Commander at L'Arbre à MOUCHES. Bad day, very cold & rainy.	
12/11/15	-do-	Inspect C.I.H. A & Machine Gun Section sick	
13/11/15	-do-	C.I.H. at BROCOURT. Issue of 10% Mud proof footwear, which I give out to the British, do not understand why issue cannot be made to whole Section, as all are in need of this, as it is Transport drivers have with the Indians to do without, am informed it is not possible to get more.	

R. J. Davis Capt. AVC
O.C. Mob. Vet. Sect
MHOW Bdge

(73989) W4141—463. 400,000. 9/14. H.&J.Ltd. Forms/C. 2118/10.

Instructions regarding War Diaries and Intelligence Summaries are contained in F. S. Regs., Part II. and the Staff Manual respectively. Title pages will be prepared in manuscript.

WAR DIARY
or
INTELLIGENCE SUMMARY.
(*Erase heading not required.*)

Army Form C. 2118.

Hour, Date, Place	Summary of Events and Information	Remarks and references to Appendices
14/11/15 SELINCOURT	Nothing to report.	
15/11/15 —do—	Inspect sick at BROCOURT & VILLERS. Evacuate 8 horses from LONGPRE Weather turns very cold & snow falls to a depth of 3 inches.	
16/11/15 —do—	Roads very hard & slippery, so stop exercise, no frost nails or cogs are to be obtained.	
17/11/15	Inspect C.H. at FRESNEVILLE, CAMPSART, & VILLERS but roads are not safe. Men are instructed in rifle & use thereof, by instructor from 6th Inniskilling Dragoons, twice a week. I have arranged for this. Capt Barton goes on leave & I take over his work.	
18/11/15	Mess cart to be painted, Pte Turner A.V.C. late for stables fined 4 days pay, he applies for transfer which is forwarded & refused. Roads too bad to go out so I arrange programme of work & clear up correspondence	
19/11/15	Inspect sick of 6th Inniskilling Dragoons at HORNOY. Accident case admitted	
20/11/15	Inspect sick of 2nd Lancers. AUMONT. BROMESNIL. HALLIVILLERS. Evacuate 8 horses from LONGPRE.	
21/11/15	Accident case dies. P.M. reveals nothing but fractured navicular, local farmer takes the carcase for dogs. R.S. Davis Capt A.V.C. O.C. Mob Vet. Sect. MHOW. Cav. Bde.	

(73989) W4141—463. 400,000. 9/14. H.&J.Ltd. Forms/C. 2118/10.

Instructions regarding War Diaries and Intelligence Summaries are contained in F. S. Regs., Part II. and the Staff Manual respectively. Title pages will be prepared in manuscript.

WAR DIARY
or
INTELLIGENCE SUMMARY.
(*Erase heading not required.*)

Army Form C. 2118.

Hour, Date, Place	Summary of Events and Information	Remarks and references to Appendices
22/11/15 SELINCOURT.	Inspect whole Regimental sick C.I.H. Still very cold misty & hoar frost, ABDUL SHAKUR 2nd Lancers dislocates his shoulder & is sent to hospital	
23/11/15 —do—	Inspect sick Inniskillings & attend to correspondence	
24/11/15 —do—	Draw 520 francs from Field Cashier & pay men. Inspect 2nd Lancers sick. Orders arrive to transfer Sgt. J. F. Ledwith to No 5 Vety Hospital	
25/11/15 —do—	Inspect Sick horses C.I.H. Sgt Harrison arrives from No 26 M.V.S.	
26/11/15 —do—	Sgt Ledwith goes. Inspect sick of Inniskillings	
27/11/15 —do—	Inspect sick of 2nd Lancers Evacuate 7 horses from LONGPRE	
28/11/15 —do—	Capt Barton returns from leave & resumes his duties	
29/11/15 —do—	Inspect sick of Central India Horse, Saddlery & Rifle inspection of Section.	
30/11/15	Inspect C.I.H. Villers & FRESNEVILLE, apply for leave.	

R. T. Davis Capt AVC

OC MVS
Mhow Cav Bdge

SERIAL NO. 201

Confidential

War Diary

of

Mobile Veterinary Section, Mhow Cavalry Brigade.

FROM 1st December 1915 TO 31st December 1915

Instructions regarding War Diaries and Intelligence Summaries are contained in F. S. Regs., Part II. and the Staff Manual respectively. Title pages will be prepared in manuscript.

WAR DIARY
or
INTELLIGENCE SUMMARY.
(Erase heading not required.)

Army Form C. 2118.

Hour, Date, Place	Summary of Events and Information	Remarks and references to Appendices
SELINCOURT 1/12/15	I receive warrant to go on leave Capt. Barton takes over in absence	
" 2/12/15	Eight horses sent to hospital via Longpré	
" 3/12/15	Nominal roll of mules, stating unit & disease, sent to ADVS. evacuated since Jan 1st 1915.	
" 4/12/15	Capt Barton inspects sick horses of C.I.H.	
" 5/12/15	" " Saddlery & Rifles of MVS.	
" 6/12/15	Nothing to report.	
" 7/12/15	Nothing to report. C.I.H. inspected	
" 8/12/15	Capt Barton draws ~~[illegible]~~ money & pays MVS. 8 horses sent to ABBEVILLE from LONGPRE, and one horse lost from MVS. reported to police and description given, but no trace found of it.	
" 9/12/15	Memo from ADVS. re Chloral Hydrate etc which has already been answered. C.I.H. inspected	
" 10/12/15	Nominal roll of natives serving with MVS. sent off, these are continually being prepared & sent off to various people.	
" 11/12/15	Capt Davis reports extension of leave granted to 19th	
" 12/12/15	Nothing to report. C I H inspected.	
" 13/12/15	Seven horses & one mule prepared for despatch. It appears that the number of mules evacuated is increasing greatly, & they chiefly suffer from ringbones.	

R. S. Davis
OC. MVS

(73989) W4141—463. 400,000. 9/14. H.&J.Ltd. Forms/C. 2118/10.

Instructions regarding War Diaries and Intelligence Summaries are contained in F. S. Regs., Part II. and the Staff Manual respectively. Title pages will be prepared in manuscript.

WAR DIARY
or
INTELLIGENCE SUMMARY.
(Erase heading not required.)

Army Form C. 2118.

Hour, Date, Place	Summary of Events and Information	Remarks and references to Appendices
SELINCOURT. 14/12/15	Seven horses & 1 mule despatched to ABBEVILLE via LONGPRE	
15/12/15	Instructions received for move to VALINES no room for horse rugs which are taken to Brigade Transport & refused by the Officer there so they are then dumped & fetched later. I have written several times pointing out the inadequacy of transport in Indian Mob Vet Sections	
16/12/15	March to VALINES via OISEMONT.	
VALINES 17/12/15	Settle billets for men & horses & get straightened up.	
18/12/15	Capt. Davis returns to duty.	
19/12/15	Inspect. MVS billets, horses, saddlery rifles etc & clear up correspondence	
20/12/15	Evacuate 9 horses & 4 mules by road to ABBEVILLE 17 kilometers this is not so far as the journey to LONGPRE was & the evacuating party are back in time for dinner midday, find out Units & receive instructions as to malleining BH. & Brigade H^d Q^s.	
21/12/15	Inspect Section, question of men's pay as to how they stand. examine books etc.	
22/12/15	Examine B.H.Qs horses & C.I.H at FRESENNVILLE	
23/12/15	Draw. 700 francs from Field Cashier & arrange programme of malleining pay men.	Ch. 637 7/1/16

[signature] Davis
O.C. M.V.S.

Army Form C. 2118.

Instructions regarding War Diaries and Intelligence Summaries are contained in F. S. Regs., Part II. and the Staff Manual respectively. Title pages will be prepared in manuscript.

WAR DIARY
or
INTELLIGENCE SUMMARY.

(Erase heading not required.)

Hour, Date, Place	Summary of Events and Information	Remarks and references to Appendices
VALINES 24/12/15	Mallein Section horses by new method. Inspect Saddlery & Rifles	Up to date I have malleined 602 horses & 62 mules, and in the great majority of cases I find that the lower eyelids puffs up within the 1st 24 hours, that a small amount of muco purulent discharge may be noticed in some cases, but that in very few cases does it affect the horse in any way, one & two only in each squadron may go slightly off their feeds. The swelling of the lower lid may continue to the 48th hour, or even longer, I have in no case as yet seen what is described as a typical reaction & have only put back two as doubtfuls. The cylinder of my syringe broke once & the fit of the new one was not satisfactory
" 25/12/15	Report cases of mange occurring in C.I.H. & evacuate 3 as suspicious	
	Inspect Section horses. no reaction	
" 26/12/15	Test A squadron C.I.H. & examine section horses	
" 27/12/15	Test B " " " " A squadron	
" 28/12/15	" C " " " " " & B squadron	
" 29/12/15	" D " " " " B " " C "	
" 30/12/15	" Machine Gun Sect " " " C " " D "	
" 31/12/15	" Headquarters C.I.H. & ½A & ½B echelon & examine D " & Machine Gun Section, more cases of mange reported ADVS comes round with me & we evacuate all cases I have picked out	

R H Davis
O.C. Mob Vet Section
Mhow Cav Bdge

(73989) W4141—463. 400,000. 9/14. H.&J.Ltd. Forms/C. 2118/10.

SERIAL NO. 201

Confidential

War Diary

of

Mobile Veterinary Section, Mhow Cavalry Brigade

FROM 1st January 1916 TO 31st January 1916.

Instructions regarding War Diaries and Intelligence Summaries are contained in F. S. Regs., Part II. and the Staff Manual respectively. Title pages will be prepared in manuscript.

WAR DIARY
or
INTELLIGENCE SUMMARY.
(*Erase heading not required.*)

Army Form C. 2118.

Hour, Date, Place		Summary of Events and Information	Remarks and references to Appendices
VALINES	1/1/16	Continue my examination of malleined horses at 38th C. I. Horse and pass the Machine Gun Section. Inspect the sick. Evacuate by road to ABBEVILLE eight sick horses all suspected mange.	
"	2/1/16	Mallein the other half of A&B Echelons, make an inventory of equipment & find the Section short of several things.	
"	3/1/16	Inspect ½ A&B Echelons no reactors. Receive instructions as to treatment of mange which I have already carried out at HAVRE last year.	
"	4/1/16	Mallein Brigade H^d Q^s at 10.30. Inspect Echelons C.I.H & pass them free. Evacuate 12 horses to ABBEVILLE	
	5/1/16	Inspect. Brig H^d Q^s put 2 back as doubtful. Inspect C.I.H	
	6/1/16	A.D.V.S. comes over to see the 2 horses I put back and agrees that they should be done again. SAUCOURT.	
	7/1/16	Inspect C.I.H sick & evacuate 10 horses to ABBEVILLE.	
	8/1/16	Office, Correspondence on various matters appears to be greatly on the increase and it takes 3 or 4 hours to clear it all up, is it necessary.	
	9/1/16	Nothing to report today	
	10/1/16	Inspect C.I.H. sick & receive instructions as to ringworm treatment	
	11/1/16	Inspect C.I.H. sick, special inspection of B squadron, who bring up some suspected mange cases which I turn down as lice only.	

R J Davis
O.C. Mhow. Mob. Vet Sect

Army Form C. 2118.

Instructions regarding War Diaries and Intelligence Summaries are contained in F. S. Regs., Part II. and the Staff Manual respectively. Title pages will be prepared in manuscript.

WAR DIARY
or
INTELLIGENCE SUMMARY.

(*Erase heading not required.*)

Hour, Date, Place		Summary of Events and Information	Remarks and references to Appendices
VALINES	12/1/16	Considerable amount of time wasted at C.I.H. in obtaining the description of in contact mange cases	
	13/1/16	Inspect Section rifle and saddlery & billets. C.I.H. sick & office in afternoon	
	14/1/16	Inspect C.I.H. sick & take over Aux Horse Transport during Farr Major Woolley's absence on leave	
	15/1/16	Inspect B.H.Q's horses & evacuate 10 cases to ABBEVILLE, receive instructions as to properly labelling describing & evacuating horses	
	16/1/16	Sergt. Harrison returns from leave. inspect C.I.H.	
	17/1/16	Inspect C.I.H. sick. Office Mallein returns etc	
	18/1/16	Inspect C.I.H. sick & B.H.Q's. One horse Aux Horse Transport dies, from what appears to be impaction	
	19/1/16	Inspect C.I.H. sick & P.M. the Aux Horse Transport animal. Office	
	20/1/16	Mallein 4 horses put back, inspect C.I.H. & horses for evacuation	
	21/1/16	A.D.V.S. inspects horses for evacuation rejects 3, evacuate 17 to ABBEVILLE	

R. J. Davis
OC M.V.S.
Mhow Cav. Bde

(73989) W4141—463. 400,000. 9/14. H.&J.Ltd. Forms/C. 2118/10.

Instructions regarding War Diaries and Intelligence Summaries are contained in F. S. Regs., Part II. and the Staff Manual respectively. Title pages will be prepared in manuscript.

WAR DIARY
or
INTELLIGENCE SUMMARY.
(Erase heading not required.)

Army Form C. 2118.

Hour, Date, Place	Summary of Events and Information	Remarks and references to Appendices
VALINES 22/1/16	Sergt. Harrison promoted & ordered to No. 7 Vety Hospital for duty. Two horses C.I.H. react to 2nd test & I arrange for burial	
" 23/1/16	Inspect C.I.H. notify A.D.V.S. of destruction of 2 horses, put off however by local mayor.	
" 24/1/16	Inspect. C.I.H. Mayor makes a lot of trouble about burying 2 horses finally decided on 28th/1/16.	
" 25/1/16	Interview A.D.V.S. re Mallein returns & disposal of reactors at DARGNIES	
" 26/1/16	SAUCOURT Draw 430 francs from Field Cashier. Sergt ~~Blum~~ Blum from 29 Mob Vety Section reports for duty notify A.D.V.S. of his arrival & S.Sgt Harrisons departure	
" 27/1/16	Pay men & ~~vi~~ visit C.I.H. burial fixed up & put off again of above 2 horses	
" 28/1/16	Visit A.D.V.S. at DARGNIES re 2 glanders cases, meet him at 3 pm & get it fixed up once more.	
" 29/1/16	Inspect C.I.H. and Post Mortem 2 horses reacting to Mallein test, find one small nodule in the left lung of one nothing in the other.	
" 30/1/16	Inspect. C.I.H. & mens billets.	
" 31/1/16	Mallein horses pending evacuation to ABBEVILLE inspect. C.I.H.	

R.J. Davis
O.C. Mob. Vet. Sect.
[illegible] Cav. Bde.

C.R. 750 6/2/16

(73989) W4141—463. 400,000. 9/14. H.&J.Ltd. Forms/C. 2118/10.

SERIAL NO 201

Confidential

War Diary

of

Mobile Veterinary Section, Mhow Cavalry Brigade

FROM 1st February 1916 TO 29th February 1916

Instructions regarding War Diaries and Intelligence Summaries are contained in F. S. Regs., Part II. and the Staff Manual respectively. Title pages will be prepared in manuscript.

WAR DIARY
or
INTELLIGENCE SUMMARY.
(Erase heading not required.)

Army Form C. 2118.

Hour, Date, Place	Summary of Events and Information	Remarks and references to Appendices
VALINES 1/2/16	Inspect sick C.I. Horse & Section. Advised of inspection by ADVS at 11 am tomorrow	During this month I am instructed that the Canadian Division will use this Section for evacuation purposes until they get one of their own. I receive several Mange cases from them to be clipped out & dressed. I am sharpening a large number of heads for clipping machines here.
" 2/2/16	ADVS 1st Ind Cav. Div. inspects Section, expresses his great satisfaction as to keep of saddlery, carts & rifles, suggests some of the men might have new tunics. C.I. Horse in afternoon.	
" 3/2/16	Evacuate 14 horses to ABBEVILLE to see how things are arranged take them in myself, find it takes 3 hours to walk in, hand them over to Major Hobday	
" 4/2/16	Inspect C.I.H. sick, Pte Pippin goes on leave. Canadian Ammunition Supply Column arrives in the village & their O.C. is made Camp Commandant & supplies police with Base Horse Transport.	
" 5/2/16	Inspect C.I.H. sick nothing else to report. ADVS's office at DARGNIES	
" 6/2/16	Nothing to report	
" 7/2/16	Inspect C.I.H. sick & go on to Sully to confer with Capt O'Gogarty there re sending horses in to me.	
" 8/2/16	I ask the ADVS. to come over & see some of the Canadian horses sent to me as I do not consider they are sending them in correctly. Evacuate 14 horses to ABBEVILLE	
" 9/2/16	Draw 370 francs for mens pay. ADVS. comes over with Major Thurston C.A.V.C. 4 of their horses are returned	

R L Davis Capt. AVC
O.C. Mob. Vet. Sect. MHOW Cav Bde

(73989) W4141—463. 400,000. 9/14. H.&J.Ltd. Forms/C. 2118/10.

Instructions regarding War Diaries and Intelligence Summaries are contained in F. S. Regs., Part II. and the Staff Manual respectively. Title pages will be prepared in manuscript.

Army Form C. 2118.

WAR DIARY
or
INTELLIGENCE SUMMARY.
(*Erase heading not required.*)

Hour, Date, Place	Summary of Events and Information	Remarks and references to Appendices
VALINES. 10/2/16	Inspect sick of C.I. Horse & evacuate 8 Canadian horses to ABBEVILLE	
" 11/2/16	Inspect sick of C.I. Horse, evacuate one case of suspected mange sent up from Remounts. Canadian mange horses clipping proceeds	
" 12/2/16	Visit ADVS at DARGNIES re AF. B213 he informs me that I am to be transferred to Divl. Ammn. Column & that Capt. Maynard will visit me ~~tomorrow~~ re taking over the Section.	
" 13/2/16	Capt Maynard arrives and I give him all information he desires. ADVS. visit re Canadian Mange cases, instructs me to send them all to Hospital without evacuation roll etc etc.	
" 14/2/16	Inspect sick C.I.H. Instructed to take over 'A' Battery at NIBAS. Evacuate 8 Clipped Canadian horses (mange) and 7 other cases to ABBEVILLE. Sergeant Blunn E.J. goes on leave.	
" 15/2/16.	Inspect sick C.I.H. & Remounts issued to them. pass them	
" 16/2/16	Inspect sick C.I.H. Remounts. Office	
" 17/2/16	Visit. OFFEUX to inspect horses of Headquarters of Indian R.H.A. send 2 animals away.	
" 18/2/16	Visit C.I.H. Office. ADVS. at Lucknow. to discuss the duties of a Mob. Vet Section for instructing the Division	

R.J. Davis Capt AVC.
OC. Mob Vety Secn
Mhow. Cav. Bdge

(73989) W4141—463. 400,000. 9/14. H.&J.Ltd. Forms/C. 2118/10.

Army Form C. 2118.

Instructions regarding War Diaries and Intelligence Summaries are contained in F. S. Regs., Part II. and the Staff Manual respectively. Title pages will be prepared in manuscript.

WAR DIARY
or
INTELLIGENCE SUMMARY.
(Erase heading not required.)

Hour, Date, Place	Summary of Events and Information	Remarks and references to Appendices
VALINES 19/2/16	Office answering correspondence & making out returns. Evacuate 2 horses by motor ambulance	
" 20/2/16	Capt. Maynard comes over re taking over. Evacuate 19 horses. Office	
" 21/2/16	Visit ADVS at DARGNIES re taking over & go on to BEAUCHAMPS to Capt. Maynard to look round his units.	
" 22/2/16	Inspect sick C. I Horse & Auxiliary Horse Transport, having taken over the latter for a week under orders from ADVS.	
" 23/2/16	Discussion with DAA & QMG as to duties of Mob Vety Section & B.V.O. in a cavalry advance, instructive in that, the conclusion come to in working out a scheme, is that, the O.C. Mob Vet Sect at the end of the 1st day would only have his transport left, his personnel being away evacuating sick horses. Evacuate 23 horses.	
" 24/2/16	Visit FEGQUIERES to see Capt Barlow re conference in afternoon. Receive 14 horses from Canadian Conference at Lucknow Mob Vet Sect FRANLEU with ADVS – re the shoeing in the Brigade, classes are to be formed & instructed by V.Os.	

R J Davis Capt AVC.
O.C. Mob Vet Sect
Mhow Cav Bge

(73989) W4141—463. 400,000. 9/14. H.&J.Ltd. Forms/C. 2118/10.

Instructions regarding War Diaries and Intelligence Summaries are contained in F.S. Regs., Part II. and the Staff Manual respectively. Title pages will be prepared in manuscript.

WAR DIARY
or
INTELLIGENCE SUMMARY.
(Erase heading not required.)

Army Form C. 2118.

Hour, Date, Place	Summary of Events and Information	Remarks and references to Appendices
25/2/16. VALINES.	Inspect sick C.I.H. & Auxiliary Horse Transport. Evacuate 16 horses to ABBEVILLE	
26/2/16 "	Office work clearing up correspondence. Sgt Chum returns from leave.	
27/2/16 "	Nothing to report.	
28/2/16 "	Inspect C.I.H. & Bge Hd Qrs go on to DARGNIES to see ADVS. receive instructions to attend to 1st Indian. R.H.A. Hd Qrs.	
29/2/16	Visit. OFFEUX. R.H.A. Hd Qrs. Inspect sick C.I.H. & Office. Heavy falls of snow occurred during the last five days & frost on top of this made roads impassable for 3 days.	
	R [illegible] Capt. AVC. O.C.	

(73989) W4141—463. 400,000. 9/14. H.&J.Ltd. Forms/C. 2118/10.

SERIAL NO 201

Confidential

War Diary

of

Mobile Veterinary Section, Mhow Cavalry Brigade

FROM 1st March 1916 TO 31st March 1916.

Army Form C. 2118.

Instructions regarding War Diaries and Intelligence Summaries are contained in F. S. Regs., Part II. and the Staff Manual respectively. Title pages will be prepared in manuscript.

WAR DIARY
or
INTELLIGENCE SUMMARY.
(Erase heading not required.)

Hour, Date, Place	Summary of Events and Information	Remarks and references to Appendices
VALINES 1/3/16	Inspect sick C.I. Horse. Draw 500 francs for pay from Field Cashier. Pay men, make out evacuation rolls etc.	Confidential
" 2/3/16	Inspect. C.I.H. + Brigade Headquarters. Evacuate 19 horses to No 22 Vety Hospital ABBEVILLE.	
" 3/3/16	A.D.V.S. at DARGNIES. D.D.V.S. inspects and instructs me to lessen my equipment. Prepare evacuation rolls + returns for Saturday	
" 4/3/16	Evacuate 13 horses to ABBEVILLE + office.	
" 5/3/16	Inspect. C.I. Horse. limber washed for painting, shelvings sanctioned for Mob. Vet. Sections.	
" 6/3/16	Inspect C.I. Horse, pack saddles improvised.	
" 7/3/16	Inspect Headquarters R.H.A. + C.I. Horse. + office. Evacuate 15 horses	
" 8/3/16	Office. A.D.V.S. inspects + instruction re mange cases	
" 9/3/16	Inspect. horses for casting from C.I.H. + Brigade No 9 ? sick, Evacuate 12 horses	
" 10/3/16	Proceed to ABBEVILLE for purchase of iron for shelvings to limber	
" 11/3/16	Inspect. sick C.I.H. 2 cases evacuated by motor ambulance. Evacuation rolls prepared + office	
" 12/3/16	Evacuate 13 horses to ABBEVILLE	

R.S. Davis Capt. AVC
OC. Mhow. Mob. Vety Sect.

(73989) W4141—463. 400,000. 9/14. H.&J.Ltd. Forms/C. 2118/10.

Instructions regarding War Diaries and Intelligence Summaries are contained in F. S. Regs., Part II. and the Staff Manual respectively. Title pages will be prepared in manuscript.

WAR DIARY
or
INTELLIGENCE SUMMARY.
(*Erase heading not required*.)

Army Form C. 2118.

Hour, Date, Place	Summary of Events and Information	Remarks and references to Appendices
VALINES 13/3/16	Inspect sick C.I.H. & Brigade H^d Q^rs	
" 14/3/16	A.D.V.S. at DARGNIES re Cast horses & office	
" 15/3/16	Proceed by Supply Car to ABBEVILLE for exchange of bolts for limber Evacuation rolls prepared & office	
" 16/3/16	Evacuate 12 cases to ABBEVILLE & draw 4 mules from Remounts	
" 17/3/16	Inspect R.H.A. Headquarters. Brigade H^d Q^rs etc & evacuate 8 horses One mule proves useless & vicious	
" 18/3/16	Office clearing correspondence & returns. In endeavouring to train mule Sgt. Chun is kicked and admitted to Hospital.	
" 19/3/16	A.D.V.S. inspects and censures me, I object explaining, conditions etc, and consider that under the circumstances my Section is as good as any to be found.	
" 20/3/16	Inspect C.I.H & Brig H^d Q^rs. Driver Turner goes on leave. Evacuate 8 horses	
" 21/3/16	Inspect route for move into new area & office. Evacuation rolls etc	
" 22/3/16	Evacuate 11 horses, draw 1000 francs from Cashier, paymen etc.	
" 23/3/16	Orders to move to New Area, clean up billets & prepare generally Evacuate 2 horses by ambulance.	

R L Davis
Capt. A.V.C.
O.C. Mhow. M.V.S.

(73989) W4141—463. 400,000. 9/14. H.&J.Ltd. Forms/C. 2118/10.

Instructions regarding War Diaries and Intelligence Summaries are contained in F. S. Regs., Part II. and the Staff Manual respectively. Title pages will be prepared in manuscript.

WAR DIARY
or
INTELLIGENCE SUMMARY.
(Erase heading not required.)

Army Form C. 2118.

Hour, Date, Place	Summary of Events and Information	Remarks and references to Appendices
VALINES 24/3/16	Orders to move cancelled presumably on account of heavy fall of snow. Office & C.I.H. in afternoon. Evacuation rolls & returns. ~~Inspect sick C.I.H. Evacuate 16 horses~~	
" 25/3/16	Move to ONEUX via ABBEVILLE at 10 am, arriving 5.15	
" 26/3/16	Leave ONEUX at 9.45 arrive MAIZICOURT 1.15 pm. arrange billets etc	
27/3/16	Settle in billets, arrange for pasture to take sick horses	
28/3/16	Inspect C.I.H. at MAISON EN PONTHIEU finding roads etc, office	
29/3/16	Field Cashier & C.I.H. ride to AUXI LE CHATEAU and arrange with R.T.O for evacuating sick horses. Evacuation rolls etc	
30/3/16	AUXI LE CHATEAU with sick horses. Evacuate 10.	
31/3/16	Inspect C.I.H. Instructed to take over The Machine Gun Sections. I am now O.C. Mobile Vety Section & doing the veterinary work for Brigade Headquarters, 38th C.I. Horse & Machine Gun Section. Sgt TURNER returns from leave	

R J Davis
Capt. AVC
O.C. Mobile Vety Section
Mhow Cav. Bde

(73989) W4141—463. 400,000. 9/14. H.&J.Ltd. Forms/C. 2118/10.

Instructions regarding War Diaries and Intelligence Summaries are contained in F. S. Regs., Part II. and the Staff Manual respectively. Title pages will be prepared in manuscript.

WAR DIARY
or
INTELLIGENCE SUMMARY.
(*Erase heading not required*.)

Army Form C. 2118.

Hour, Date, Place	Summary of Events and Information	Remarks and references to Appendices
VALINES 1/3/16	Inspect sick C. I. Horse. Draw 500 francs for pay from Field Cashier. Pay men, make out evacuation rolls etc.	
2/3/16	Inspect B. I. H. & Brigade Headquarters. Evacuate 19 horses to No 22 Vety Hospital ABBEVILLE.	
3/3/16	A. D. V. S. at DARGNIES. A. D. V. S. inspects and instructs me to lessen my equipment. Prepare evacuation rolls & returns for Saturday	
4/3/16	Evacuate 13 horses to ABBEVILLE & office.	
5/3/16	Inspect C. I. Horse. Limber washed for painting, shelvings sanctioned for Mob Vet Sections	
6/3/16	Inspect C. I. Horse. pack saddles improvised.	
7/3/16	Inspect Headquarters R. H. A. & C. I. Horse. & office. Evacuate 15 horses	
8/3/16	Office. A. D. V. S. inspects & instruction re mange cases	
9/3/16	Inspect horses for casting from C. I. H. & Brigade No 6th sick. Evacuate 12 horses }	
10/3/16	Proceed to ABBEVILLE for purchase of iron for shelvings to limber	
11/3/16	Inspect sick C. I. H. 2 cases evacuated by motor ambulance. Evacuation rolls prepared & office	
12/3/16	Evacuate 13 horses to ABBEVILLE	

R. J. Bawn Capt AVC.
O.C. Mhow. Mob. Vety Sect.

Instructions regarding War Diaries and Intelligence Summaries are contained in F. S. Regs., Part II. and the Staff Manual respectively. Title pages will be prepared in manuscript.

WAR DIARY
or
INTELLIGENCE SUMMARY.
(*Erase heading not required.*)

Army Form C. 2118.

Hour, Date, Place		Summary of Events and Information	Remarks and references to Appendices
YALINES	13/3/16	Inspect sick G.I.N. & Brigade H^d Q^rs.	
"	14/3/16	ADVS. at DARGNIES re Cast horses & office	
"	15/3/16	Proceed by Supply Car to ABBEVILLE for exchange of bolts for limber. Evacuation rolls prepared & office	
"	16/3/16	Evacuate 12 cases to ABBEVILLE & draw 4 mules from Remounts.	
"	17/3/16	Inspect R.N.A. Headquarters. Brigade H^d Q^rs etc & evacuate 8 horses. One mule proves useless & vicious.	
"	18/3/16	Office clearing correspondence & returns. In endeavouring to train mule Sgt. Chun is kicked and admitted to Hospital.	
"	19/3/16	ADVS inspects and censures me. I object explaining conditions etc, and consider than under the circumstances my Section is as good as any to be found.	
"	20/3/16	Inspect G.I.N. & Brig H^d Q^rs. Driver Turner goes on leave. Evacuate 8 horses	
"	21/3/16	Inspect route for move into new area & office. Evacuation rolls etc	
"	22/3/16	Evacuate 11 horses, draw 1000 francs from Cashier, pay men etc.	
"	23/3/16	Orders to move to New Area, clean up billets & prepare generally. Evacuate 2 horses by ambulance.	

R. L. Davis
Capt. AVC.
O.C. Mhow. M.V.S

(73989) W4141—463. 400,000. 9/14. H.&J.Ltd. Forms/C. 2118/10.

Army Form C. 2118

Instructions regarding War Diaries and Intelligence Summaries are contained in F. S. Regs., Part II. and the Staff Manual respectively. Title pages will be prepared in manuscript.

WAR DIARY
or
INTELLIGENCE SUMMARY.

(*Erase heading not required.*)

Hour, Date, Place	Summary of Events and Information	Remarks and references to Appendices
VALINES 24/3/16	Orders to move cancelled presumably on account of heavy fall of snow. Office & C.I.H. in afternoon. Evacuation rolls & returns. ~~Inspect sick B.I.H. Evacuate 16 horses~~	
" 25/3/16	Move to ONEUX via ABBEVILLE at 10 am arriving 5.15.	
26/3/16	Leave ONEUX at 9.45 arrive MAIZICOURT 1.15 pm. arrange billets etc	
27/3/16	Settle in billets, arrange for pasture to take sick horses	
28/3/16	Inspect B.I.H. at MAISON EN PONTHIEU finding roads etc, office.	
29/3/16	Field Cashier & C.I.H. ride to AUXI LE CHATEAU and arrange with R.T.O for evacuating sick horses. Evacuation rolls etc	
30/3/16	AUXI LE CHATEAU with sick horses. Evacuate 10.	
31/3/16	Inspect B.I.H. Instructed to take over The Machine Gun Section. I am now O.C. Mobile Vety Section & doing the veterinary work for Brigade Head quarters, 35th C.I. Horse & Machine Gun Section. Pte TURNER returns from leave	

R J Davies
Capt. AVC
OC Mobile Vety Section
Mhow Cav. Bge

(73989) W4141—463. 400,000. 9/14. H.&J.Ltd. Forms/C. 2118/10.

SERIAL NO 201

Confidential

War Diary

of

Mobile Veterinary Section, Mhow Cavalry Brigade

FROM 1st April 1916 TO 30th April 1916

Army Form C. 2118.

Instructions regarding War Diaries and Intelligence Summaries are contained in F. S. Regs., Part II. and the Staff Manual respectively. Title pages will be prepared in manuscript.

WAR DIARY
or
INTELLIGENCE SUMMARY.
(Erase heading not required.)

Hour, Date, Place	Summary of Events and Information	Remarks and references to Appendices
1/4/16 MAIZICOURT	Inspect Machine Gun Section sick & office Cpl H Brown on leave	
2/4/16 —do—	Machine Gun Section, horse dies suddenly, post mortem made, result Enteritis diagnosed search made for barbs, none found.	
3/4/16 —do—	Inspect C.I.H. & Machine Gun Section Office & Section Evacuation rolls	
4/4/16 —do—	C.I.H. re Returns Evacuate 18 horses 3 by road to ABBEVILLE others by rail. Inspect A Squadron C.I.H.	
5/4/16 —do—	Field Cashier draw 600 francs. Pay men. ADVS inspects Machine Gun Squadron at HIERMONT with me. Office etc	
6/4/16 —do—	Very bad weather, laid up with lumbago. Office etc	
7/4/16 —do—	Inspect Machine Gun Section & C.I.H. saddles & rifles in Section.	
8/4/16 —do—	Office etc etc. still bad	
9/4/16 —do—	Nothing to report	
10/4/16 —do—	Inspect Mach Gun Sect & C.I.H. and in accordance with instructions attend farmers mare at AUCHEL removing dead foal	
11/4/16 —do—	Office pay Indians, Inspect Brigade H^d^ Qrs. Heavy rain & gales	
12/4/16 —do—	Nothing to report Cpl Brown returns from leave. Inspect C Squadron C.I.H.	

(73989) W4141—463. 400,000. 9/14. H.&J.Ltd. Forms/C. 2118/10.

Instructions regarding War Diaries and Intelligence Summaries are contained in F. S. Regs., Part II. and the Staff Manual respectively. Title pages will be prepared in manuscript.

WAR DIARY
or
INTELLIGENCE SUMMARY.
(Erase heading not required.)

Army Form C. 2118.

Hour, Date, Place		Summary of Events and Information	Remarks and references to Appendices
13/4/16	MAIZICOURT	Inspect C.H. Office & evacuation rolls. Evacuate horses.	
14/4/16	— do —	M. G. S. Inspected. Attend Gas demonstration.	
15/4/16	— do —	Inspect Remounts C.H. report on 3 of them. Office	
16/4/16	— do —	Nothing to report	
17/4/16	— do —	Inspect C.H. & M.G.S. Evacuate 10 horses	
18/4/16	— do —	Office & Section correspondence etc	
19/4/16	— do —	Draw 250 from Field Cashier & pay men	
20/4/16	— do —	C.H. & M.G.S. inspected. D squadron C.H. etc.	
21/4/16	— do —	Orders to move to training area pack up & clear billets	
22/4/16	— do —	Move to NOYELLE EN CHAUSSEE & evacuate 10 horses. rain all day reach billets at 1 pm settle in	
23/4/16	— do —	Settle in billets report arrival to ADVS & apply for leave,	
24/4/16	— do —	Leave granted, apply to Brigade warrant to be made out on 28th	
25/4/16	— do —	Section. Sgt Bliven reprimanded Section brought to book etc.	
26/4/16	— do —	Hand over duties to Capt Gooderidge after inspecting C.H. & M.G.S..	

(73989) W4141—463. 400,000. 9/14. H.&J.Ltd. Forms/C. 2118/10.

Army Form C. 2118.

Instructions regarding War Diaries and Intelligence Summaries are contained in F. S. Regs., Part II. and the Staff Manual respectively. Title pages will be prepared in manuscript.

WAR DIARY
or
INTELLIGENCE SUMMARY.

(Erase heading not required.)

Hour, Date, Place	Summary of Events and Information	Remarks and references to Appendices
27/4/16 NOYELLE	Leave for England return on 5th of May R G Davis Capt. AVC OC. 9/4/16	

(73989) W4141—463. 400,000. 9/14. H.&J.Ltd. Forms/C. 2118/10.

SERIAL NO 201.

Confidential

War Diary

of

Mobile Veterinary Section, Mhow Cavalry Brigade.

FROM 1st May 1916 TO 31st May 1916.

Instructions regarding War Diaries and Intelligence Summaries are contained in F. S. Regs., Part II. and the Staff Manual respectively. Title pages will be prepared in manuscript.

WAR DIARY
or
INTELLIGENCE SUMMARY.
(Erase heading not required.)

Army Form C. 2118.

Mhow Brigade
Mobile Vety Section 1st Ind. Cav. Div.

Hour, Date, Place		Summary of Events and Information	Remarks and references to Appendices
6/5/16	NOYELLE	Orders to return to old billets pack up & clean billets, also receive instructions to proceed to 4th Cav Bde. British for duty.	
7/5/16	—do—	Move to MAIZICOURT & settle in old billets	
8/5/16	—do—	Capt. Thomson AVC comes to arrange taking over Section and I clear up all correspondence, evacuate 7 horses, & generally get everything straightened up for handing over	This page was written by Capt Davis. AVC. who was O.C. Section up till the 9th May 1916 T. Thomson Capt AVC (T)

(73989) W4141—463. 400,000. 9/14. H.&J.Ltd. Forms/C. 2118/10.

Instructions regarding War Diaries and Intelligence Summaries are contained in F. S. Regs., Part II. and the Staff Manual respectively. Title pages will be prepared in manuscript.

WAR DIARY
or
~~INTELLIGENCE~~ SUMMARY.
(*Erase heading not required.*)

Army Form C. 2118.

Mhow. Cav. Bde.
Mobile Vety. Section
1st Ind. Cav. Div.

Hour, Date, Place	Summary of Events and Information	Remarks and references to Appendices
7.30 P.M. 9/5/16 : MAZICOURT.	Took over Veterinary charge of the MHOW BRIGADE Veterinary Mobile Section from Capt. DAVIS; who also handed over his veterinary chest + Wallet.	
10/5/16 IVERGNY	Marched to IVERGNY in the rear of B. ECHLON. Distance 10 miles, time taken 4 hours, arriving at 3 P.M.	
11/5/16 "	Settled in new billets + prepared sick lines.	
12/5/16 "	Took over Vety charge of the 38th (K.R.O) Horse	
13/5/16 "	Evacuated 7 Lame horses to No 22 Vety Hospital from Railhead at FREVENT. Inspected Horses for Casting of 2nd Lancers.	
14/5/16 "	Took over Vety. charge of the MHOW Bde. Machine Gun Squadron	
15/5/16 "	Got men's sleeping quarters lime washed as they had been left very dirty by Infantry.	
16/5/16 "	Examined horses of 2nd Lancers brought up by the Regt. for casting by Remount Officer	G. Thomson Capt. A.V.C. (T.F.)

Instructions regarding War Diaries and Intelligence Summaries are contained in F. S. Regs., Part II. and the Staff Manual respectively. Title pages will be prepared in manuscript.

WAR DIARY
or
INTELLIGENCE SUMMARY.
(Erase heading not required.)

Army Form C. 2118.

Lucknow Cav. Bde.
M.V.S.
1st Ind. Cav. Div.

Hour, Date, Place	Summary of Events and Information	Remarks and references to Appendices
IVERGNY		
17/5/16 "	Evacuated 6 horses to No 22 Hospital from FREVENT Station	
	Examined horses of the 6th Dragoons + 38th Central India Horse to be shown to Remount Officer.	
18/5/16 "	Received orders from A.D.V.S. for Sgt. CHUN A.V.C. to proceed to No 6. Vety Hospital ROUEN on being replaced.	
	Sgt E. SPILSTEAD No 1915 arrived to replace Sgt. CHUN.	
19/5/16 "	Evacuated 13 horses from FREVENT Station.	
	Sgt CHUN proceeded to No 6. Vety Hospital.	
	Many horses with Ringbones going lame owing to the hard ~~state~~ of the roads	
20/5/16 "	Inspected horses + men's kit of Section.	
21/5/16		G. Thomson Capt. A.V.C. (T)
22/5/16.	Inspected shoeing + sick of 38th C.I.H.	

(73989) W4141—463. 400,000. 9/14. H.&J.Ltd. Forms/C. 2118/10.

Instructions regarding War Diaries and Intelligence Summaries are contained in F. S. Regs., Part II. and the Staff Manual respectively. Title pages will be prepared in manuscript.

WAR DIARY
or
~~INTELLIGENCE~~ SUMMARY.

(*Erase heading not required.*)

Army Form C. 2118.

Mhow Cav. Bde. M.V.S. 1st Ind. Cav. Div.

Hour, Date, Place	Summary of Events and Information	Remarks and references to Appendices
IVERGNY	—	
23/5/16	Evacuated 7 horses + 1 mule from FREVENT Station.	
24/5/16 "	Inspected arms, gas helmets etc. of Section.	
25/5/16	Evacuated 6 horses to No 22 Vety Hospital from FREVENT Station	
26/5/16 "	Inspected one Section of Machine Gun Squadron.	
27/5/16		
28/5/16 "	— One suspected mange case from C.I.H. came in for evacuation.	
29/5/16		
30/5/16 "	Evacuated 8 horses + 1 mule to No 22. Hospital ABBEVILLE from FREVENT Station	
31/5/16 "	Took British units of Section out on Divisional Field Day, when we practised 1st Aid + Collection of Horses left behind by Regiments of the Brigade.	T. Thomson Capt A.V.C. (S.R.)

(73989) W4141—463. 400,000. 9/14. H.&J.Ltd. Forms/C. 2118/10.

SERIAL NO 201

Confidential

War Diary

of

Mobile Veterinary Section, Mhow Cavalry Brigade

FROM 1st June 1916 TO 30th June 1916

Instructions regarding War Diaries and Intelligence Summaries are contained in F. S. Regs., Part II. and the Staff Manual respectively. Title pages will be prepared in manuscript.

WAR DIARY
or
INTELLIGENCE SUMMARY.
(Erase heading not required.)

Army Form C. 2118.

Mobile Vety section
Mhow Cavalry Bde
1st I C Division

Hour, Date, Place	Summary of Events and Information	Remarks and references to Appendices
13.6.15 Isergny	Took over charge of mobile Vety section Mhow Bde. Vety Officer for Central India Horse, Machine gun squadron & Brigade HdQrs. Admitted 14 horses & 2 mules into section	
14.6.15	Had section paraded marching order. Inspected horses & kit. Admitted 4 horses into section	
15.6.15	Evacuated 8 horses to No 22 Vety Hospital by train from Railhead. Reported presence of mange in the units of the Brigade to ADVS.	
16.6.15	Inspected all horses of the C.I.H. for contagious disease & lameness. Admitted 3 horses into section	
17.6.15	Examined all lame horses in the C.I.H picked out the day before.	
18.6.15	Evacuated 43 horses for suspected mange by road to No 22 Vety Hospital Abbeville.	A B Bowhay Capt AVC

1

(73989) W4141—463. 400,000. 9/14. H.&J.Ltd. Forms/C. 2118/10.

Instructions regarding War Diaries and Intelligence Summaries are contained in F. S. Regs., Part II. and the Staff Manual respectively. Title pages will be prepared in manuscript.

WAR DIARY
or
INTELLIGENCE SUMMARY.
(*Erase heading not required.*)

Army Form C. 2118.

Mobile Vety Section
Mhow Cav Bde 1st IC Division

Hour, Date, Place	Summary of Events and Information	Remarks and references to Appendices
19·6·16 Iverguy –	Admitted 13 horses into section. Ordinary routine work	
20·6·16 –	Evacuated 15 horses to No 22 Vety Hospital from Railhead. Inspected all horses of the Machine Gun squadron for contagious disease & lameness. Admitted 10 horses into section	
21·6·16 "	Examined the lame horses picked out the day before – Ordinary routine work	
22 6·16 "	Evacuated 22 horses from Railhead to No 22 Vety Hospital – Inspected some suspicious cases of mange picked out at previous inspection of CIH	
23·6·16	Admitted 7 horses into section – Inspected all horses at Bde Hd Qrs for contagious disease & lameness	
24·6·16	Admitted 2 mules into section – Evacuated 5 horses & 2 mules from Railhead to No 22 Vety Hospital	HB Bowhay Capt AVC

1c

(73989) W4141—463. 400,000. 9/14. H.&J.Ltd. Forms/C. 2118/10.

Instructions regarding War Diaries and Intelligence Summaries are contained in F. S. Regs., Part II. and the Staff Manual respectively. Title pages will be prepared in manuscript.

WAR DIARY
or
~~INTELLIGENCE SUMMARY~~.
(Erase heading not required.)

Army Form C. 2118.

Mobile Vety Section
Mhow Cavalry Bde 1st I C Division

Hour, Date, Place	Summary of Events and Information	Remarks and references to Appendices
26·6·16 Ivergny	Admitted 19 horses into section - Destroyed two	
27·6·16 "	Evacuated 24 horses. from Railhead to No 22 Vety Hospital Abbeville - ordinary routine work	
28·6·16 "	Admitted 3 horses into section Ordinary routine work	
29·6·16 "	Admitted 11 horses into section Evacuated to Railhead to await trucking to No 22 Vety Hospital on the morrow - as we were under orders to move in the morning.	
30·6·16	Marched from Ivergny at 9am & arrived at Doullens at 12.30 - Admitted one horse into section.	

A B Bowhay
Capt AVC

SERIAL NO 201.

Confidential

War Diary

of

Mobile Veterinary Section, Mhow Cavalry Brigade.

FROM 1st July 1916 TO 31st July 1916.

Instructions regarding War Diaries and Intelligence Summaries are contained in F. S. Regs., Part II. and the Staff Manual respectively. Title pages will be prepared in manuscript.

WAR DIARY
or
~~INTELLIGENCE SUMMARY.~~
(Erase heading not required.)

Army Form C. 2118.

Mobile Vety Section
Mhow Cavalry Bde

Hour, Date, Place	Summary of Events and Information	Remarks and references to Appendices
1-7-16. Doullens.	Admitted five horses into section. Inspected horses of one Squadron of Central India Horse for contagious disease.	W.R.B.
2-7-16 "	Admitted seven horses into section. Received orders to move in two hours at 3.25 pm. Took thirteen sick horses to await evacuation at Bouquemaison station & then proceeded to Mazicourt. Rest of the section marched with A Echelon to Mazicourt.	W.R.B.
3-7-16 Mazicourt	Moved to more suitable billets in same village. Admitted six sick horses into section. Ordinary routine work.	W.R.B.
4-7-16 "	Admitted five sick horses into section. Inspected horses of one section in M.G. squadron for contagious disease.	W.R.B.
5-7-16 "	Admitted eight sick horses into section. Ordinary routine work. Evacuated sixteen from Auxi le Chateau station to No 22 Vety Hospital Abbeville.	W.R.B.
6-7-16 "	Admitted eight sick horses into section. Ordinary Routine work.	W.R.B.
7-7-16.	Admitted two horses into section. Ordinary Routine work.	W.R.B.

(73989) W4141—463. 400,000. 9/14. H.&J.Ltd. Forms/C. 2118/10.

Instructions regarding War Diaries and Intelligence Summaries are contained in F. S. Regs., Part II. and the Staff Manual respectively. Title pages will be prepared in manuscript.

WAR DIARY
or
~~INTELLIGENCE SUMMARY.~~
(*Erase heading not required.*)

Army Form C. 2118.

Mobile Vety Section
Mhow Cavalry Bde

Hour, Date, Place	Summary of Events and Information	Remarks and references to Appendices
8·7·16 Mazicourt	Admitted four sick horses into section. Inspected horses of one section of M.G. Squadron for contagious diseases.	ARB
9·7·16 "	Collected a horse, which was lost, from Agenville – returned same to Lucknow Bde. Admitted one sick horse into section	ARB.
10·7·16 "	Admitted five sick horses into section. Inspected horses of one Squadron of Central India Horse for contagious diseases.	ARB
11·7·16 "	Admitted two sick horses into section. Evacuated by road to No 22 Vety Hospital Abbeville twenty sick horses.	ARB
12·7·16 "	Admitted one sick horse into section. Ordinary Routine work	ARB.
13·7·16 "	Admitted one sick horse into section " "	ARB
14·7·16 "	Admitted two sick horses into section " "	ARB
15·7·16 "	Admitted twenty four sick horses into section. Evacuated by road to No 22 Vety Hospital Abbeville twenty seven sick horses. Motor Ambulance was sent from Abbeville for two horses unable to walk.	ARB

(73989) W4141—463. 400,000. 9/14. H.&J.Ltd. Forms/C. 2118/10.

Instructions regarding War Diaries and Intelligence Summaries are contained in F. S. Regs., Part II. and the Staff Manual respectively. Title pages will be prepared in manuscript.

WAR DIARY
or
~~INTELLIGENCE~~ SUMMARY.
(*Erase heading not required.*)

Army Form C. 2118.

Mobile Vety Section
Mhow Cavalry Bde

Hour, Date, Place	Summary of Events and Information	Remarks and references to Appendices
16. 7. 16 Mazicourt	Admitted four sick horses into section – Inspected horses of one Squadron of Central India Horse for contagious disease	ABB
17. 7. 16 "	Admitted one horse into section. Inspected horses of one section of M.G. Squadron for contagious diseases.	ABB
18. 7. 16 "	Admitted four horses into section. Evacuated by Road nine sick horses to No 22 Vety Hospital Abbeville.	ABB
19. 7. 16.	Marched from Mazicourt to Roellecourt with B echelon. Motor ambulance was sent from Abbeville to collect two horses unable to walk.	ABB
20. 7. 16 Roellecourt.	Admitted one horse into section – Ordinary Routine work.	ABB
21. 7. 16 "	Admitted six horses into section " "	ABB
22. 7. 16	Admitted nine horses into section. Inspected Horses of one Squadron of CIH for contagious diseases	ABB
23. 7. 16.	Admitted two horses into section. Evacuated sixteen horses to No 22 Vety Hospital from Ligny	ABB

Instructions regarding War Diaries and Intelligence Summaries are contained in F. S. Regs., Part II. and the Staff Manual respectively. Title pages will be prepared in manuscript.

WAR DIARY
or
~~INTELLIGENCE~~ SUMMARY.
(Erase heading not required.)

Army Form C. 2118.

Mobile Vety Section
Mhow Cavalry Bde

Hour, Date, Place	Summary of Events and Information	Remarks and references to Appendices
24.7.16 Roellecourt	Admitted three horses into section. Ordinary Routine work.	ABB
25.7.16 "	Nothing to note. Ordinary Routine work	ABB
26.7.16 "	Admitted five horses into section. Collected one horse which was left at Berlencourt by 4th Bde 1st I.C. Division. unable to move with troops. Inspected horses of one section of M.G. Squadron for contagious diseases.	ABB
27.7.16 "	Admitted six horses into section. Evacuated eight horses to ~~20~~ 22 Vety Hospital from Lingues	ABB
28.7.16	Admitted five horses into section. Ordinary routine work	ABB
29.7.16 "	Admitted four horses into section. Evacuated eight horses to No 22 Vety Hospital from Lingues	ABB
30.7.16 "	Admitted one horse into section. Collected two mules from Wavrans - left behind by 15th D.A.C. unable to walk	ABB
31.7.16	Inspected horses of one Squadron of CIH for contagious Diseases	ABB.

A B Bowbay Capt AVC
Oc M.V.S.
Mhow Cav Bde

(73989) W4141—463. 400,000. 9/14. H.&J.Ltd. Forms/C. 2118/10.

SERIAL NO 201.

Confidential

War Diary

of

Mobile Veterinary Section, Mhow Cavalry Brigade.

FROM 1st August 1916 TO 31st August 1916

Instructions regarding War Diaries and Intelligence Summaries are contained in F. S. Regs., Part II. and the Staff Manual respectively. Title pages will be prepared in manuscript.

WAR DIARY
or
INTELLIGENCE SUMMARY.
(*Erase heading not required.*)

Army Form C. 2118.

Mobile Vety section
Mhow Cav: Bde

Hour, Date, Place		Summary of Events and Information	Remarks and references to Appendices
1/8/16	Roellecourt	Admitted one horse into section Evacuated eight from Ligny to Abbeville	ARB
2/8/16	"	Admitted eight horses into section Inspected a section of Machine Gun Squadron for contagious disease	ARB
3/8/16	"	Admitted four horses & evacuated twelve from Ligny to No 22 Vety Hospital Abbeville	ARB
4/8/16		Admitted three horses. Ordinary Routine work.	ARB
5/8/16		Admitted two horses. Ordinary Routine work	ARB
6/8/16	"	Evacuated six horses from Ligny to No 22 Vety Hospital Abbeville	ARB
7/8/16		Inspected horses of one Squadron of Central India Horse for contagious diseases	ARB
8/8/16	"	Admitted six horses into section Ordinary Routine work	ARB
9/8/16		Admitted two horses into section Evacuated ten horses from St Pol to No 22 Vety Hospital Abbeville	ARB
10/8/16		Marched from Roellecourt to Cambligneul	ARB
11/8/16	Cambligneul	Admitted nine sick horses into section. Inspected one section of M G Sq for contagious diseases	ARB
12/8/16	"	Received orders to take over Vety charge of Sealkot Field Ambulance in addition to other duties	ARB

(73989) W4141—463. 400,000. 9/14. H.&J.Ltd. Forms/C. 2118/10.

Instructions regarding War Diaries and Intelligence Summaries are contained in F. S. Regs., Part II. and the Staff Manual respectively. Title pages will be prepared in manuscript.

WAR DIARY
or
INTELLIGENCE SUMMARY.
(Erase heading not required.)

Army Form C. 2118.

Mobile Vety Section
Mhow Cav: Bde

Hour, Date, Place	Summary of Events and Information	Remarks and references to Appendices
13/8/16. Cambligneul.	Inspected horses of one squadron of Central India Horse for contagious diseases	ARB.
14/8/16	Recommended Corporal Brown & Pte Murray for promotion	ARB.
15/8/16 "	Admitted 11 horses into section Ordinary Routine work	ARB.
16/8/16 "	Admitted 4 horses & evacuated 14 from Aubigny to No 22 Vety Hospital Abbeville	ARB.
17/8/16 "	Inspected horses of one section of M G Sq. for contagious diseases. Admitted 5 horses	ARB
18/8/16	Evacuated 8 horses from Aubigny to No 22 Vety Hospital Abbeville.	ARB.
19/8/16	Admitted 5 horses. Inspected horses of one section of the M G Sq for contagious diseases. Took over Vety charge of 278 Coy R E while billeted at Cambligneul	ARB
20/8/16	Ordinary Routine work	ARB
21/8/16	Inspected horses of one squadron of CIH for contagious diseases. Admitted 5 horses into section	ARB
22/8/16	Admitted one horse into section. Ordinary Routine work.	ARB

(73989) W4141—463. 400,000. 9/14. H.&J.Ltd. Forms/C. 2118/10.

Instructions regarding War Diaries and Intelligence Summaries are contained in F. S. Regs., Part II. and the Staff Manual respectively. Title pages will be prepared in manuscript.

WAR DIARY
or
INTELLIGENCE SUMMARY.
(*Erase heading not required.*)

Army Form C. 2118.

Mobile Vety Section
Mhow Cav Bde.

Hour, Date, Place	Summary of Events and Information	Remarks and references to Appendices
23/8/16 Cambligneul	Malleined 26 horses and two Mules – these were remounts which came from a depot where a case of glanders had afterwards been detected. No reactions	ABB
24/8/16 ..	Admitted one horse into section. Attended an inspection of Horses of Central India Horse by ADVS	ABB
25/8/16	Admitted 4 horses into section. Attended an inspection of Horses of MG Squadron by ADVS	ABB
26/8/16	Evacuated 8 horses to Hospital	ABB
27/8/16	Ordinary Routine work.	ABB
28/8/16	Admitted one horse into section. Ordinary Routine work	ABB
29/8/16	Admitted 3	
30/8/16	Ordinary Routine work.	
31/8/16	.. .. ..	

A.B. Bowhay.
Capt. AVC.

(73989) W4141—463. 400,000. 9/14. H.&J.Ltd. Forms/C. 2118/10.

SERIAL NO. 201

Confidential War Diary

of

MOBILE VETERINARY SECTION, MHOW CAVALRY BRIGADE.

FROM 1st SEPTEMBER 1916 TO 30th SEPTEMBER 1916

Instructions regarding War Diaries and Intelligence Summaries are contained in F. S. Regs., Part II. and the Staff Manual respectively. Title pages will be prepared in manuscript.

WAR DIARY
or
INTELLIGENCE SUMMARY.
(Erase heading not required.)

Army Form C. 2118.

Mobile Vety Section
Mhow Cav Bde
1 I C D

Place	Date	Hour	Summary of Events and Information	Remarks and references to Appendices
Cambligneul	1/9/16		Received orders to move tomorrow. Inspected one Squadron of horses of Central India Horse for contagious disease	ABB
Grand Camp	2/9/16		Evacuated 13 horses from Aubigny to No 22 Vety Hospital - marched from Cambligneul to Grand camp near St Pol.	ABB
Couchy sur Cauche	3/9/16		Marched from Grand camp to Couchy sur Cauche.	ABB
	4/9/16		Marched from Couchy sur Cauche to Noyelle-en-Chaussee	ABB
Noyelle en Chaussee	5/9/16		Admitted two horses into section. Inspected two sections of Machine Gun Sq. for Contagious disease	ABB
"	6/9/16		Admitted nine horses into section. Inspected two squadrons of CIH for Contagious disease	ABB
"	7/9/16		Admitted one horse into section and evacuated 13 horses by road to No 22 Vety Hospital Abbeville	ABB
"	8/9/15		Admitted seven horses into section. Took section out for Divisional manoeuvres. Rendered report on working of section to ADVS 1st ICD.	ABB

2353 Wt. W2514/1454 700,000 5/15 D. D. & L. A.D.S.S./Forms/C. 2118.

Army Form C. 2118.

WAR DIARY
or
INTELLIGENCE SUMMARY.
(*Erase heading not required.*)

Instructions regarding War Diaries and Intelligence Summaries are contained in F. S. Regs., Part II. and the Staff Manual respectively. Title pages will be prepared in manuscript.

Mobile Vety Section
Mhow Cav. Bde
1 I C D

Place	Date	Hour	Summary of Events and Information	Remarks and references to Appendices
Noyelle en Chaussee	9/9/16		Admitted one horse. Inspected one section of Machine Gun Sq for contagious disease	ABB
"	10/9/16		Evacuated seven horses by road to No 22 Vety Hospital Abbeville	ABB
Remaisnil	11/9/16		Marched from Noyelle en Chaussee to Remaisnil. Admitted 11 horses into section	ABB
Authieule	12/9/16		Marched from Remaisnil to Authieule (n' Doullens) Evacuated 12 horses from Doullens to No 22 Vety Hosp. Admitted 16 horses into section	
Querrieu	13/9/16		Evacuated 15 horses from Doullens by rail to No 22 Vety section. Marched from Authieule to Querrieu	ABB
"	14/9/16		Admitted 12 sick horses. Evacuated 9 horses from Treckencourt to No 7 Vety Hospital	ABB
Morlancourt	15/9/16		Marched from Querrieu to Morlancourt. Admitted 5 sick horses	ABB
	16/9/16		Admitted three horses. Transferred 8 horses to Lucknow Mob Vety section	ABB
	17/9/16		Admitted 4 horses & transferred them to Lucknow Mob Vety section	ABB
	18/9/16		Inspected two squadrons of Central India Horse for contagious disease	ABB
	19/9/16		Admitted one sick horse into section	ABB
	20/9/16		Inspected horses of Machine Gun squadron for contagious disease	ABB

2353 Wt. W2544/1454 700,000 5/15 D. D. & L. A.D.S.S./Forms/C. 2118.

Army Form C. 2118.

WAR DIARY
INTELLIGENCE SUMMARY

(Erase heading not required.)

Instructions regarding War Diaries and Intelligence Summaries are contained in F. S. Regs., Part II. and the Staff Manual respectively. Title Pages will be prepared in manuscript.

Mobile Vet. Section
Mhow Cav. Bde
1st I.C.D.

Place	Date	Hour	Summary of Events and Information	Remarks and references to Appendices
Morlancourt	21.9.16		Admitted 5 sick horses into section & transferred them to Lucknow M.V.S	ARB
	22.9.16		" 1 " " " Ordinary Routine work.	ARB
	23.9.16		" 5 " " " Transferred one to Lucknow M.V.S	ARB
	24.9.16		" 13 " " " Transferred fifteen to "	ARB
Mametz	25.9.16		Marched from Morlancourt for Mametz acting as advanced mob. Vet. Sect. Admitted one sick horse. Received orders not to move until receiving orders from A.D.V.S	ARB
Morlancourt	26.9.16		Marched from Mametz to Morlancourt. Transferred one sick horse unable to march to No 33 Vet. Mob. Sect. On arriving at Morlancourt received orders to march to a new area - proceeded about 3 kilos & then received orders to return. Admitted 8 sick horses	ARB
Bussy les Daours	27.9.16		Evacuated 8 sick horses from Méricourt to No 7 Vet. Hospital. Marched from Morlancourt to Bussy les Daours. Admitted one horse	ARB
Belloy sur Somme	28.9.16		Marched from Bussy les Daours to Belloy. Admitted two horses from 1st Brit Cav Div. aux horse transport.	ARB
Vauchelles les Domart	29.9.16		Marched from Belloy sur Somme to Vauchelles les Domart.	ARB
Domart	30.9.16		Marched from Vauchelles les Domart to Domart. Attended to one horse with Ruptured artery on the Road & handed over to Transport Officer 10th Lancaster Fusiliers, until collected by the 14th Divn M.V.S	ARB

A.R. Bowker Capt. A.V.C.

2449 Wt. W14957/M90 750,000 1/16 J.B.C. & A. Forms/C.2118/12.

SERIAL NO. 201

Confidential

War Diary

of

Mobile Veterinary Section, Mhow Cavalry Brigade.

FROM 1st October 1916 TO ~~31st October~~ 30th November 1916.

Army Form C.2118.

WAR DIARY
or
~~INTELLIGENCE SUMMARY~~

(Erase heading not required.)

Instructions regarding War Diaries and Intelligence Summaries are contained in F. S. Regs., Part II. and the Staff Manual respectively. Title Pages will be prepared in manuscript.

Mobile Vet. Sectn. Mhow Cavalry Bgde. 1st I.C. Division

Place	Date	Hour	Summary of Events and Information	Remarks and references to Appendices
Bouviez	1/10/16		Capt. Barton on leave took over charge of VI Dragoons + 2nd Lancers admitted 13 sick horses	
"	2/10/16		Admitted 7 sick horses inspected 2 sections of machine gun sqdn for contagious diseases	
"	3/10/16		Admitted 3 sick horses into Section; ordinary routine work —	
"	4/10/16		Evacuated 21 sick horses from Beaurainville to No 7. Vet. H. Forges-le-Eau admitted one sick horse.	
"	5/10/16		Detailed one man to Division to take charge of float — Inspected 1 Sqdn 38th C.I.H for contagious diseases —	
"	6/10/16		Collected one sick horse from Raye-sur-Authie left behind by 1st I.C. Divisional Ammunition Column! R.H.A —	
"	7/10/16		Admitted one horse to Section —	
"	8/10/16		Admitted one sick horse to Section Routine work as usual	
"	9/10/16		Admitted one horse, inspected one sqdn C.I.H. for contagious diseases	
"	10/10/16		Evacuated 7 horses by rail from Beaurainville to No 7 Vet. H. Forges-le-Eau.	
"	11/10/16		Admitted 5 sick + 11 cast horses from D.A.D.R	

2449 Wt. W14957/M90 750,000 1/16 J.B.C. & A. Forms/C.2118/12.

Army Form C. 2118.

Instructions regarding War Diaries and Intelligence Summaries are contained in F. S. Regs., Part II. and the Staff Manual respectively. Title Pages will be prepared in manuscript.

WAR DIARY
or
INTELLIGENCE SUMMARY
(Erase heading not required.)

~~Wilson~~ Mobile Vet^y Section
Mhow Cavalry Bg^de
1st I.C. Division

Place	Date	Hour	Summary of Events and Information	Remarks and references to Appendices
Douriez	12/10/16		Evacuated 21 horses by rail from Beaurainville to No 7 Vet^y H. Forges-les-Eaux.	
"	13/10/16		Admitted 2 sick horses. Had inspection of Section by D.D.V.S.	
"	14/10/16		Admitted 2 sick horses. inspected one Sq^dn of 38th C.I.H. for contagious diseases	
"	15/10/16		General Routine work –	
"	16/10/16		Inspected one section of Machine Gun Sq^n for contagious diseases	
"	17/10/16.		Capt Bowby went Hospital. Capt Barton in charge. admitted 2 sick horses	ChmB
	18/10/16		Inspection of section & general clear up..	
	19/10/16.		Admitted 5 sick horses. General routine work.	ChmB
	20/10/16.		Evacuated 11 sick horses from Beaurainville.	ChmB
	21/10/16.		Lieut Stevens in charge of Section	ChmB
	22/10/16		Inspection 1 Squad. C.I.H.	ChmB
	23/10/16.		Admitted 8 sick horses	ChmB
	24/10/16		Evacuated 11 sick horses. Capt Barton visited Section.	ChmB
	25/10/16.		Admitted 6 sick horses	ChmB
	26/10/16.		Admitted 2 sick horses. evacuated 5 by Road to Abbeville	ChmB
	27/10/16.		Inspected 2 squad. Inniskillings	ChmB

2449 Wt. W14957/M90 750,000 1/16 J.B.C. & A. Forms/C.2118/12.

Army Form C. 2118.

Instructions regarding War Diaries and Intelligence Summaries are contained in F. S. Regs., Part II. and the Staff Manual respectively. Title Pages will be prepared in manuscript.

WAR DIARY
or
INTELLIGENCE SUMMARY
(Erase heading not required.)

Mobile Vet^y Sect^n Mhow. Cav. Bg^de 1st I. C. Div

Place	Date	Hour	Summary of Events and Information	Remarks and references to Appendices
28/10/16.	Doniez.		Inspected Section + had general parade admitted 2 sick horses	GHB
29/10/16	"		D.D.V.S visited section + inspected equipment + men's quarters	GHB
30/10/16	"		Inspected Machine Gun Sq^dn + admitted six sick horses to Section	GHB
31/10/16	"		Inspected 1 Sq^dn C.I.H for contagious disease. Evacuated 8 sick horses by road to Abbeville + was under orders to move	
			admitted 6 horses from D.A.D.R for casting + 2 from 2nd Lancers	GHB

G H Bennet
Lt. A.V.C

2449 Wt. W14957/M90 750,000 1/16 J.B.C. & A. Forms/C.2118/12.

Confidential.

WAR DIARY
of
Mobile Veterinary Section
MHOW Cavalry Brigade.
for
November. 1916.

Instructions regarding War Diaries and Intelligence Summaries are contained in F. S. Regs., Part II. and the Staff Manual respectively. Title pages will be prepared in manuscript.

WAR DIARY
or
~~INTELLIGENCE~~ SUMMARY.
(Erase heading not required.)

Army Form C. 2118.

Mhow Mobile Veterinary Section

Place	Date	Hour	Summary of Events and Information	Remarks and references to Appendices
DOURIEZ	1·11·16		March from DOURIEZ via CRECY to BELLOY. sur MER. attended to sick horse on line of march otherwise a successful journey. Evacuated four horses & five mules en-route to 22 Vet. H.P.	G.H.B.
BELLOY	2·11·16		Arranged billets for horses and men Admitted one sick horse.	G.H.B.
"	3·11·16		Visited 38th C.I.H at NIBAS. and Machine Gun Squadn. at OFFEUX. Admitted one sick horse	G.H.B.
"	4·11·16		General inspection of arms and Equipment, visited C.I.H at OCHANCOURT	G.H.B.
"	5·11·16		Inspected one section of Machine Gun Squadron for contagious diseases, ordinary routine work as usual.	G.H.B.
"	6·11·16		Admitted two sick horses	G.H.B.
"	7·11·16		Admitted three sick horses, visited C.I.H, at NIBAS inspected one Squadron for contagious diseases.	G.H.B.
"	8·11·16		Evacuated six sick horses by road to No 22 Vety Hospital ABBEVILLE, received visit from A.D.V.S to inspect, horses, men billets equipment &c	G.H.B.
"	9·11·16		Admitted 3 sick horses + inspected sick horses of C.I.H at OCHANCOURT. Made Post mortem on one horse sent in with colic & diagnosed incarceration of bowel.	G.H.B.
"	10·11·16		Evacuated one sick horse by road to 22 Vety. H.P. ABBEVILLE routine work as usual.	G.H.B.

Instructions regarding War Diaries and Intelligence Summaries are contained in F. S. Regs., Part II. and the Staff Manual respectively. Title pages will be prepared in manuscript.

WAR DIARY
or
~~INTELLIGENCE SUMMARY.~~
(Erase heading not required.)

Mhow Mobile Veterinary Section

Army Form C. 2118.

Place	Date	Hour	Summary of Events and Information	Remarks and references to Appendices
BELLOY	11-11-16		Admitted one sick horse and inspected one section of Machine Gun Squadron for contagious diseases.	G.H.B.
"	12-11-16		Private Mitchell arrived from Base to complete Establishment. Admitted one sick horse. Ordinary Routine Work.	G.H.B.
"	13-11-16		Inspected new stables of Machine Gun Squadron at OFFEUX and had an inspection of head quarter horses as regards shoeing	G.H.B.
"	14-11-16		Admitted one horse to Section for treatment in Section & inspected D. Squadron C.I.H for contagious diseases.	G.H.B.
"	15-11-16		Had a rifle inspection and marching order parade of Mobile Section, routine work as usual.	G.H.B.
"	16-11-16		Admitted 2 sick horses & arranged Extension ~~for~~ of sick lines for animals remain under treatment.	G.H.B.
"	17-11-16		Inspected one section of Machine Gun Squadron for contagious diseases.	G.H.B.
"	18-11-16		Routine Work as usual.	
"	19-11-16		Held a shoeing board at OFFEUX and qualified one farrier and inspected sick animals of Machine Gun Squadron at same time	G.H.B.

Army Form C. 2118.

Instructions regarding War Diaries and Intelligence Summaries are contained in F. S. Regs., Part II. and the Staff Manual respectively. Title pages will be prepared in manuscript.

WAR DIARY
or
~~INTELLIGENCE~~ SUMMARY.
(Erase heading not required.)

Mhow Mobile Veterinary Section

Place	Date	Hour	Summary of Events and Information	Remarks and references to Appendices
BELLOY	20.11.16		Visited C.I.H at NIBAS and OCHANCOURT and inspected shoeing re. prevention of picked up nails	G.H.B.
"	21.11.16		Inspected sick horses at OFFEUX. Routine work as usual	G.H.B.
"	22.11.16		Admitted one sick horse from C.I.H. Inspected 1 Squadron C.I.H for contagious diseases	G.H.B.
"	23.11.16		Evacuated four sick horses by road to 22 Vet. H. Havre. Routine work as usual	G.H.B.
"	24.11.16		Had kit inspection and read extracts from General Routine Orders to men	G.H.B.
"	25.11.16		Inspected one section Machine Gun Squadron at OFFEUX for contagious diseases	G.H.B.
"	26.11.16		Visited sick horses C.I.H at NIBAS. Routine work as usual	G.H.B.
"	27.11.16		Admitted 2 sick horses for treatment in Section. Inspected new billets	G.H.B.
"	28.11.16		Gave orders re. road cleaning in village. Inspected sick horses at OCHANCOURT.	G.H.B.
"	29.11.16		Inspected 1 squadron C.I.H at NIBAS for contagious diseases, visited sick horses at OCHANCOURT	G.H.B.
"	30.11.16		Routine work as usual & had a general parade of men + horses.	G.H.B.

Geoffrey H. Bennet
Lt. A.V.C.

T2134. Wt. W708–776. 500000. 4/15. Sir J. C. & S.

SERIAL NO. 201

Confidential

War Diary

of

Mobile Veterinary Section, Mhow Cavalry Brigade.

FROM 1st December 1916 TO 31st December 1916

Instructions regarding War Diaries and Intelligence Summaries are contained in F. S. Regs., Part II. and the Staff Manual respectively. Title pages will be prepared in manuscript.

WAR DIARY
or
INTELLIGENCE SUMMARY.
(Erase heading not required.)

Army Form C. 2118.

MHOW. MOBILE VETERINARY SECTION

Place	Date	Hour	Summary of Events and Information	Remarks and references to Appendices
BELLOY	1.12.16		Routine work as usual	GHB.
"	2.12.16		Inspected Shoeing, Brigade Headquarters horses, inspected sick horses A & C ~~horses~~ Squadron C.I.H. (GHB)	GHB.
"	3.12.16		Inspected sick horses B & D Squadrons C.I.H & Machine Gun Squadron	GHB.
"	4.12.16		Inspected one sectn Machine Gun Squad. for contagious diseases & shoeing.	GHB.
"	5.12.16		Inspected one squadron C.I.H for Contagious Diseases & shoeing	GHB.
"	6.12.16		Inspected sick horses A & C squadron C.I.H.	GHB.
"	7.12.16		Admitted one sick horse. Routine work as usual	GHB.
"	8.12.16		Took over veterinary charge of Auxiliary Horse Transport & gave up C.I.H to Capt Williams	GHB.
"	9.12.16		Admitted one sick horse, routine work as usual.	GHB.
"	10.12.16		Admitted 3 sick horses visited Aux Horse Transport & inspected sick horses.	GHB.
"	11.12.16		Admitted 1 sick horse inspected dip & billets for horses & met at Friville	GHB.
"	12.12.16		Admitted 1 sick horse, evacuated 5 sick to No. 22. Vety. H. ABBEVILLE by road. visited	GHB.
"			machine gun squadron & inspected sick horses & one section for contagious diseases.	
"	13.12.16		Inspected one section Machine Gun Squadron for Shoeing & Contagious diseases & admitted	GHB.
"			four sick horses.	

G H Bennet Lt A.V.C

T2134. Wt. W708-776. 500000. 4/15. Sir J. C. & S.

Instructions regarding War Diaries and Intelligence Summaries are contained in F. S. Regs., Part II. and the Staff Manual respectively. Title pages will be prepared in manuscript.

WAR DIARY or INTELLIGENCE SUMMARY. MHOW MOBILE VETERINARY SECTION

(Erase heading not required.)

Army Form C. 2118.

Place	Date	Hour	Summary of Events and Information	Remarks and references to Appendices
BELLOY	14.12.16		Inspected AUX. Horse Transport for Contagious Diseases + Shoeing also Sick horses. recommended Machine Gun Squadron to use linseed cake for fifty horses if possible.	G.H.B.
"	15.12.16		Admitted 3 sick horses. Routine work as usual.	G.H.B.
"	16.12.16		Routine Work as usual.	G.H.B.
"	17.12.16		Rifle inspection + dismounted drill	G.H.B.
"	18.12.16		Eight sick horses evacuated to No. 22 Veterinary Hospital ABBEVILLE	G.H.B.
"	19.12.16		Inspected one sectn Machine Gun Squadron for contagious diseases + Shoeing + visited "dip"	G.H.B.
"	20.12.16		Took over Veterinary charge of C.I.H + admitted one sick horse.	G.H.B
"	21.12.16		Visited C.I.H at Vibras + Ochancourt + inspected one squadron for Shoeing	G.H.B.
"	22.12.16		Admitted 2 sick horses, inspected whole of Machine Gun Squadron for contagious diseases + Shoeing also B + D Squadron C.I.H at OCHANCOURT.	G.H.B.
"	23.12.16		Inspected sick horses AUX. Horse Transport also 50 horses for contagious diseases + Shoeing	G.H.B
"	24.12.16		Routine work as usual. Evacuated four horses by road to ABBEVILLE	G.H.B
"	25.12.16		Routine work.	
"	26.12.16		Admitted 2 sick horses, reported outbreak of 2 cases Pink Eye Aux. Horse Transport	G.H.B
"			Inspected remainder for contagious diseases.	

G H Bennet Lt. A.V.C

T.134. Wt. W708-776. 500000. 4/15. Sir J. C. & S.

Army Form C. 2118.

Instructions regarding War Diaries and Intelligence Summaries are contained in F. S. Regs., Part II. and the Staff Manual respectively. Title pages will be prepared in manuscript.

WAR DIARY
or
INTELLIGENCE SUMMARY. Mhow Mobile Veterinary Section.
(Erase heading not required.)

Place	Date	Hour	Summary of Events and Information	Remarks and references to Appendices
BELLOY	27·12·16		Admitted 2 sick horses + inspected Brigade Transport Horses for shoeing.	G.H.B
	28·12·16		Admitted 1 sick horse + inspected sick horses AUX. Horse Transport.	G.H.B
	29·12·16		Inspected B o D. Squadron C.I.H for contagious diseases + shoeing also sick horses.	G.H.B
	30·12·16		Inspected sick horses Machine Gun Squadron also one Sectn for shoeing	G.H.B
	31·12·16		Routine work as usual. Inspected progress with "D.I.P."	G.H.B.

O.C

MOBILE VETERINARY SECTION
31.12.16
MHOW BRIGADE

G.H. Bennet
Lt. A.V.C

T.2134. Wt. W708–776. 500000. 4/15. Sir J. C. & S.

Instructions regarding War Diaries and Intelligence Summaries are contained in F. S. Regs., Part II. and the Staff Manual respectively. Title pages will be prepared in manuscript.

WAR DIARY
or
INTELLIGENCE SUMMARY.
(Erase heading not required.)

Army Form C. 2118.

MHOW MOBILE VETERINARY SECTION

Place	Date	Hour	Summary of Events and Information	Remarks and references to Appendices
BELLOY	1.12.16		Routine work as usual	GHB
"	2.12.16		Inspected [illegible] Brigade Headquarters horses, inspected sick horses A & C ~~[illegible]~~ Squadron C.I.H.	GHB
"	3.12.16		Inspected sick horses B & D Squadron C.I.H. & Machine Gun Squadron	GHB
"	4.12.16		Inspected [illegible] Machine Gun Squadron for contagious disease & [illegible]	GHB
"	5.12.16		Inspected [illegible] Squadron C.I.H. for contagious diseases & [illegible]	GHB
"	6.12.16		Inspected sick horses A & C Squadron C.I.H.	GHB
"	7.12.16		Admitted [illegible] sick horses. Routine work as usual	GHB
"	8.12.16		Took over veterinary charge of Brigade Horse Transport [illegible] C.I.H. [illegible]	GHB
"	9.12.16		Admitted [illegible] sick horse. Routine work continued	GHB
"	10.12.16		Admitted [illegible] sick horses [illegible] Horse Transport & inspected sick horses	GHB
"	11.12.16		Admitted 1 sick horse. Inspected [illegible] billets for horses [illegible]	GHB
"	12.12.16		Admitted 1 sick horse, evacuated 5 [illegible] to 22 V.E.S. [illegible] [illegible] Machine Gun Squadron & inspected sick horses [illegible] for contagious diseases	GHB
"	13.12.16		Inspected [illegible] Machine Gun Squadron for [illegible] & contagious diseases & admitted four sick horses	GHB

G H Bennett [illegible]

T.134. Wt. W708-776. 500000. 4/15. Sir J. C. & S.

Army Form C. 2118.

Instructions regarding War Diaries and Intelligence Summaries are contained in F. S. Regs., Part II. and the Staff Manual respectively. Title pages will be prepared in manuscript.

WAR DIARY
or
INTELLIGENCE SUMMARY.
(Erase heading not required.)

MHOW MOBILE VETERINARY SECTION

Place	Date	Hour	Summary of Events and Information	Remarks and references to Appendices
BELLOY	14.12.16		Inspected Aux. Horse Transport for Contagious Diseases & Shoeing, also Sick horses; recommended Machine Gun Squadron to have linseed cake for fifty horses if possible	G.H.B.
"	15.12.16		Admitted 3 sick horses. Routine work as usual.	G.H.B.
"	16.12.16		Routine work as usual.	G.H.B.
"	17.12.16		Rifle inspection + dismounted drill	G.H.B.
"	18.12.16		Eight sick horses evacuated to No. 22 Veterinary Hospital ABBEVILLE	G.H.B.
"	19.12.16		Inspected the [illegible] Machine Gun Squadron for contagious diseases & shoeing, [illegible] dip	G.H.B.
"	20.12.16		Took over Veterinary charge of C.I.H. & admitted one sick horse.	G.H.B.
"	21.12.16		Visited C.I.H. at [illegible] & [illegible]court & inspected one Squadron for shoeing	G.H.B.
"	22.12.16		Admitted 2 sick horses, inspected [illegible] Machine Gun Squadron for contagious diseases & shoeing, also B & D Squadrons C.I.H. at [illegible]COURT.	G.H.B.
"	23.12.16		Inspected sick horses Aux. Horse Transport also 50 horses for contagious diseases & shoeing,	G.H.B.
"	24.12.16		Routine work as usual. Evacuated four horses by road to ABBEVILLE	G.H.B.
"	25.12.16		Routine work.	
"	26.12.16		Admitted 2 sick horses, reported outbreak of 2 cases Pink Eye Aux. Horse Transport. Inspected remainder for contagious disease.	G.H.B.

G H Bennet Lt. A.V.C.

T2134. Wt. W708—776. 500000. 4/15. Sir J. C. & S.

Instructions regarding War Diaries and Intelligence Summaries are contained in F. S. Regs., Part II. and the Staff Manual respectively. Title pages will be prepared in manuscript.

WAR DIARY
or
INTELLIGENCE SUMMARY.
(Erase heading not required.)

Army Form C. 2118.

Mhow Mobile Veterinary Section

Place	Date	Hour	Summary of Events and Information	Remarks and references to Appendices
BELLOY	27.12.16		Admitted 2 sick horses & inspected Brigade Transport horses for disease	9.H.B
	28.12.16		Admitted 1 sick horse & inspected sick horses A.V.& horse transport	9.H.B
	29.12.16		Inspected B. D. Squadron C. I. H. for contagious diseases. Slung also sick horses.	9.H.B
	30.12.16		Inspected sick horses Machine Gun Squadron also the Sect[n] for skin [illegible]	9.H.B
	31.12.16		Routine work as usual. Inspected progress with "D.I.P"	9.H.B.

OC

MOBILE VETERINARY SECTION 31.12.16 MHOW BRIGADE

G.H. Bennet
Lt. A.V.C.

T.2134. Wt. W708-776. 500000. 4/15. Sir J. C. & S.

B.E.F

1 IND CAV DIV

MHOW Bde

SUPPLY OFFICER

1915 SEPT to 1916 SEPT

NO BOX

Army Form C. 2118

Instructions regarding War Diaries and Intelligence Summaries are contained in F. S. Regs., Part II. and the Staff Manual respectively. Title pages will be prepared in manuscript.

WAR DIARY
of
~~INTELLIGENCE~~ SUMMARY.
(Erase heading not required.)

Capt J.R. BRUNKER Brigade Supply Officer MHOW CAV^d B^de

Hour, Date, Place 1915	Summary of Events and Information	Remarks and references to Appendices
VILLERS-SOUS-AILLY 16th Sept	Supply Estab of AMBALA Brigade is transferred to MHOW B^de & remaining in present billets - a complete exchange of all documents being made by the two Supply Estabs, that formerly belonging to MHOW B^de now becoming AMBALA B^de; to adjust ration issues lorries of MHOW B^de from 2nd Div Supply Column delivering rations here on 15th readjustment of lorry loads for 16th Sept being made at Rail head -	
VILLERS-SOUS-AILLY	Capt Hunter proceeds of 5-days leave to England on very urgent private affairs.	JRB
16th Sept:	Rations for Brigade delivered by lorries of 2nd Div Supply Column - all correct.	JRB
" 17th Sept	Ration issue now normal. local purchase of fuel + fodder -	JRB

Army Form C. 2118.

Instructions regarding War Diaries and Intelligence Summaries are contained in F. S. Regs., Part II. and the Staff Manual respectively. Title pages will be prepared in manuscript.

WAR DIARY
of
~~INTELLIGENCE SUMMARY.~~

(Erase heading not required.)

CAPT. J. R. BRUNKER Supply Officer MHOW. Cav. Brigade

Place	Date	Hour	Summary of Events and Information	Remarks and references to Appendices
VILLERS SOUS AILLY	18/9/15		Routine work & local purchases – nothing to record	JB
do	19/9/15		do do do	JB
do	20/9/15		do do – Capt Brunker returned from leave –	JB
do	21/9/15		Routine work – nothing to record –	JB
do	22/9/15	7.30 Am	Orders received from 1st Ind Cav. Div. that Div would move to new billeting area. MHOW Brigade marched at 12 noon to BOURNEVILLE The whole Brigade being close billetted in the one village – Supply Rendezvous was at 3-30 pm at X road 2¼ miles S. S E of BOURNEVILLE – Units were in receipt of rations by 4.30 Pm. I arranged, prior to leaving VILLERS, to borrow a Lorry from 4 H.Q. Ammn Column & in this brought along 2 days supply of potatoes & one days coal fuel. So that the same was available for issue immediately on arrival of the troops – At the same time,	

2353 Wt. W2544/1454 700,000 5/15 D. D. & L. A.D.S.S./Forms/C. 2118.

Army Form C. 2118

Instructions regarding War Diaries and Intelligence Summaries are contained in F. S. Regs., Part II. and the Staff Manual respectively. Title pages will be prepared in manuscript.

WAR DIARY
or
~~INTELLIGENCE SUMMARY.~~
(Erase heading not required.)

Capt. J. R. Brunker. B.S.O. [illegible] Cavalry Brigade.

Place	Date	Hour	Summary of Events and Information	Remarks and references to Appendices
	1915			
BOURNAVILLE	22/9		Instructed to rail-head one days supply of potatoes, to be brought forward in the lorries of the Column on 24th inst.	[initials]
BERNAVILLE	23/9		Supply rendezvous is fixed for same place & time as on 22nd inst. I find that there are shortages through wastage of iron rations for animals in the Bde & am making urgent arrangements for the replacement thereof. A stock of 3 tons of coal from balance in hand was left at VILLERS in charge of the Mayor & the matter reported by me to the S.S.O. 1st Cav. Div. Rations delivered under normal conditions. Fuel purchased (wood) at 15 F per 1000 kilos. This however exhausts the local resources.	
" do	24/9		Coal fuel purchased at 63 F per 1000 kilos after failing to procure it at rail head. Rations delivered to units at 3.45 P.M. Emergency rations to make good deficiencies were ~~[illegible]~~ demanded from Rail head.	
		7.30 P.M.	Orders received for Brigade to be ready to move at 2 hours notice from 6 A.M. 25th inst. I completed all necessary arrangements for work in the event of extemporised horse train or Pack animal convoy for rations (emergency) becoming necessary ~~on~~ a push forward where lorries cannot go	[initials]

2353 Wt. W2514/1454 700,000 5/15 D. D. & L. A.D.S.S./Forms/C. 2118.

Instructions regarding War Diaries and Intelligence Summaries are contained in F. S. Regs., Part II. and the Staff Manual respectively. Title pages will be prepared in manuscript.

WAR DIARY
or
~~INTELLIGENCE SUMMARY.~~
(Erase heading not required.)

Army Form C. 2118.

Capt. J. M. [illegible] Brig Supply Officer MHOW Cav. Brigade

Place	Date	Hour	Summary of Events and Information	Remarks and references to Appendices
	1915			
BERNAVILLE	25/9		Brigade ready to move at 2 hours notice. All units are clearly instructed in supply arrangements for a push forward with horse train or pack transport. "B" echelon wagons 16 in no. with 2 drivers & 2 loaders per wagon accompanied by 1 S&T NCO (S. Sergt NEWMAN) & 1 S&T agent sent to railhead after dumping all kits & baggage with local mayor, at 7 P.M. where the wagons were loaded up with two days iron rations for men & 2 days grain for animals & then formed into an extemporised Div Horse train.	
		2 P.M.	Brigade now on 1 hours notice to move. Supplies delivered by Supply Column at 3.30 but Lorries ordered to stand fast in Brigade area till 5 P.M. – units were warned to have rations cooked & ready for cook carts in event of a move. Grain put into nose bags but hay left, except little amount required for immediate use, at unit offloading points ready for Lorries to pick up & bring along in event of move. I proceeded to Railhead at 5 P.M. to supervise loading of extemporised train.	
do.	26/9		Brigade standing to at 1 hours notice. All men now in possession of 3 days iron rations by 1 day on man & 2 days on extemporised pack animals.	
		1.30 P.M.	Orders received from 1st I.C. Div. placing Brigade on 2½ hours notice to move. Nothing further to record.	

2353 Wt. W2514/1454 700,000 5/15 D. D. & L. A.D.S.S./Forms/C. 2118.

Army Form C. 2118.

Instructions regarding War Diaries and Intelligence Summaries are contained in F. S. Regs., Part II. and the Staff Manual respectively. Title pages will be prepared in manuscript.

WAR DIARY
of
~~INTELLIGENCE SUMMARY.~~

(Erase heading not required.) Capt. J. R. Brunker. Brigade Supply Officer. MHOW Cav[l] Brigade

Place	Date 1915	Hour	Summary of Events and Information	Remarks and references to Appendices
BERNAVILLE	27.9		Brigade still at 2½ hours notice – Ration issued from Supply Column at 3.30 P.m, cooked at once & made ready for ark carts. Local purchase of coal fuel – The Wagon train rejoined the Brigade at 3 P.m being treated as a separate unit under command of the B. Tpt officer.	JRB
do	28.9	9 A.m	Brigade still in close billets – arrangements made for local purchase of one days green vegetables – also coal fuel; purchase will be completed & no more take place prior to issue of rations –	
–		3.30 P.m	Rations issued to all units correct. No further remarks	JRB
do	29.9		Brigade still in close billets. Purchase of wheat & oat straw to complete authorised fodder ration for animals – also local purchase of coal & potatoes for one days issue –	
do	30.9		Nothing to record. Brigade still in billets.	JRB
do	do	7.45 P.m	Orders received that Brigade would march at 9 a.m on 1/10/15 to new billets which would be allotted on ground by A.Q. M.G.	

J. R. Brunker Captain
Brigade Supply Officer
Mhow Cav[l] Brigade

2353 Wt. W2514/1454 700,000 5/15 D. D. & L. A.D.S.S./Forms/C. 2118.

Serial No. 250.

Confidential

War Diary

of

Brigade Supply Officer; Mhow Cavalry Brigade.

FROM 1st October 1915 TO 31st October 1915

1st Ind CAV DIV

Army Form C. 2118.

WAR DIARY

of

INTELLIGENCE SUMMARY.

Instructions regarding War Diaries and Intelligence Summaries are contained in F. S. Regs., Part II. and the Staff Manual respectively. Title pages will be prepared in manuscript.

CAPT. J. R. Brunker Brigade Supply Officer (Erase heading not required.) MHOW. CAV. BDE IEF "A"

Place	Date 1915	Hour	Summary of Events and Information	Remarks and references to Appendices
BERNAVILLE	1 Oct	9.30 AM	Brigade marched to join in Divisional Tactical scheme - echelon A transport accompanying. Horse extemporised train & dismounted men of units marched to LE MEILLARD to await orders. I accompanied G.O.C. on march. Brigade moved N. across L'AUTHIE river arriving at point 1 mile SW of VILLERS L'HOPITAL at 3.30 P.M. - Brigade billeting area was given by A.Q. 2.G reaching Brigade Report Centre at 3-50 P.M. - area for Brigade being WAVANS - Ch. de BEAUVOIR - FROHEN LE GRAND and VILLERS L'HOPITAL - I now proceeded by car to cross road N of OCCOCHES where I met Supply Column & directed Lorries to unit areas. Thence to Supply Column H.Q. at exchange 3316 with Column Supply officer. Much difficulty is being experienced in procuring fuel. All coal has already been used up by French troops & wood is practically unobtainable. Units in receipt of rations by 6.0 P.M.	
Ch. de BEAUVOIR	2 Oct		Surrounding country has been reconnoitred by B. Reg. officer & a small quantity of fuel sufficient for cooking only procured for today - but no further quantity is forthcoming. Arrangements now being made to dig potatoes from fields close by. Rations in hands of units by 4.30 P.M.	
do	3 Oct		Brigade still in close billets now at 4 hours notice. Local purchase of coal (at DOULLENS) & potatoes, latter dug in fields by troops at 5 francs per 100 kilos. Nothing further to record	

53

2353 Wt. W2514/1454 700,000 5/15 D. D. & L. A.D.S.S./Forms/C. 2118.

Army Form C. 2118.

WAR DIARY
of
INTELLIGENCE SUMMARY.

(Erase heading not required.)

Instructions regarding War Diaries and Intelligence Summaries are contained in F. S. Regs., Part II. and the Staff Manual respectively. Title pages will be prepared in manuscript.

Capt J.R. Brunker - Supply Officer MHOW CAV. BRIGADE

Place	Date 1915	Hour	Summary of Events and Information	Remarks and references to Appendices
Ch de BEAUVOIR	4 Oct.		Local purchase of potatoes dug from fields, this is found to be by far the most economical method of purchase - reducing the price from 30 to 25 per cent. purchase of coal at DOULONS - price 60 f per 1000 kilos - usual ration arrangements -	
do do	5th Oct		Nothing to record -	
do	6th Oct		Routine work, coal fuel was delivered from Rail head by Supply Column. Local purchase of potatoes for 7th & 8th units - orders issued to the effect that units will cease making any local purchases & that the Requisitioning Officer will henceforth make all purchases including extra fodder, straw etc & deliver to units, this I found necessary owing to large fluctuations of prices paid -	
do	7th Oct		Local purchase of oat fodder & dry clover for 6th Inniskillings & [illegible] extra fodder for 7th & 8th at 2 lbs per horse. Routine work - nothing to record.	
do	8th Oct		Routine work, nothing to record - local purchase of fodder & wood fuel for 2 Lancers & 38th C.I.H. for 8th & 9th inst -	
do	9 Oct		Nothing to record	
do	10th Oct		Local Purchases - Nothing to record	

2353 Wt W2544/1454 700,000 5/15 D. D. & L. A.D.S.S./Forms/C. 2118.

Army Form C. 2118.

WAR DIARY
or
INTELLIGENCE SUMMARY.
(Erase heading not required.)

Instructions regarding War Diaries and Intelligence Summaries are contained in F. S. Regs., Part II. and the Staff Manual respectively. Title pages will be prepared in manuscript.

Capt. J. R. BRUNKER – Supply Officer MHOW. CAVY. BRIGADE.

Place	Date	Hour	Summary of Events and Information	Remarks and references to Appendices
	1915			
Ch. de BEAUVOIR	11th Oct		BRIGADE in billets – local purchase of Fuel Potatoes & Clover hay – Routine work.	JRB
do	12 Oct –		Orders received that Brigade will move to BERNEUIL & surrounding villages on 13/10/15.	JRB
do	13 Oct		Brigade moved to new area H^d Quarters & 2nd Lancers to BERNEUIL 6th Inniskillings to FRANQUEVILLE & SURCAMPS. A Batty. R.H.A. to St HILAIRE. 38th C I H to GORGES & VACQUERIE.	
do	"	1 pm	Brigade arrived in billets. Local purchase of wood & Potatoes – owing to high prices lately given to French troops difficulty is found in purchasing at our late rates. Coal is now coming daily 1½ tons per day from Rail head –	JRB JRB
BERNEUIL do	14 Oct.		Divisional Supply Park &c. [illegible] allotted to FIENVILLERS – where I met lorries & conducted them to H^d Qrs from where guides from units conducted the lorries to Regtl. areas – owing to very scattered billets of 6th Dragoons & Central India Horse	

WAR DIARY

or

INTELLIGENCE SUMMARY.

(Erase heading not required.)

Army Form C. 2118.

Instructions regarding War Diaries and Intelligence Summaries are contained in F. S. Regs., Part II. and the Staff Manual respectively. Title pages will be prepared in manuscript.

Capt. J. R. Brenker Supply Officer MHOW Cav" Brigade

Place	Date	Hour	Summary of Events and Information	Remarks and references to Appendices
	1915			
BERNEVIL	14 Oct		I have arranged for lorries after delivering full rations at, in the first case SURCAMPS & in the second VACQUERIE. To in the case of Inniskillings lift the Hay & grain of two Squadrons to FRANQUEVILLE & in the case of the C.I.H. to lift the grain & Hay of one Squadron to GORGES, in each case this being done on their return run. This procedure was found necessary by owing to units being, at present, without their Scheme "B" transport, they have not the lifting power for the above – All rations issued by 5 P.M. – local purchase of fuel & potatoes also Hay for all units –	
do	15 Oct.		Routine work nothing to record ——	JRB
do	16 Oct.		do do – orders received at 9 P.M. that Brigade Hd. Quarters will move to FIENVILLERS at 10.30 AM on 17.10.15 –	JRB

WAR DIARY

Army Form C. 2118.

or ~~INTELLIGENCE SUMMARY.~~

(Erase heading not required.)

Instructions regarding War Diaries and Intelligence Summaries are contained in F. S. Regs., Part II. and the Staff Manual respectively. Title pages will be prepared in manuscript.

Capt T. R. [illegible] Supply Officer MHOW CAV^y B^de

Place	Date 1915	Hour	Summary of Events and Information	Remarks and references to Appendices
FIENVILLERS	17 Oct	12 am	Brigade Head Quarters arrived & went into billets. Much difficulty in watering as practically speaking there is no water except wells & the latter are very dry. Remainder of Brigade in same area. The local resources of the area in fodder, fuel etc are becoming very scarce	[illegible]
do	18 Oct		Corps Tactical day - Routine work, nothing to record.	[initials]
do	19th & 20th Octr		Routine work, nothing to record	[initials]
do	21st Octr		Routine work. Orders received that the Corps will move to new billeting area South of R. SOMME.	[initials]
SELINCOURT	22nd Octr		Brigade marched off at 7 a.m. arriving in new area at noon. The whole of the Transport in by 5.30 p.m. Divisional rendezvous was 2.30 p.m. at PICQUINGY. Rations all issued by 7 p.m.	[initials]
do	23rd Octr		Reconnoitring of roads of Brigade Area, fixing Regimental Off-loading points. Divisional Rendezvous same hour and place as yesterday. Owing to extended area Units empowered to make own purchases, B.R.O assisting O's C units by interviewing principal farmers, ascertaining quantities available and settling rates beforehand. Local purchases for Head Quarter details of Potatoes at 9 francs per 100 Kilos, Firewood at 2 francs per 100 Kilos and Dry Clover at 7 francs per 100 kilos. Coal is now being brought daily from Railhead, thus reducing purchases of wood of which there is not an abundant stock.	[initials]

2353 Wt. W2514/1454 700,000 5/15 D. D. & L. A.D.S.S./Forms/C. 2118.

Army Form C. 2118.

WAR DIARY

of

~~INTELLIGENCE SUMMARY.~~

(Erase heading not required.)

Instructions regarding War Diaries and Intelligence Summaries are contained in F. S. Regs., Part II. and the Staff Manual respectively. Title pages will be prepared in manuscript.

CAPT. J. R. BRUNKER Supply Officer, MHOW CAVALRY BRIGADE.

Place	Date	Hour	Summary of Events and Information	Remarks and references to Appendices
	1915			
SELINCOURT	24th Octr.		Routine work: Brigade settled down. Supplies now delivered direct to Units by Supply lorries at midday. Local purchases of Potatoes and wood and Dry Clover for Brigade Headquarters & details at same rates as yesterday.	Ad.
do.	25th Octr.		Routine work: nothing to record except local purchases as yesterday.	Ad.
do	26th Octr.		Divisional Rendezvous at CONDÉ FOLIE at 11 a.m. Routine work. Purchases of Potatoes, Firewood and Dry Clover for Brigade Headquarters and details	Ad.
do	27th Octr.		Divisional Rendezvous same place and time as yesterday. Intimation from S.S.O. that Supply rendezvous will cease from to-day & that S.O's of Echelons will visit each Brigade to settle accounts. Supply lorries proceeding direct to Regimental Off-loading points. Local purchases the same as yesterday.	Ad.
do	28th–31st Octr.		Routine work: nothing to record.	Ad.

A Richards[?] Lt.

for Brigade Supply Officer

Mhow Cavalry Brigade.

2353 Wt. W2544/1454 700,000 5/15 D. D. & L. A.D.S.S./Forms/C. 2118.

Army Form C. 2118.

CR/64.

WAR DIARY
of
~~INTELLIGENCE SUMMARY~~.
(Erase heading not required.)

Instructions regarding War Diaries and Intelligence Summaries are contained in F. S. Regs., Part II. and the Staff Manual respectively. Title pages will be prepared in manuscript.

CAPT. J. R. Brunker Brigade Supply Officer MHOW. CAV^Y. B^DE I.E.F. "A"

Place	Date 1915	Hour	Summary of Events and Information	Remarks and references to Appendices
BERNAVILLE	1 Oct.	9.30 AM.	Brigade marched to join in Divisional Tactical Scheme. Echelon A transport accompanying. Horse extemporised train & dismounted men of units marched to LE MEILLARD to await orders. I accompanied G.O.C. on march. Brigade moved N. across L'AUTHIE river arriving at point 1 mile SW of VILLERS L'HOPITAL at 3.30 P.M. Brigade billeting area was given by A.Q.M.G. reaching Brigade Report Centre at 3-50 P.M. Area for Brigade being WAVANS – Cte de BEAUVOIR – FROHEN LE GRAND – and VILLERS L'HOPITAL. I now proceeded by car to cross roads N of OCCOCHES where I met Supply Column & directed Lorries to unit areas. Thence to Supply Column H^d Q^rs [illegible] with Column Supply Officer. Much difficulty is being experienced in procuring fuel. All coal has already been used up by French troops & wood is practically unobtainable. Units in receipt of rations by 6.0 P.M.	JB
Cte de BEAUVOIR	2 Oct.		Surrounding country has been reconnoitred by B. Req. Officer & a small quantity of fuel, sufficient for cooking only, procured for today – but no further quantity is forthcoming. Arrangements now being made to dig potatoes from fields close by. Rations in hands of units by 4.30 P.M.	JB
do	3 Oct		Brigade still in same billets now at 4 hours notice. Local purchase of coal (at DOULLONS) & potatoes, latter dug in fields by troops at 5F per 100 kilos. Nothing further to record.	JB

2353 Wt. W2544/1454 700,000 5/15 D. D. & L. A.D.S.S./Forms/C. 2118.

Instructions regarding War Diaries and Intelligence Summaries are contained in F. S. Regs., Part II. and the Staff Manual respectively. Title pages will be prepared in manuscript.

WAR DIARY of INTELLIGENCE SUMMARY.

(Erase heading not required.)

Army Form C. 2118.

Capt. T. R. Brunker - Supply Officer MHOW CAV[Y] BRIGADE

Place	Date	Hour	Summary of Events and Information	Remarks and references to Appendices
Chde BEAUVOIR	4 Oct. 1915.		Local purchase of potatoes dug from fields, this is found to be by far the most economical method of purchase - reducing the price from 20 to 25 per cent. Purchase of coal at DOULLENS - price 60 f per 1000 kilos. Usual [illegible] among units -	
do do	5 Oct		Nothing to record -	
do	6 Oct		Routine work, coal fuel was delivered from Rail head by Supply Column. Local purchase of potatoes for 7 & 8th units - Orders issued to the effect that units will cease making any local purchases & that the Requisitioning Officer will henceforth make all purchases including extra fodder, straw etc & deliver to units, this I found necessary owing to large fluctuations of prices paid -	
do	7 Oct		Local purchase of oat fodder & dry clover for 6th Inniskillings & [illegible] extra fodder for 7th & 8th at 2 lbs per horse. Routine work - nothing to record.	
do	8 Oct		Routine work, nothing to record - local purchase of fodder & wood fuel for 2 Lancers & 38th C.I.H for 8th & 9th [illegible] -	
do	9 Oct.		Nothing to record	
do	10 Oct		Local Purchases - Nothing to record -	

2353 Wt. W2514/1454 700,000 5/15 D. D. & L. A.D.S.S./Forms/C. 2118.

Instructions regarding War Diaries and Intelligence Summaries are contained in F. S. Regs., Part II. and the Staff Manual respectively. Title pages will be prepared in manuscript.

WAR DIARY
or
INTELLIGENCE SUMMARY.
(Erase heading not required.)

Army Form C. 2118.

Capt T.R. BRUNKER. Supply officer MHOW CAV^Y BRIGADE.

Place	Date	Hour	Summary of Events and Information	Remarks and references to Appendices
	1915			
Ch^teau de BEAUVOIR	11th Oct		BRIGADE in billets. Local purchase of fuel, potatoes & clover hay – Routine work.	[illegible]
do	12 Oct		Orders received that Brigade will move to BERNEUIL & surrounding villages on 13/10/15.	[illegible]
do	13 Oct		Brigade moved to new area. H^d Quarters & 2^d Lancers to BERNEUIL. 6th Inniskilling to FRANQUEVILLE & SURCAMPS. A Batt^y R.H.A. to St HILAIRE. 38th C I H to GORGES & VACQUERIE.	[illegible]
do	do	10am	Brigade arrived in billets. Local purchase of wood & potatoes – owing to high prices lately given to French troops, difficulty is found in purchasing at our table rates. Coal is now coming daily 1½ tons per day from Rail head –	[illegible]
BERNEUIL do^s	14 Oct		Divisional Supply Conference attended at FIENVILLERS – then I met lorries & conducted them to 1st H^d Q^rs from where guides from units conducted the lorries to Regt^l Areas – Owing to very scattered billets of 6th Dragoons & Central India Horse	

2353 Wt. W2544/1454 700,000 5/15 D. D. & L. A.D.S.S./Forms/C. 2118.

Instructions regarding War Diaries and Intelligence Summaries are contained in F. S. Regs., Part II. and the Staff Manual respectively. Title pages will be prepared in manuscript.

Army Form C. 2118.

WAR DIARY
or
INTELLIGENCE SUMMARY.
(Erase heading not required.)

Capt. J. R. Brewster Supply Officer MHOW Cav" Brigade

Place	Date	Hour	Summary of Events and Information	Remarks and references to Appendices
	1915			
BERNEVIL	14 Oct		I have arranged for lorries after delivering full rations etc, in the first case SURCAMPS & in the second VACQUERIE – to in the case of Inniskillings lift the Hay & grain of two Squadrons to FRANQUEVILLE & in the case of the C.I.H. to lift the grain & Hay of one Squadron to GORGES, in each case this being done on their return run. This procedure was found necessary, owing to units being, at present without their Echelon "B" transports, they have not the lifting power for the above – All rations issued by S.O. – local purchase of fuel & potatoes also Hay for all units –	
do	15 Oct.		Routine work nothing to record ——	
do	16 Oct.		do do – orders received at 9 p.m. that Brigade Head Quarters will move to FIENVILLERS at 10.30 am on 17.10.15 –	

2353 Wt. W2544/1454 700,000 5/15 D. D. & L. A.D.S.S./Forms/C. 2118.

Instructions regarding War Diaries and Intelligence Summaries are contained in F. S. Regs., Part II. and the Staff Manual respectively. Title pages will be prepared in manuscript.

Army Form C. 2118.

WAR DIARY
of
~~INTELLIGENCE SUMMARY.~~
(Erase heading not required.)

Capt T. R. [illegible] Supply Officer MHOW CAV^Y B^DE

Place	Date 1915	Hour	Summary of Events and Information	Remarks and references to Appendices
FIENVILLERS	17 Oct	12 noon	Brigade Head Quarters arrived & went into billets. Much difficulty in watering as practically speaking there is no water except wells & the latter are very dry. Remainder of Brigade in same area. The local resources of the area in fodder, fuel etc are becoming very scarce	[initials]
do	18 Oct		Corps Tactical day - Routine work, nothing to record.	[initials]
do	19th & 20th Oct		Routine work nothing to record	[initials]
do	21st Oct		Routine work. Orders received that the Corps will move to new billeting area South of R. SOMME.	[initials]
SELINCOURT	22nd Oct		Brigade marched off at 7 a.m. arriving in new area at noon. The whole of the Transport in by 5.30 p.m. Divisional rendezvous was 2.30 p.m at PICQUIGNY. Rations all issued by 7 p.m.	[initials]
do	23rd Oct		Reconnoitring of roads of Brigade Area, fixing Regimental Off loading points. Divisional Rendezvous same hour and place as yesterday. Owing to extended area Units empowered to make own purchases, B.R.O assisting O/C units by interviewing principal farmers ascertaining quantities available and settling rates beforehand. Local purchases for Head Quarter details of Potatoes at 9 francs per 100 Kilos, Firewood at 2 francs per 100 Kilos and Dry Clover at 7 francs per 100 kilos. Coal is now being brought daily from Railhead, thus reducing purchases of wood of which there is not an abundant stock.	[initials]

2353 Wt. W2514/1454 700,000 5/15 D. D. & L. A.D.S.S./Forms/C. 2118.

Army Form C. 2118.

WAR DIARY
of
~~INTELLIGENCE~~ SUMMARY.

(Erase heading not required.)

Instructions regarding War Diaries and Intelligence Summaries are contained in F. S. Regs., Part II. and the Staff Manual respectively. Title pages will be prepared in manuscript.

CAPT J. R. BRUNKER Supply Officer. MHOW CAVALRY BRIGADE

Place	Date	Hour	Summary of Events and Information	Remarks and references to Appendices
	1915			
SELINCOURT	24th Octr		Routine work: Brigade settled down. Supplies now delivered direct to Units by Supply Lorries at mid day. Local purchases of Potatoes and Wood and Dry Clover for Brigade Headquarters & details at same rates as yesterday.	Ad.
do	25th Octr		Routine work: nothing to record except local purchases as yesterday.	Ad.
do	26th Octr		Divisional Rendezvous at CONDÉ FOLIE at 11 a.m. Routine work. Purchases of Potatoes Firewood and Dry Clover for Brigade Headquarters and details	Ad.
do	27th Octr		Divisional Rendezvous same place and time as yesterday. Intimation from S.S.O. that Supply rendezvous will cease from to-day & that S.O's of Echelons will visit each Brigade to settle accounts. Supply lorries proceeding direct to Regimental Off-loading points. Local purchases the same as yesterday.	Ad.
do	28th-31st Octr.		Routine work nothing to record.	Ad.

A Wichard
2/Lt
for Brigade Supply Officer
Mhow Cavalry Brigade.

2353 Wt. W2544/1454 700,000 5/15 D. D. & L. A.D.S.S./Forms/C. 2118.

(9)

Serial No. 250.

121/7780

Confidential

War Diary

of

Supply Officer, Mhow Cavalry ~~Division~~ Brigade.

FROM 1st November 1915 TO 30th November 1915

1st Ind Cav Div

Instructions regarding War Diaries and Intelligence Summaries are contained in F. S. Regs., Part II. and the Staff Manual respectively. Title pages will be prepared in manuscript.

WAR DIARY

Supply Officer Mhow Cavalry Brigade

~~INTELLIGENCE SUMMARY.~~

(Erase heading not required.)

Army Form C. 2118.

7

Place	Date	Hour	Summary of Events and Information	Remarks and references to Appendices
SELINCOURT	1915 1st Nov to 3rd "		Brigade remains in same billets. routine duties, nothing to record.	Ad.
do.	4th Nov		Routine duties. B.R.O. has arranged to supply from an adjacent forest the wood fuel requirements ~~of~~ of the units in bulk at a very favourable rate. Nothing further to record.	Ad.
do.	5th " to 8th Nov		Routine duties; nothing to record.	Ad.
do	9th Nov.		Routine duties. purchases of Oat Fodder (unthrashed Oats) to supplement hay ration now being made in bulk at a rate of Francs Ninety per 1000 kilos being about 25-30 % cheaper than the price a year ago.	Ad.
do	10th to 14th Nov		Routine duties; nothing to record.	Ad.
do	15th & 16th Nov		Routine duties; nothing to report.	Ad.
do	17th Nov.		Routine duties. Divisional Rendezvous this day at CONDÉ FOLIE at 12 noon. Captain L. St. J. WRIGHT S&T Corps. assumed the duties of Brigade Supply Officer MHOW CAVALRY BRIGADE from the afternoon of the 17th November 1915	Ad. Aw

76

2353 Wt. W2544/1454 700,000 5/15 D. D. & L. A.D.S.S./Forms/C. 2118.

/11

WAR DIARY
or
~~INTELLIGENCE~~ SUMMARY.

Supply Officer Lucknow Cavalry Brigade

(*Erase heading not required.*)

Army Form C. 2118.

Instructions regarding War Diaries and Intelligence Summaries are contained in F. S. Regs., Part II. and the Staff Manual respectively. Title pages will be prepared in manuscript.

Place	Date	Hour	Summary of Events and Information	Remarks and references to Appendices
SELINCOURT.	18th Nov.	11 AM 5 PM	Rendezvous at AIRAINES - Routine duties. Went to Divisional Head Quarters to discuss scheme of supply arrangements for the proposed "dismounted" Division - Reported to SSO that no salt for animals had been received - (Supply column informed me none had been received at Railhead)	ASJ
SELINCOURT	19th "		Routine duties - visited all units in the Brigade	
SELINCOURT	20th		Routine duties. Visited 38th Central Horse - 6th Innis Killing Dragoons & "A" Battery RHA re figures of men and animals going up to trenches and those remaining behind if scheme SA 606 comes into force.	ASJ
SELINCOURT	21st-28th		Routine duties	ASJ
SELINCOURT	29th		Went to BOIS DE GUIBERMESNIL with Lieut Richards the Brigade Requisitioning Officer and Interpreter QUANTIN & the Brigade Transport Officer Lieut Price, made arrangements for purchase of cut wood at rate of eighteen francs per one thousand kilos - the average distance from units of this wood is about 6 kilometres. The stock of wood already cut and stacked will last the Brigade about one month.	ASJ
SELINCOURT	30th		Routine -	ASJ

A St John Wright Captain
Brigade Supply Officer
Lucknow Cavalry Brigade
1st Indian Cavalry Division

SELINCOURT
30-11-15.

for Q.G.
JMO
2-1-16

Instructions regarding War Diaries and Intelligence Summaries are contained in F. S. Regs., Part II. and the Staff Manual respectively. Title pages will be prepared in manuscript.

Army Form C. 2118.

CR. 418 6/12/15

WAR DIARY
or
~~INTELLIGENCE SUMMARY.~~
(Erase heading not required.)

Supply office Mhow Cav Bde

Place	Date	Hour	Summary of Events and Information	Remarks and references to Appendices
SELINCOURT	1915 1st Nov to 3rd		Brigade remains in same billets - routine duties, nothing to record	Ad
do.	4th Nov		Routine duties. B.R.O. has arranged to supply from an adjacent forest the wood fuel requirements of the units in bulk at a very favourable rate. Nothing further to record.	Ad
do.	5th to 8th Nov		Routine duties, nothing to record.	Ad
do	9th Nov		Routine duties, purchases of Oat Fodder (unthrashed Oats) to supplement hay ration now being made in bulk at a rate of Francs ninety per 1000 kilos being about 25-30% cheaper than the price a year ago.	Ad
do	10th to 14th Nov		Routine duties; nothing to record	Ad
do	15th & 16th Nov		Routine duties; nothing to report	Ad
do	17th Nov		Routine duties. Divisional Rendezvous this day at CONDÉ FOLIE at 12 noon. Captain A. St. J. WRIGHT S. & T. Corps. assumed the duties of Brigade Supply Officer MHOW CAVALRY BRIGADE from the afternoon of the 17th November 1915.	Ad / AW

II

Army Form C. 2118.

Instructions regarding War Diaries and Intelligence Summaries are contained in F. S. Regs., Part II. and the Staff Manual respectively. Title pages will be prepared in manuscript.

WAR DIARY or ~~INTELLIGENCE SUMMARY.~~ Supply Office Ambala? Cav. Bde

(Erase heading not required.)

Place	Date	Hour	Summary of Events and Information	Remarks and references to Appendices
SELINCOURT	18th Nov.	11 am	Rendezvous at AIRAINES - Routine duties.	
		5 pm	[illegible]	Ary
SELINCOURT	19th "		Routine duties - visited all units in the Brigade.	
SELINCOURT	20th		Routine duties. Visited 3rd Cavalry [illegible] "A" Battery RHA [illegible]	Ary
SELINCOURT	21-24		Routine [illegible]	
SELINCOURT	25th		[illegible]	Ary
SELINCOURT	26th		Routine.	Ary

A. St. [illegible] Captain

Brigade Supply Officer

[illegible] Cavalry Brigade

1st Indian Cavalry Division

SELINCOURT 30-11-15.

2353 Wt. W2544/1454 700,000 5/15 D. D. & L. A.D.S.S./Forms/C. 2118.

Serial No. 250.

Confidential

War Diary

of

Supply Officer, Mhow Cavalry Brigade.

FROM 1st December 1915 TO 31st December 1915

Army Form C. 2118.

Instructions regarding War Diaries and Intelligence Summaries are contained in F. S. Regs., Part II. and the Staff Manual respectively. Title pages will be prepared in manuscript.

WAR DIARY
or
~~INTELLIGENCE SUMMARY.~~ Supply officer [illegible] Cav. Bde

(Erase heading not required.)

– 1st Indian Cavalry Division –

Place	Date 1915	Hour	Summary of Events and Information	Remarks and references to Appendices
SELINCOURT.	December 1st to 15th	—	Nothing of interest to record.	
VALINES	16th		Brigade moved from SELINCOURT area to new billetting area roughly 20 miles North-West from SELINCOURT area. Biletting area allotted as follows. Brigade Head Quarters – SAUCOURT Supply Head Quarters – VALINES Mobile Veterinary Section – VALINES. Post office – VALINES Transport of Bde. Hd. Qrs – VALINES. "A" Battery R.H.A. – VALINES (Battery is at present away from the Brigade) 6th Inniskilling Dragoons FOUQUIERES 2nd Lancers CHÉPY 38th C.I.H. FRESSENNEVILLE. Auxiliary Horse Transport Company A.S.C is attached to this Brigade for rations and is billeted at St MARR. ——— No divisional rendezvous was fixed for the Supply Column Motor Lorries, each Brigade fixing its own. I fixed this Brigade's for the 16th & 17th at a well marked cross road South of VALINES at 12 midday on both dates and had a representative from each unit to guide the lorries to their respective units. On the 16th rations were handed over at units head Quarters to the biletting parties who had arrived a couple of days in advance. Brigade arrived about 5 pm on evening of 16th in new biletting area. I arranged for sufficient firewood locally to cook evening meal & breakfasts on 17th and located sources of supply of local fodder. Firewood appeared very scarce.	C.R. 624 [630] 6/1/16

A. St. John [illegible] Capt.

2353 Wt. W2544/1454 700,000 5/15 D. D. & L. A.D.S.S./Forms/C. 2118.

(1)

WAR DIARY
or
~~INTELLIGENCE SUMMARY.~~

Supply Officer Meerut(?) Cavalry Brigade.
— 1st Indian Cavalry Division —

(*Erase heading not required.*)

Army Form C. 2118.

Instructions regarding War Diaries and Intelligence Summaries are contained in F. S. Regs., Part II. and the Staff Manual respectively. Title pages will be prepared in manuscript.

Place	Date 1915.	Hour	Summary of Events and Information	Remarks and references to Appendices
VALINES	DEC 17th		Rendezvous for lorries same place as on 16th	
VALINES	18th		Lorries proceeded direct to units, & Brigade Head Quarter Lorries to VALINES. rations for SAUCOURT I arranged should be sent daily to SAUCOURT from VALINES (in a Brigade Head Quarter G.S. wagon) after distribution at VALINES.	
VALINES	15th 19–31st		Most of the time taken up with interviewing the Maires of the several communes in the area for the purpose of arranging local supplies as economically as possible. Found stocks moderately plentiful but rates as certified by the Maires as necessary to remunerate farmers higher than those paid by us in the past, averaging approximately as follows- Wheat Straw --- Frcs 65 to 70 per 1000 kilos Oat Straw --- " 45 – 50 " " " Clover --- " 70 – 75 " " " Oat fodder --- 100 – 150 " " " Potatoes --- 90 — " " " (best red variety plentiful) The reasons for higher prices is probably due to the large purchases made by No 9 Commission of Supplies of the French Army in this area last year, also the fact that the district is largely manufacturing, the people are strongly socialiste and do not see why the British Army should pay lower prices than the French Army do. Firewood is practically non-existent – I had great difficulties in obtaining even day to day supplies. The coal ration which had been reduced to half – increased our requirements.	

CR 594 3/1/16.

2353 Wt. W2544/1454 700,000 5/15 D. D. & L. A.D.S.S./Forms/C. 2118.

(2)

Army Form C. 2118.

Instructions regarding War Diaries and Intelligence Summaries are contained in F. S. Regs., Part II. and the Staff Manual respectively. Title pages will be prepared in manuscript.

WAR DIARY
or
~~INTELLIGENCE~~ SUMMARY.

(*Erase heading not required.*)

Supply Officer
Mhow Cavalry Brigade
1st Indian Cav Division

Place	Date	Hour	Summary of Events and Information	Remarks and references to Appendices
			On the 24th December the coal ration was increased to the full ration of 1½ LBS per man per day plus 200 LBS per week for office fire places. This reduced the requirements of firewood, and by an arrangement of "meeting convoys" between the Meerut Reserve Park & the Auxiliary Horse Transport Coy A.S.C (attached to 1st Indian Cavalry Division) a Divisional dump at CHEPY under my control was started – half the Divisions requirements are met from this dump and the other half from wood cut by fatigue parties arranged by the Requisitioning & Supply Officer of the Divisional Troops at DARGNIES. The wood brought to the dump is from the forest D'EU about 18 miles away. This wood is dry & costs Frcs 37 per 1000 kilos. The loading of the wagons and despatch of wood was superintended by Sergeant BREWSTER S.T.C of this Brigade – 1000 kilos of wood made a suitable load for a G.S. wagon.	
			On 24th December permission was granted by S.S.O for the purchase of small quantities of local hay at Frcs 75–80 per 1000 kilos to supplement the hay ration brought up by the Supply Column. Previously the purchase of hay was forbidden. This permission is only to buy when the farmers are willing to part with it.	
			In addition to my duties as Brigade Supply Officer Mhow Cav. Bde. I had the duties of O.C. Divisional Coal Dump – where the coal – wood & emergency ration (iron rations) are dumped.	
			A St John Wright Capt S.S.O. MHOW BDE	

2353 Wt. W2514/1454 700,000 5/15 D. D. & L. A.D.S.S./Forms/C. 2118.

SERIAL NO 250.

Confidential

War Diary

of

Supply Officer, Mhow Cavalry Brigade.

FROM 1st January 1916 TO 31st January 1916.

January 1916

Instructions regarding War Diaries and Intelligence Summaries are contained in F. S. Regs., Part II. and the Staff Manual respectively. Title pages will be prepared in manuscript.

WAR DIARY

of Supply officer MHOW CAVALRY BRIGADE. – 1st Indian Cavalry Division –

~~INTELLIGENCE SUMMARY.~~

(Erase heading not required.)

Army Form C. 2118.

Place	Date	Hour	Summary of Events and Information	Remarks and references to Appendices
VALINES	1-1-16	...	Duties in connection with Divisional wood Supply of wood near BLANGY.	
VALINES	2-1-16	–	Sub Cond STONEHAM STC returned from leave from United Kingdom. Sergeant BREWSTER STC " " duties in connection with wood supply from forest near BLANGY.	
VALINES	3-1-16	6.15am	Capt A. ST JOHN WRIGHT STC left to take up (temporarily) duties in 1st Indian Cavalry Division Supply Column – in relief of Capt A.E. BYRCH STC who (temporarily) takes over duties of BRIGADE Supply officer of this Brigade.	
VALINES	4-1-16		2 Lieut Richards carried on the duties of Brigade Supply Officer temporarily pending the arrival of Captain A. E. B. Byrch –	
VALINES	5-1-16		Captain A. E. B. Byrch took over duties of Brigade Supply officer from Lieut Richards, in the afternoon. – Reported to Brigade Major at Brigade Headquarters. –	
VALINES	6-1-16		Present at the issue of rations at Brigade Headquarters. – Visited the Coal & wood dump at CHEPY, under Sergt Harvey. – Sergt BREWSTER. STC left the Brigade on eight days leave to United Kingdom. –	
VALINES	7-1-16		Interviewed G.O.C the Bde. – Sent in report to O.C. ASC with reference to employment of G.S. regimental wagons for carting supplies from Brigade Headquarters to units. –	

January 1916

Instructions regarding War Diaries and Intelligence Summaries are contained in F. S. Regs., Part II. and the Staff Manual respectively. Title pages will be prepared in manuscript.

WAR DIARY of Supply Officer Mhow Cavalry Brigade
INTELLIGENCE SUMMARY. 1st Indian Cavalry Division

(Erase heading not required.)

Army Form C. 2118.

Place	Date	Hour	Summary of Events and Information	Remarks and references to Appendices
VALINES	9-1-16		Present at issue of rations to 2nd Lancers.-	
			Letter received from S.S.O 1st Ind: Cav: Div:- regarding the shortage of hay from Railhead, & ordered to make arrangements to make up shortage of 6 lbs per animal by local purchase.-	
			With Lieut Richards & the Interpreter, I interviewed the mayors of the following places:- VALINES, CHEPY, FEUQUIERES & FRESSENNEVILLE & asked them to let me have the amount of dry fodder they could produce.- The reports were promised by the 11th Inst.-	
			The minimum amount of fodder required was worked out on a basis of 9 lbs per animal for 16 days, this is to enable me to form the dump of 50 tons of baled hay at CHEPY by about the 25th of this month.-	
			I intend taking 3 lbs per animal of baled hay from each unit, & placing this amount in the CHEPY Dump.- This 3 lbs thus deducted from each unit, will be replaced by local purchase plus six lbs per horse due to shortage from Railhead.-	
			It was found that several of the Mayors had already received a letter from the French authorities asking for the amount of supplies available in the MHOW Bde area.-	
			This was reported to the S.S.O 1st Ind Cav Div, with a request that steps be taken to stop requisitioning by other formations in this Brigade area.-	

2353 Wt. W2544/1454 700,000 5/15 D. D. & L. A.D.S.S./Forms/C. 2118.

January 1916.

Instructions regarding War Diaries and Intelligence Summaries are contained in F. S. Regs., Part II. and the Staff Manual respectively. Title pages will be prepared in manuscript.

WAR DIARY
of Supply officer Mhow Cavalry Brigade
INTELLIGENCE SUMMARY.
1st Indian Cavalry Division

(Erase heading not required.)

Army Form C. 2118.

Place	Date	Hour	Summary of Events and Information	Remarks and references to Appendices
VALINES	10-1-16		Went round the Brigade & explained to units the arrangements made to meet the Shortage of hay, & impressed on them the necessity for making a small regimental Reserve in case supply of hay failed.-	
			Interviewed OC-A.S.C. & S.S.O with regard to the above.-	
			Arranged with O.C Divisional Supply Clm to send hay from Railhead on alternate days to units & dump at CHEPY.-	
			Informed units that the 6 lbs hay ration received to-morrow, will be a two days supply, & that no baled hay will be received by them on 12th.-	
			Made arrangements with Mayor of CHEPY for the temporary loan of wooden beams on which to place the baled hay at the Dump.-	
VALINES	11-1-16		Received letter No S.S.0843 / 10-1-16 from S.S.O informing that following reserve of fodder to be arranged:-	
			a/. Divisional Dump at CHEPY 48 lbs per animal.-	
			b/. Unit Charge in billets 36 " " "	
			c/. Reserve in Bde area 36 " " "	
			TOTAL = 120 lbs	

2353 Wt. W2544/1454 700,000 5/15 D. D. & L. A.D.S.S./Forms/C. 2118.

January 1916.

Instructions regarding War Diaries and Intelligence Summaries are contained in F. S. Regs., Part II. and the Staff Manual respectively. Title pages will be prepared in manuscript.

WAR DIARY
of Brigade Supply Officer Mhow Cavalry Brigade
INTELLIGENCE SUMMARY.
1st Indian Cavalry Division

(Erase heading not required.)

Army Form C. 2118.

Place	Date	Hour	Summary of Events and Information	Remarks and references to Appendices
VALINES	12-1-16		Visited all units in the Brigade.-	
			Arrangements are being made in each unit to form a regimental Reserve of 3 days at 12lbs per animal, of hay.-	
			Received reports from the Mayors of VALINES, FRESSENNEVILLE & FEUQUIÈRES, that the following amounts of dry fodder are available:-	
			(a) VALINES 23000 Kilos	
			(b) FRESSENNEVILLE 35000	
			(c) FEUQUIÈRES 35000	
			(d) CHEPY 27600	
			Of the above:	
			(a) is 1000 over requirements	
			(b) 11000 under requirements	
			(c) 10 000 under "	
			(d) 16500 under "	
VALINES	13-1-16		Routine duties.-	
			Fatigue Party sent out under Brigade arrangements, to cut wood in the Mhow Brigade area.-	

2353 Wt. W2544/1454 700,000 5/15 D. D. & L. A.D.S.S./Forms/C. 2118.

January 1916

Instructions regarding War Diaries and Intelligence Summaries are contained in F. S. Regs., Part II. and the Staff Manual respectively. Title pages will be prepared in manuscript.

WAR DIARY
INTELLIGENCE SUMMARY.

of Brigade Supply Officer, Mhow Cavalry Brigade 1st Indian Cavalry Division –

(Erase heading not required.)

Army Form C. 2118.

Place	Date	Hour	Summary of Events and Information	Remarks and references to Appendices
VALINES	13-1-16	-16-1-16.	Routine duties. –	
"	17-1-16		11,050 kilos of hay obtained from HOCQUELUS. –	
"	18-1-16	-19-1-16	Routine duties. –	
			All wood cut in VALINES wood. –	
			Report received that 500 tons of cut wood are available at OCHANCOURT. – As the place is not in the Mhow Bde area, permission ~~was asked~~ to remove the wood, was asked for from ~~ADT~~ OC. A.S.C. —	
			Capt. Wright. S.T.C. took over duties of B.S.O Mhow Bde from Capt. Pyrch S.T.C. –	
VALINES	20.1.16	–	Fatigue party cutting wood for the brigade at VALINES.	
	21.1.16		Ref report of 500 tons of cut wood. at OCHANCOURT – on investigation it was found that there was only 20 tons of cut wood which had been already taken over by the LUCKNOW BRIGADE – the remainder, being uncut wood, the owner of the wood refused to part with.	AW
VALINES	22.1.16		Capt. WRIGHT S.T.C. proceeded on leave to the United Kingdom. 2/Lt A. Richards S.T.C (I.A.R) assumed duties of B.S.O. Mhow Bde. in addition to his own of Requisitioning Officer. Routine duties in billets: nothing to record. Difficulty experienced in obtaining necessary firewood. Went to the BOIS D'ARREST in search thereof & interviewed the GARDE CHAMPÊTRE who stated he had none for disposal.	
ditto	23.1.16		Routine duties in billets: nothing to record.	AR
"	24.1.16		Routine duties. Went to NIBAS and saw Adjoint (Maire being mobilised) with regard to possible supplies of fodder at SAUCOURT (Bde H.Q.) he promised to send GARDE & let me have the amounts available & names of farmers. Arranged with B.S.O. LUCKNOW Bde to draw balance of cut wood, about 15 tons remaining	AR

2353 Wt. W2514/1454 700,000 5/15 D. D. & L. A.D.S.S./Forms/C. 2118.

Army Form C. 2118.

Instructions regarding War Diaries and Intelligence Summaries are contained in F. S. Regs., Part II. and the Staff Manual respectively. Title pages will be prepared in manuscript.

WAR DIARY
or
INTELLIGENCE SUMMARY.
(Erase heading not required.)

Place	Date	Hour	Summary of Events and Information	Remarks and references to Appendices
VALINES	24.1.16		remaining at OCHANCOURT, as he (B.S.O.–Lucknow Bde) had found another source of supply.	
– ditto –	25.1.16		Routine duties. Went to NIBAS and interviewed a M. BILLOT who is "Receveur" to an Estate there having possible supplies of wood. M. BILLOT was unable to give a decision but referred me to a M. CHOPIN living at ST. VALERIE S/SOMME and I arranged to go over there in the afternoon. Went on to OCHANCOURT & arranged with M. MALLABAT, the owner, to draw wood (10 tons) for the Brigade tomorrow – the price of the wood, which comprises much brushwood, works out at about Fcs 15 per 1000 kilos – a very favourable rate. In the afternoon went to ST. VALERIE S/SOMME & interviewed M. CHOPIN. He gave me a letter to his representative at FEUQUIERES the spirit of which will enable me to draw on the wood when I require it, but as the price is high, about Fcs 30 per 1000 kilos I shall only do so in extremis.	[initials]
– ditto –	26.1.16		Routine duties. Went to NIBAS & saw Adjoint who stated that the GARDE CHAMPETRE had only succeeded in obtaining 500 Ks. of Fodder from SAUCOURT so gave instructions for him to go again and find 20,000 kilos. Sent 15 G.S. wagons to OCHANCOURT and drew 10 tons of firewood for the Brigade. Canadian Cavalry Brigade arrives in FRIVILLE and adjoining villages: being attached to the 1st Indian Cavalry Division for "training and administration". Supply administration under the Supply Officer, Divisional Troops.	[initials]
– ditto –	27.1.16		Drew 3,500 kilos of Oat Fodder from FRESSENNEVILLE, giving 2,500 kilos to the 2nd Lancers at CHEPY (in whose village the supply of fodder is practically exhausted) and the remaining 1000 to Bde H.Q. Drew the attention of the SSO 1st I.C.D. to the state of affairs at the 2nd Lancers hay is still arriving at railhead at 6 lbs per animal daily: out of this the necessary reserves have to be accumulated thus making a great drain on local resources.	[initials]

2353 Wt. W2544/1454 700,000 5/15 D. D. & L. A.D.S.S./Forms/C. 2118.

Army Form C. 2118.

WAR DIARY
or
INTELLIGENCE SUMMARY.
(*Erase heading not required.*)

Instructions regarding War Diaries and Intelligence Summaries are contained in F. S. Regs., Part II. and the Staff Manual respectively. Title pages will be prepared in manuscript.

Place	Date	Hour	Summary of Events and Information	Remarks and references to Appendices
VALINES	28.1.16		Went round Units. Then went to ACHEUX and saw B.S.O. SIALKOT BDE with a view to obtaining supplies of fodder from his area, but found the same difficulty of securing sufficient stocks existing there also. In the afternoon I went over to OARGNIES and saw the Senior Supply Officer, 1st I.C.D. and explained to him our difficulty in obtaining sufficient supplies for our units - pointing out that the Area is largely industrial having many factories and munition workers. I drew particular attention to the case of the 2nd Lancers at CHEPY who had consumed all available local fodder. The SSO agreed that failing exterior sources of supply they would have to break into their regimental reserves which they had saved from their 12 lb-per-animal ration. 8.30 p.m. received two wires from the S.S.O. 1st I.C.D. (1) asking me to arrange for the supply tomorrow morning without fail of 10 tons of coal from the CHEPY dump to the Canadian Cavalry Brigade. and (2) to obtain the figures from Units of the personnel proceeding with the Trench Digging Party and to prepare an AF 3316 for same & hand it to S. Sgt NEWMAN at the Lucknow Bde. as soon as possible. With regard to (1) I went and saw the OC Auxiliary Horse Transport Coy at St. MARC & arranged with him for 9 carts to be at the dump at CHEPY tomorrow morning at 10 a.m. Then for (2) I went round Units, obtained the necessary figures from the Adjts prepared AF 3316 & handed it to S. Sgt NEWMAN at FRANLEU at 11 p.m.	[illegible]
– ditto –	29.1.16		The Machine Gun Sections in the Brigade are to be formed into a M.G. Squadron under Captn HUMFREY - 6th Inniskilling Dgns. It is to be a separate unit located at HOCQUELUS and a lorry will be set apart for conveying its rations. Went round Units	[illegible]

2353 Wt. W2544/1454 700,000 5/15 D. D. & L. A.D.S.S./Forms/C. 2118.

Army Form C. 2118.

Instructions regarding War Diaries and Intelligence Summaries are contained in F. S. Regs., Part II. and the Staff Manual respectively. Title pages will be prepared in manuscript.

WAR DIARY
or
INTELLIGENCE SUMMARY.

(Erase heading not required.)

Place	Date	Hour	Summary of Events and Information	Remarks and references to Appendices
VALINES	29.1.16	(Contd)	Units to obtain figures of sections joining the M.G. Squadron. The squadron would move into its new billets on Monday next. It would take the current days rations from its respective regiment. The first lorry (containing the next days rations) would arrive on Monday morning. Gave the ~~O.C.~~ 2nd Supply Officer 1st Echelon SCSC the strength of this new unit. Arranged with the O.C. M.G. Section to have one of my agents to assist in the taking over and issue of the rations for the first few days until things had got into working order & arranged also to come over myself to give any help needed. Went on to ACHEUX & saw B.S.O. SIALKOT BDE with a view to our purchasing & cutting a wood near for the joint use of the two Brigades. Word received that fifty horses from each ~~Unit~~ Ind Regiment are to be lent on Monday next to the Canadian Cavalry Brigade so adjust AF 3316 for that day accordingly.	AA
-ditto-	30.1.16		Went to FRESSENNEVILLE & saw a farmer who has 5000 kilos of oat fodder for sale. Our maximum price for this commodity is Fcs 90 per 1000 & the owner will not accept less than Fcs 120. I must not requisition so am unable to secure the fodder which is most urgently needed if we are to conserve our baled fodder. The result is that the 2nd Lancers have to draw on their regimental reserve. Then on to CHEPY: arranged to take over another piece of land for a Dump at the same pute as the original dump and adjacent thereto. In the afternoon I went reconnoitring for possible supplies of wood and found a small wood near VALINES. The owner lives at AMIENS but the "Receveur" charged with the affairs of the Estate, a M. ALEXANDRE, lives at ABBEVILLE. Decide to visit M ALEXANDRE	AA

2353 Wt. W2544/1454 700,000 5/15 D. D. & L. A.D.S.S./Forms/C. 2118.

Instructions regarding War Diaries and Intelligence Summaries are contained in F. S. Regs., Part II. and the Staff Manual respectively. Title pages will be prepared in manuscript.

WAR DIARY
or
INTELLIGENCE SUMMARY.
(Erase heading not required.)

Army Form C. 2118.

Place	Date	Hour	Summary of Events and Information	Remarks and references to Appendices
			tomorrow.	
VALINES	31-1-16		Interviewed the Maire of VALINES who shewed me a letter he had received from "L'Officier d'Administration de 1ère classe Duranel de la Région du Nord chargé de l'Exploitation des Fourrages at SAINT VALERY s/SOMME", dated 29th January 1916, wherein it states that on no account are the farmers to sell straw, fodder, oats and cattle, especially to the British Army, as it is required by the French 19th Army, and that he (the Maire) is to make this known to all the inhabitants. In view of the shortage of baled hay arriving this makes the position of the Units in this Brigade very serious as we shall be precluded from purchasing local fodder to supplement and the reserve we have been able to accumulate is small. Moreover we shall not be able to obtain relief from outside the area. I immediately went over to the H.Q. 1st I.C.D. at DARGNIES and saw the O.C., A.S.C. stating the purport of the letter the Maires in my Area had received and the seriousness of our position. Went on to the M.G. ~~Section~~ 1st Squadron at HOCQUELUS and purchased 2000 kilos of Oat Fodder which I handed over to them to supplement the Hay ration: The Reserve of Fodder accumulated for this Brigade now stands as follows: (1) CHEPY DUMP – 48 lbs per animal (2) In Units' Charge – approximately 36 lbs per animal, but one Unit (2nd Lancers) has already been compelled to draw on this. (3) In Brigade Area in Supply charge – 6 lbs per animal excluding Battery ("A") or 5 lbs per animal including Battery.	Ad

2353 Wt. W2514/1454 700,000 5/15 D. D. & L. A.D.S.S./Forms/C. 2118.

Instructions regarding War Diaries and Intelligence Summaries are contained in F. S. Regs., Part II. and the Staff Manual respectively. Title pages will be prepared in manuscript.

WAR DIARY
or
INTELLIGENCE SUMMARY.
(Erase heading not required.)

Army Form C. 2118.

Place	Date	Hour.	Summary of Events and Information	Remarks and references to Appendices
VALINES	31.1.16 Contd		Handed over duties of B.S.O. Mhow Bde to Captn WRIGHT on his return from leave this day	AW.
			A Wright Capt S.F.C. B.S.O. Mhow Cav. Bde. 1/2/16	

2353 Wt. W2544/1454 700,000 5/15 D. D. & L. A.D.S.S./Forms/C. 2118.

SERIAL NO. 250

Confidential

War Diary

of

Supply Officer, Mhow Cavalry Brigade

FROM 1st February 1916 TO 29th February 1916

Page ONE

Instructions regarding War Diaries and Intelligence Summaries are contained in F. S. Regs., Part II. and the Staff Manual respectively. Title pages will be prepared in manuscript.

WAR DIARY of Supply Officer MHOW Cavalry BRIGADE 1st Indian Cavalry Division

~~INTELLIGENCE SUMMARY.~~

(Erase heading not required.)

Army Form C. 2118.

I DIV

Place	Date	Hour	Summary of Events and Information	Remarks and references to Appendices
February 1916			Nothing important to report–	128
VALINES	1 to 27th		The French authorities have forbidden the local farmers to sell fodder to us– therefore the horses of the Brigade are being fed on baled hay received daily from the Supply Column Motor Lorries– at the scale of ten pounds per animal– During the period that only six pounds was coming up from Railhead– I made the ration up to ten pounds by drawing daily on the "dump" at CRESY– which is now reduced to 35,000 pounds– Firewood for the Brigade was obtained by fatigue parties cutting from two woods– one at ACHEUX and the other at FEUQUIERES– Ready cut dry wood is unobtainable as it is reserved for the French bakeries	AY
VALINES	28th–29th & 1st March		"Thaw Scheme" came into effect– owing to roads being impossible for motor lorries rations (exclusive of fodder) was delivered by horse transport– at a divisional rendezvous by Mecurt Reserve Park wagons– from whence Brigade transport delivered to units. Hay was consumed from the "Regimental Reserve" which had been previously collected and amounted to 30 lbs per animal (3 days ration) this reserve was in units own charge.	AY

A. St. John Wright Capt. B.S.O. S. and T. Corps

Transferred to Col Menneer [illegible] 27.3.16

SERIAL NO 250.

Confidential

War Diary

of

Supply Officer, Mhow Cavalry Brigade.

FROM 1st March 1916 TO 31st March 1916.

1 DIV

~~do~~ (35)

Army Form C. 2118.

WAR DIARY
~~or~~ of Brigade Supply Officer
~~INTELLIGENCE SUMMARY.~~
MHOW Cavalry Brigade
- 1st Indian Cavalry Division -

(Erase heading not required.)

Instructions regarding War Diaries and Intelligence Summaries are contained in F. S. Regs., Part II. and the Staff Manual respectively. Title pages will be prepared in manuscript.

Place	Date - 1916 -	Hour	Summary of Events and Information	Remarks and references to Appendices
VALINES	1st March		As everything points to a more shortly - orders were issued to units to consume any surplus hay over from the "regimental reserve" remaining, if necessary by increasing the ration from 10 to 12 lbs. Stocks of vegetables were ordered to be reduced to three days. The wood cutting was regulated so as to have three days in hand only.	avy
VALINES	2nd March		All the iron Rations of the Division which had been dumped at CHEPY were re-issued to Brigades. I have 2 days iron rations now at VALINES for the Brigade stacked separately for units of this Brigade. which will be disposed of according to Indian Cavalry Corps Secret No Q.5573 of 27.2.16. The Indian troops iron ration, of gur and Biscuits keeps, well - as does the British except for the OXO cubes which melt and leak and spoil the tea and Sugar. I personally went through all the British rations and found a great many of the grocery rations spoiled because of this - have reported it to the Senior Supply Officer - and indented for replacements.	avy
VALINES	2nd to 16th		Nothing particular to report. As potatoes are scarce I purchased mixed vegetables consisting of potatoes - carrots - and turnips @ 18 francs 50 centimes per 100 kilos. I also discontinued the wood cutting fatigues - as the sap is rising in the trees and the wood is very wet and does not burn well. I managed to find a saw mill at ABBEVILLE (17 kilometres away) from whom I have arranged to draw my requirements for the Brigade (21 tons a month) @ 25 to 30 francs per 1000 kilos - arranged with the Brigade Transport Officer to draw in G.S. wagons 3 days at a time.	avy
VALINES	17th & 18th		Went round all units of the Brigade and got them to give me in detail their feeding strengths under four heads as follows (1) actual fighting troops. (2) "A" Echelon Transport (3) "B" Echelon Transport (4) Dismounted men. Each sub-head sub-divided into - British. Mahomedans. Hindus & animals. Sent a compiled statement for the Brigade to the Division.	avy

2353 Wt. W2514/1454 700,000 5/15 D. D. & L. A.D.S.S./Forms/C. 2118.

(11)

Instructions regarding War Diaries and Intelligence Summaries are contained in F. S. Regs., Part II. and the Staff Manual respectively. Title pages will be prepared in manuscript.

WAR DIARY
or
INTELLIGENCE SUMMARY.
(Erase heading not required.)

Army Form C. 2118.

Place	Date – March 1916 –	Hour	Summary of Events and Information	Remarks and references to Appendices
VALINES	19th to 24th		– Routine duties –	avy
(line of march)	25th	10 AM	Brigade marched from VALINES area via ABBEYVILLE en route to new area – Went on ahead with requisitioning officer (Lieut Richards I.A.R.) and arranged for a kilo of firewood per man at each of the headquarters of units halting place for the night. Units arrived about 2-30 pm in St RIQUIER area and were billeted for night of 25/26 as follows – Brigade Head Quarters at ONEUX. Inniskilling Dragoons at St RIQUIER. 'A' Battery R.H.A at St RIQUIER. 2nd Lancers at ONEUX and NEUVILLE. 38th C.I.H. at NEUF MOULIN. Machine Gun Squadron at NEUF MOULIN. Rendezvous for Supply Column lorries on main ABBEYVILLE – St RIQUIER Road at 2 pm at cross road just S.W of St RIQUIER – Rations delivered correctly to all units including coal and vegetables to scale which had been laid aside at VALINES and handed over to Supply Column – Went on ahead in car to permanent billeting area at 5 pm same evening –	avy
MAIZICOURT	26th		Went round to each head quarter billet of units in new area – and arranged for wood and to reconnoitre roads for the Supply Column lorries to units head quarters. Rendezvous for Supply Column lorries at 2 pm at cross roads ¾ mile S.W of HIERMONT ~~at 2 pm~~ Arranged for an intelligent representative from each unit to be present at rendezvous to direct units lorries to respective headquarters – which are as below – Brigade Head Quarters including Supply & Transport & Mobile Veterinary Section = MAIZICOURT – Inniskilling Dragoons WAVANS & BEAUVOIR RIVIERE. 2nd Lancers. BEALCOURT. St ACHEUL & FROHEN-LE-PETIT. 38th C.I.H. MAISON-PONTHIEU & St LOT. Machine Gun Squadron HIERMONT. 'A' Battery R.H.A. BERNATRE. Railhead for the 1st Indian Cavalry Division AUXI-LE-CHATEAU. Besides the above units the 13th Battn The Rifle Brigade, The Cadet School, and the Field Squadron and Divisional Supply Column all at AUXI-LE-CHATEAU are attached to this Brigade for rations.	avy
MAIZICOURT	27th		Double issue of rations this day –	
MAIZICOURT	28th – 31st		All units of this Brigade drew rations on their horse transport wagons from railhead – rendezvous 8-30 am daily until further notice at AUXI-LE-CHATEAU railway station.	avy avy

2353 Wt. W2514/1454 700,000 5/15 D. D. & L. A.D.S.S./Forms/C. 2118.

Instructions regarding War Diaries and Intelligence Summaries are contained in F. S. Regs., Part II. and the Staff Manual respectively. Title pages will be prepared in manuscript.

III

WAR DIARY
or
INTELLIGENCE SUMMARY.
(Erase heading not required.)

Army Form C. 2118.

Place	Date	Hour	Summary of Events and Information	Remarks and references to Appendices
			Resources of this area –	
			Interviewed all the Maires of the Communes in this area and Requisitioning Officer gave them the forms which he has himself drawn up for them to fill in to show the amounts of various commodities the local farmers possess and the amounts which the Mayor in his capacity as local civil authority considers the farmer should part with – Straw and forage appears very scarce. as previous to the occupation by us of this area General Conneau's Cavalry Corps was billeted here for over six months – followed by French Heavy Artillery, and extensive requisitioning was done by the French from one village alone (BEALCOURT) 40,000 tons of straw and fodder were drawn.	
			Potatoes are the most plentiful a six weeks stock @ from 11 to 13 francs per 100 kilos was easily found. Firewood is fairly plentiful a three weeks supply at full winter scale has been found at REMAISNIL. @ 25 francs per 1,000 kilos. The country is thickly wooded but stocks of cut wood are below normal on account of scarcity of labour	AW
			Prices of the small stock of straw available is from 45 to 55 francs per 1000 kilos. Clover about 80 francs per 1000 kilos. Beetroot in small quantities (only about three tons in the area) is obtainable at francs 20 per thousand kilos. These amounts already found and declared by Maires are no doubt a very small portion of the resources of the area – as it takes time (and prompt payment) to reveal willing vendors – but judging from previous experience this area appears from the supply point of view good – and local Maires (with the exception of one) all willing to help us.	
			Only other item to report is that sanction has been given to continue winter scale of fuel up to 30th April or until further notice.	
			A. St. John Knight Captain Brigade Supply Officer	31/3/16

2353 Wt. W2544/1454 700,000 5/15 D. D. & L. A.D.S.S./Forms/C. 2118.

SERIAL NO 250.

Confidential

War Diary

of

Supply Officer, Mhow Cavalry Brigade

FROM 1st July 1916 TO 31st July 1916.

Page ONE

Army Form C. 2118.

31

Instructions regarding War Diaries and Intelligence Summaries are contained in F. S. Regs., Part II. and the Staff Manual respectively. Title pages will be prepared in manuscript.

JULY 1916

WAR DIARY
or
~~INTELLIGENCE SUMMARY.~~
(Erase heading not required.)

of Supply Officer "MHOW CAVALRY BRIGADE
1ST INDIAN CAVALRY DIVISION
FRANCE.

Place	Date July 1916	Hour	Summary of Events and Information	Remarks and references to Appendices
DOULLENS	1st		Brigade Head Quarters at DOULLENS where Supply depôt was fixed. Units of the Brigade were all in close billets at AUTHIEULE (about 3 miles S.E of DOULLENS) grazing was plentiful and I purchased no green fodder to supplement the baled hay ration. Located a supply of firewood at Mairie at AUTHIEULE which was sufficient for units during period we were there. Wood for Brigade Head Quarters was obtained from DOULLENS.	AVG
MAIZICOURT (3 miles S. of AUXI-LE CHATEAU	2nd to 18th		Brigade Head Quarters (including Supply) and 2nd Lancers at MAIZICOURT. INNISKILLING DRAGOONS at BEALCOURT 38th CENTRAL INDIA HORSE at ST ACHEUL, Machine gun Squadron first few days at MAIZICOURT afterwards moved to BERNATRE. As we had been in this same area in March, April and May the arranging of local supplies was easy. During this time viz July 2nd to 18th we were on short notice to move varying from 2 to 6 hours. Horse transport was not used. Supply Column delivering direct to units from Railhead which changed during this time between AUXI-LE CHATEAU. FRENENT & PETIT HOUVIN. During this period I gave a lecture to the Supply Establishment on "duties of Brigade Supply office & his subordinates" dealing especially with work we have to do during an advance. A précis of the lecture was circulated for notes to be taken. One point which especially strikes me is the weak link in our chain viz Indian agents. They work hard. But they are handicapped for instance in not being able to ride. They are suited to depôt work which is stationary and does not demand hard physical exertion. I would personally (from the point of view of a Cavalry Brigade Supply officer) prefer a British rank who could be relied upon to put his back into his work under any conditions. I quite anticipate losing my Indian Establishment during an advance (if they go with "A" Echelon) and therefore am keeping the majority of them back with "B" Echelon. The menial establishment are very useful when we are in billets and "depôt work" is being done. But to expect this class of man to keep up on a bicycle with "A" Echelon is, I consider, too much. Even from the point of view of depôt work the menial establishment cannot be compared to what British ranks would do. I personally consider I could get the depôt work done just as quickly and thoroughly with half the number of British ranks. There is very little work indeed for the two Indian agents to do, I do not use them (as has been suggested can be done) as "go-betweens" between the Indian Regiments and me, as I prefer to deal direct with O.Cs and Quarter Masters of Regiments. As I have a British officer (Requisitioning officer) a British W.O and a British staff Sergeant we four can visit units at ration hours.	AVG

2353 Wt. W2544/1454 700,000 5/15 D. D. & L. A.D.S.S./Forms/C. 2118.

Page Two.

July 1916. **WAR DIARY** of Supply Officer MHOW CAVALRY BRIGADE

~~or~~ **~~INTELLIGENCE SUMMARY.~~** 1st INDIAN CAVALRY DIVISION

(*Erase heading not required.*) FRANCE

Army Form C. 2118.

32

Instructions regarding War Diaries and Intelligence Summaries are contained in F. S. Regs., Part II. and the Staff Manual respectively. Title pages will be prepared in manuscript.

Place	Date July 1916	Hour	Summary of Events and Information	Remarks and references to Appendices
ROELLECOURT	19th to	31st	Brigade Head Quarters (with Supply) and 38th C.I.H. at ROELLECOURT. Inniskilling Dragoons at St MICHEL Machine Gun Squadron between these two places. 2nd Lancers at GRAND CAMP about 2 miles N of Brigade Head Quarters. The Brigade is in a very compact area just E of St POL. During this month 'A' Battery R.H.A. has been detached from the Brigade. The over-averaging of baled hay received from the Base through the Supply Column is a cause of some worry. The Supply Column have to accept these bales as way-billed from the base and I as B.S.O. have to accept them from the Supply Column at way-billed weights. A circular letter from G.H.Q. lays down the necessity for "averaging" and states that it lays with Supply Officers at points of issue to ensure that units get their fair proportion. As one unit in this Brigade received over 20% short on three separate issues within 8 days it follows that the baled hay is considerably over-averaged. I have put the matter up to the S.S.O. The replacement of short issues by local purchase (of green fodder or straw) is at this particular time of year difficult. We are forbidden to buy hays ~~and~~ the first crop of green clover is finished and the second is not quite ready. As thrashing has not yet commenced straw is very scarce. Regiments are expected to accept oat sacks and hay bales as way-billed - and not quibble about actual weight - but I personally consider that to expect them to accept 20% or 25% shortages as "full ration of 10 lbs" is unreasonable. Nine hundred men of this Brigade (300 from each Regiment) proceeded to trench area as working parties on 29th 30th & 31st (destination region of NEUVILLE St VAST). I fixed rendezvous for lorry at MAROEUIL at which place 38th C.I.H take off their rations - lorry then proceeds to BOIS DE BRAY (MOUNT St ELOY) where rations for Inniskilling Dragoons and 2nd Lancers are put on light railway which delivers to these units in trenches after dark. 38th C.I.H rations are taken up on G.S. Limber Wagon from MAROEUIL after dark to unit. One pound of coal is sent up daily. I have arranged wood locally. Staff Sergeant BREWSTER S.T.C. and two Indian Establishment remain at MAROEUIL during these operations. I attend rendezvous and distribution of rations daily. A Wright Capt. S.&T. Corps.	?W

2353 Wt. W2514/1454 700,000 5/15 D. D. & L. A.D.S.S./Forms/C. 2118.

SERIAL NO 250.

Confidential

War Diary

of

Supply Officer, Mhow Cavalry Brigade.

FROM 1st August 1916 TO 31st August 1916

Army Form C. 2118.

31

Instructions regarding War Diaries and Intelligence Summaries are contained in F. S. Regs., Part II. and the Staff Manual respectively. Title pages will be prepared in manuscript.

WAR DIARY

~~or~~

~~INTELLIGENCE SUMMARY.~~

(Erase heading not required.)

of Brigade Supply Officer MHOW CAVALRY BRIGADE. 1st Indian Cavalry Division

Place	Date August	Hour 1916	Summary of Events and Information	Remarks and references to Appendices
ROELLECOURT	1st to 9th		Nothing important to report - except that the purchase of green fodder became easier - and by purchasing a large field of green clover (2nd crop) I was able to supply all units of the Brigade - and also make up any serious shortage received from railhead - Vegetables and firewood were found in sufficient quantities.	
CAMBLIGNEUL	10th	—	Brigade Head Quarters and 38th Central India Horse and Machine Gun Squadron moved to CAMBLIGNEUL (4 miles NW of MOUNT ST ELOY). 2nd Lancers to MAGNICOURT SUR CANCHE and the 6th Inniskilling Dragoons to PENIN. Firewood and green fodder was arranged without much difficulty	
CAMBLIGNEUL	14th	—	All units of the Brigade started drawing on horse transport from Railhead at TINQUES.	
CAMBLIGNEUL	18th	—	Captain A St J. WRIGHT. S.T.C proceeded to Divisional Head Quarters for duty as adjutant to O.C A.S.C (temporarily) handing over B.S.O's work to Lieut A RICHARDS (I.A.R att S.T.C) the Brigade Requisitioning Officer.	
CAMBLIGNEUL	20th	~~2.15~~	T/Lieut F.E LUPTON. A.S.C posted temporarily as Requisitioning Officer as long as Capt Wright is away.	
CAMBLIGNEUL	31st		During this month the Brigade is still in the trenches (in NEUVILLE - ST VAST area) strength 300 men per Regiment. Rations arrive at MORDEUIL in lorry for 38th C I H from there after dark they are sent up to trench party in G.S. Limber. Rations for Inniskillings & 2nd Lancers are delivered by lorry to BOIS DE BRAY (MT ST ELOY) and are sent up to trench party after dark on light Railway. Firewood arranged locally for all units. Reliefs of these parties of 300 men take place every 5 days - relieved and relieving parties taking with them the unexpended portion of their days ration	

A St J Wright Captain
Bde Supply Officer

2353 Wt. W2544/1454 700,000 5/15 D. D. & L. A.D.S.S./Forms/C. 2118.

SERIAL NO. 250.

Confidential

War Diary

of

SUPPLY OFFICER, MHOW CAVALRY BRIGADE.

FROM 1st SEPTEMBER 1916 TO 30th SEPTEMBER 1916

Instructions regarding War Diaries and Intelligence Summaries are contained in F. S. Regs., Part II. and the Staff Manual respectively. Title Pages will be prepared in manuscript.

WAR DIARY

~~or~~

~~INTELLIGENCE SUMMARY~~

(*Erase heading not required.*)

Army Form C. 2118.

29.

Place	Date	Hour	Summary of Events and Information	Remarks and references to Appendices
	1916			
CAMBLIGNEUL	1st September		Units continue in same billets, i.e. Brigade Headquarters ..... } at CAMBLIGNEUL 38th (K.G.O.) Central India Horse } *Machine Gun Squadron ..... } 6th Inniskilling Dragoons .. " PENIN 2nd Lancers .... " MONTS EN TERNOIS *M.G.S. with detachment at LA BELLE ÈPINE as before.	
			The Brigade Trench Digging Party re-joined us to-day and its rations were delivered in billets. Preliminary orders received that Brigade will move to new area to-morrow (2nd inst). There was no issue of rations to-day (except for Digging Party) as Units have been drawing on Horse Transport and have rations for to-day and to-morrow.	AL
GRAND CAMP (nr ST POL)	2nd September		Brigade moved to new area, occupying billets as follows. Brigade Headquarters ...... GRAND CAMP 38th (K.G.O.) Central India Horse } ST MICHEL Machine Gun Squadron .... } The 6th Inniskillings and 2nd Lancers did not move.	

2449 Wt. W14957/M90 750,000 1/16 J.B.C. & A. Forms/C.2118/12.

Instructions regarding War Diaries and Intelligence Summaries are contained in F. S. Regs., Part II. and the Staff Manual respectively. Title Pages will be prepared in manuscript.

WAR DIARY
or
INTELLIGENCE SUMMARY
(Erase heading not required.)

Army Form C. 2118.

30.

Place	Date	Hour	Summary of Events and Information	Remarks and references to Appendices
GRAND CAMP	1916 2nd September (Contd)		The detachment from M.G.S. re-joined its Unit to-day. Fixed Supply Rendezvous for Brigade at TINCQUES at 11 a.m: rations ready for troops on their arrival in new billets. Local purchases of wood. Visited units in new billets.	[initials]
CONCHY SUR CANCHE	3rd September		Brigade moved to new area occupying billets as follows: Brigade Headquarters - - - - CONCHY SUR CANCHE 6th Inniskillings - - - - - - BOUBERS SUR CANCHE 2nd Lancers - - - - - - - - - - LIGNY SUR CANCHE 38th (K.G.O.) C.I.H - - - - - - CONCHY SUR CANCHE Machine Gun Squadron - - MONCHEL. Supply Rendezvous for Brigade - LIGNY S/CANCHE at 3.30 p.m. Local purchases of wood to complete fuel ration. Visited all Units.	[initials]
NOYELLES-EN-CHAUSSÉE	4th September		Brigade moved to new area as follows: Brigade Headquarters - - - - NOYELLES EN CHAUSSÉE 6th Inniskillings - - - - - - - GUESCHART - Western portion. 2nd Lancers - - - - - - - - - - - - - ditto - - Eastern " 38th (K.G.O.) C.I.H. - - - - - - MAISON PONTHIEU Machine Gun Squadron - - NEUILLY LE DIEU	[initials]

2449 Wt. W14957/M90 750,000 1/16 J.B.C. & A. Forms/C.2118/12.

Army Form C. 2118.

31

Instructions regarding War Diaries and Intelligence Summaries are contained in F. S. Regs., Part II. and the Staff Manual respectively. Title Pages will be prepared in manuscript.

WAR DIARY
or
INTELLIGENCE SUMMARY

(Erase heading not required.)

Place	Date	Hour	Summary of Events and Information	Remarks and references to Appendices
NOYELLES-EN-CHAUSSÉE	4th September	Contd.	Supply Rendezvous for Brigade at GUESCHART at 4 p.m. Local purchases of wood for all Units to complete fuel ration – 1 lb Coal per man arriving on Lorries. Visited all Units. The Dismounted men of the Brigade marched to BUIRE-AU-BOIS (joining up with the other D.M. of the Division) & are removed from my sphere until they rejoin. Took over a dump of Coal at GUESCHART from S.S.O. 56th Division – Contents approximately ten tons – for issue to Units of this Brigade.	[initials]
ditto	5th September		Brigade remains in same area for training. Brigade Supply Rendezvous at the X roads AUXI LE CHATEAU – ABBEVILLE and YVRENCH – DOMQUEUR (Chaussee) Main Roads at 3 p.m. Visited all Units. Issued Coal from Dump at GUESCHART at 1 lb per man for all Units except 6th Inniskillings who received full fuel ration in Coal (1½ lbs per man) & Local purchases of wood (at 1 lb per man) for all Units (exc. Inniskillings.) Discovered quantity of stores such as tinned meat, biscuits etc left behind by outgoing Unit in billets occupied by Inniskillings. Reported matter to S.S.O. and arranged for collection of Stores for return to Railhead.	[initials]
ditto	6th September to 10th September		Routine duties, nothing to record	

2449 Wt. W14957/M90 750,000 1/16 J.B.C. & A. Forms/C.2118/12.

Instructions regarding War Diaries and Intelligence Summaries are contained in F. S. Regs., Part II. and the Staff Manual respectively. Title Pages will be prepared in manuscript.

WAR DIARY
or
INTELLIGENCE SUMMARY
(Erase heading not required.)

Army Form C. 2118.

32

Place	Date	Hour	Summary of Events and Information	Remarks and references to Appendices
	1916			
REMAISNIL	11th September		Brigade moved to new area occupying billets as follows: Brigade Headquarters — REMAISNIL 6th Inniskillings — BARLY 2nd Lancers — MEZEROLLES (North Bank of River) Machine Gun Squadron — ditto — (South " " ") 38th (K.G.O) C. I. H. — OUTREBOIS (North " " ")	
			Supply R.V. for Brigade — FROHEN LE GRAND Time — 3 p.m.	
			Local Purchases of wood to complete Fuel Ration.	[initials]
AUTHIEULE near DOULLENS	12th September		Brigade moved to new area occupying billets as follows:- Brigade Headquarters — AUTHIEULE 38th (K.G.O) C.I.H — AMPLIER (Eastern end) 2nd Lancers — ditto — (Western ") 6th Inniskillings — ORVILLE M. G. S — AUTHIEULE	
			Divisional Supply R.V — LE COLLEGE STATION near DOULLENS Time — 3 p.m.	
			Local purchases of wood to complete Fuel ration.	[initials]

2449 Wt. W14957/M90 750,000 1/16 J.B.C. & A. Forms/C.2118/12.

Army Form C. 2118.

33.

Instructions regarding War Diaries and Intelligence Summaries are contained in F. S. Regs., Part II. and the Staff Manual respectively. Title Pages will be prepared in manuscript.

WAR DIARY
or
INTELLIGENCE SUMMARY

(Erase heading not required.)

Place	Date	Hour	Summary of Events and Information	Remarks and references to Appendices
QUERRIER.	1916 13th September,		Brigade moved to new area as follows: Brigade Headquarters, less Supply Establishment and Mobile Veterinary Section — ALLONVILLE 6th Inniskillings, 2nd Lancers, 38th C.I.H. + M.G.S. — near QUERRIER in bivouacs. Divisional Supply R.V. — near X roads N. of ST. GRATIEN Time — 4 p.m. In this instance I detached Supply Establishment from Brigade Headquarters and placed it in close proximity to the 3 regiments + the Machine Gun Squadron, thus facilitating supervision of supply arrangements for the Brigade. There was on this occasion a certain "Stickiness" with the Supply Column who had received orders to dump supplies where the lorries stood. No regimental transport being available it would have been a question of man-handling a distance of nearly three kilometres for the Brigade. The roads were in perfect condition + lorries could have travelled almost anywhere. Eventually the Supply Column was prevailed upon to allow the supply lorries to proceed nearer to units and rations were issued at 7.30 p.m. The attitude of the Supply Column + its lack of Elasticity in such an emergency will be duly reported to the O.C. A.S.C. 1st I.C.D.	[illegible]

Instructions regarding War Diaries and Intelligence Summaries are contained in F. S. Regs., Part II. and the Staff Manual respectively. Title Pages will be prepared in manuscript.

WAR DIARY
or
INTELLIGENCE SUMMARY
(Erase heading not required.)

Army Form C. 2118.

34.

Place	Date	Hour	Summary of Events and Information	Remarks and references to Appendices
	1916			
QUERRIER	14th Septr.		Brigade remains in same bivouac. S. Sgt. BREWSTER detailed from Supply Est. of this Brigade to be in supply charge of Loads with limbered train formed for the 1st I.C.D. Reported to O.C. A.S.C. "Mishaps" of Supply Column in dealing with yesterday situation and action duly taken. "B" Echelon remaining behind divisionalized, sent figures of strengths to S.O. D.S.C. and S.O. ~~Div~~ "B" Echelon troops. Rations delivered to Units this afternoon.	[initials]
MORLANCOURT	15th September		Brigade ^less "B" Echelon^ moved to fresh bivouac near MORLANCOURT. Divisional Supply R.V. — Forked Roads North of DERNANCOURT Time — 4 p.m. As only 5 lbs of Hay per animal sent up on lorries, requirements completed by local grazing. Sanction given by "Q" that lorries might discharge at 7 p.m.	
— ditto —	16th Septr.		As Units bivouacing amongst Crops I had orders published through Brigade that on no account whatever were Units to take possession of or in any way interfere with the Crops, pointing out that all arrangements for the local purchase of fodder to supplement Hay Ration arriving from Railhead were in the hands of the Brigade Requisitioning Officer who only is authorised to take over these supplies. Units are warned that they will be held directly responsible for	[initials]

2449 Wt. W14957/M90 750,000 1/16 J.B.C. & A. Forms/C.2118/12.

Army Form C. 2118.

35

WAR DIARY
or
INTELLIGENCE SUMMARY

(Erase heading not required.)

Instructions regarding War Diaries and Intelligence Summaries are contained in F. S. Regs., Part II. and the Staff Manual respectively. Title Pages will be prepared in manuscript.

Place	Date	Hour	Summary of Events and Information	Remarks and references to Appendices
MORLANCOURT (Contd)	16th September (Contd)		for any Claims preferred against them through any infringement of this order.	
			Ration lorries proceeded under direction of SSO, 1st I.C.B. and dispersed to Brigades and Units as yesterday. R.V. not nominated. Met SSO at O.C. ASC's bivouac at 3.30 p.m. Arranged local grazing to complete Hay ration.	
— ditto —	17th to 24th September		Brigade remains in same bivouacs near MORLANCOURT. Owing to bad weather and men being exposed an issue of Rum was made. Local purchases of Vegetables + Grazing. Fuel arriving in sufficient quantities on lorries. Attended Divisional Supply R.V. daily at the Fork Road North of the C of DERNANCOURT (Ref. AMIENS map $\frac{1}{100,000}$). Three dismounted men from the 6th Inniskillings detailed on the 23rd to join Divisional Supply Column to be in charge of dumps of Hay for the 3 Regiments (with M.G. Troops) on a basis of 5 lbs per animal which will be dumped in positions in forward area on the 25th inst.	
MAMETZ	25 September		Brigade moved to forward area as follows: Report Centre — MONTAUBAN 'A' Echelon TRANS — MAMETZ.	

2449 Wt. W14957/M90 750,000 1/16 J.B.C. & A. Forms/C.2118/12.

Army Form C. 2118.

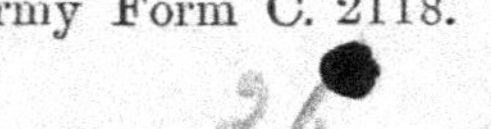

WAR DIARY
or
INTELLIGENCE SUMMARY

(Erase heading not required.)

Instructions regarding War Diaries and Intelligence Summaries are contained in F. S. Regs., Part II. and the Staff Manual respectively. Title Pages will be prepared in manuscript.

Place	Date	Hour	Summary of Events and Information	Remarks and references to Appendices
MAMETZ (Contd)	1916 25th September		6th Inniskilling Dragoons – near BERNAFRAY WOOD 2nd Lancers 38th (K.G.O.) C.I.H. – POMMIERS REDOUBT Supply Establishment – MAMETZ (Machine Gun Squadron was split up into troops, 1 of each being attached to each Unit) Five lbs of Hay per animal dumped near BERNAFRAY WOOD, POMMIERS REDOUBT & MAMETZ under representatives duly taken over by Units on arrival. In the afternoon "A" Echelon ordered to move up and join Brigade, but later on Brigade received orders to return to bivouac near MORLANCOURT. Ration lorries proceeded to MORLANCOURT at 9.30 p.m. & dumped rations ready for issue to troops early next morning. Brigade arrived back at 11 p.m.	
MORLANCOURT	26th September		Rations issued at 7 a.m. in bivouacs near MORLANCOURT. "A" Battery joins the Brigade. Supply lorries came out direct to Units at 5.30 p.m. & rations for to-morrow (27th) issued.	[illegible initials]
BUSSY-LES-DAOURS	27th September		Brigade marched at 12 mid-day to-day to bivouac near BUSSY-LES-DAOURS Divisional Supply R.V. – On road QUERRIEUX – BUSSY – West of River HALLYE.	[illegible initials] [illegible initials]

2449 Wt. W14957/M90 750,000 1/16 J.B.C. & A. Forms/C.2118/12.

Army Form C. 2118.

37

Instructions regarding War Diaries and Intelligence Summaries are contained in F. S. Regs., Part II. and the Staff Manual respectively. Title Pages will be prepared in manuscript.

WAR DIARY
or
INTELLIGENCE SUMMARY
(Erase heading not required.)

Place	Date	Hour	Summary of Events and Information	Remarks and references to Appendices
	1916			
BELLOY SUR SOMME	28th Sept.		Brigade marched to new Area occupying billets as follows:	
			Brigade H.Q. ---------- } – BELLOY SUR SOMME "A" Batty. R.H.A ---------- }	
			6th Inniskillings – TIRANCOURT	
			2nd Lancers ---------- } 38th C. I. H ---------- } – LA CHAUSSÉE near PICQUIGNY M. G. S ---------- }	
			Divisional Supply R.V. – E. entrance to PICQUIGNY Time – 11 a.m.	
			Brigade Supply R.V. – S (River Road) Entrance to LA CHAUSSÉE Time – 12 mid day	
			Local purchases of wood to complete Fuel Ration.	
VAUCHELLES LES-DOMART	29 September		Brigade marched to new Area occupying billets as follows:	
			Brigade HQ ---------- } M. G. S ---------- } VAUCHELLES LES DOMART	
			6th Inniskillings ---------- BRUCAMPS	
			38th C. I. H ---------- VILLERS SOUS AILLY	
			2nd Lancers ---------- BOUCHON	
			"A" Batty R. H. A ---------- MOUFLERS	

2449 Wt. W14957/M90 750,000 1/16 J.B.C. & A. Forms/C.2118/12.

Instructions regarding War Diaries and Intelligence Summaries are contained in F. S. Regs., Part II. and the Staff Manual respectively. Title Pages will be prepared in manuscript.

WAR DIARY
or
INTELLIGENCE SUMMARY
(Erase heading not required.)

Army Form C. 2118.

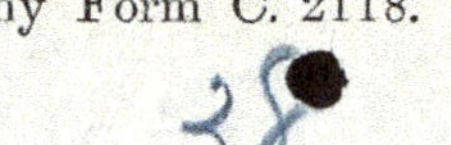

Place	Date	Hour	Summary of Events and Information	Remarks and references to Appendices
VAUCHELLES LES DOMART (Contd)	1916 29th September (Contd)		Divisional Supply R.V. – AILLY LE HAUT CLOCHER Time – 10 a.m. As the Brigade's billets for Units were not known at the time of Divisional Supply R.V. & only Brigade area was given to me – I fixed a Brigade Supply R.V. at the road junction 1 mile S.E. of AILLY LE HAUT CLOCHER on main MOUFLERS – AILLY road – obtained billeting list from Staff Captain & directed lorries to Units. Local purchases of wood to complete fuel ration.	[illegible]
DOURIEZ	30th September		Brigade marched to new area occupying billets as follows: Brigade HQ ------- } – DOURIEZ 38th C.I.H. ------- } 6th Inniskillings – DOMPIERRE SUR AUTHIE 2nd Lancers – PONCHES M.G.S. – HAMEL LES PONCHES "A" Batty, RHA – ESTRUVAL Supply R.V. for Brigade – DOMPIERRE Time – 12 noon	[illegible]

2449 Wt. W14957/M90 750,000 1/16 J.B.C. & A. Forms/C.2118/12.

Army Form C. 2118.

39

Instructions regarding War Diaries and Intelligence Summaries are contained in F. S. Regs., Part II. and the Staff Manual respectively. Title Pages will be prepared in manuscript.

WAR DIARY
or
INTELLIGENCE SUMMARY
(Erase heading not required.)

Place	Date	Hour	Summary of Events and Information	Remarks and references to Appendices
DOURIEZ (contd)	1916 30 Sept (contd)		Local purchases of wood to complete Fuel Ration.	

Field
30th September 1916

[illegible]
Lieut.
B.S.O.
Mhow Cavalry Brigade

2449 Wt. W14957/M90 750,000 1/16 J.B.C. & A. Forms/C.2118/12.

BEF

1 IND. CAV. DIV.

MHOW BDE.

BDE TRANSPORT OFFICER

1916 JULY to 1916 ~~DEC~~ SEP

SERIAL NO. 269.

Confidential

War Diary

of

Transport Officer, Mhow Cavalry Brigade

FROM 1st July 1916 TO 31st July 1916

B.139 Original

Instructions regarding War Diaries and Intelligence Summaries are contained in F. S. Regs., Part II, and the Staff Manual respectively. Title pages will be prepared in manuscript.

WAR DIARY July 1916 ~~or INTELLIGENCE SUMMARY.~~

(Erase heading not required.)

Army Form C. 2118. (37)

I. A. Haig. Lieut.
B.T.O. Mhow: Cav: Bde:
1st Ind: Cav: Div: –

1916. Hour. Date. Place.	Summary of Events and Information.	Remarks and references to Appendices.
July. 1st Doullens.	Ordinary routine	
2nd Doullens till 6.30 p.m. and Maizicourt 10.45 p.m.	Division marched at moments notice. B. Echelon left Doullens 6.30 and arrived Maizicourt 10.45 p.m. All well no casualties.	
3rd to 11th Maizicourt	Ordinary routine.	
12th Maizicourt	6th Inniskilling Dgs: Horse Show. I judged pack Horses mules & transport.	
13th to 18th Maizicourt	Ordinary routine.	
19th Maizicourt till 8.30 a.m. Rollecourt and: 4.45 p.m.	B. Echelon left Maizicourt about 8.30 a.m. composed of B.H.Q. part of 2nd Lancers – M.V.S. joining up with remaining Squads: 2nd Lancers, 6th Dgs: & C.I.H. at Auxi-le-Chateau about 10.30 a.m. – Column rested an hour at Ligny-s-Canche, watered & fed and Rollecourt about 4.45 p.m. All well – no casualties.	
20th Rollecourt	Ordinary routine.	
21st "	As instructed inspected all vehicles in Transport especially wheels. Result as per Report B 139 dated 21.VIII.16. submitted	
22nd to 31st	Ordinary routine – all vehicles being camouflaged.	

I. A. Haig. Lieut.
B.T.O.

SERIAL NO. 269.

Confidential

War Diary

of

Transport Officer, Mhow Cavalry Brigade.

FROM 1st August 1916 TO 31st August 1916

B 204

Instructions regarding War Diaries and Intelligence Summaries are contained in F. S. Regs., Part II. and the Staff Manual respectively. Title Pages will be prepared in manuscript.

WAR DIARY
or
INTELLIGENCE SUMMARY

(Erase heading not required.)

Army Form C. 2118.

35

J. A. Haig. Lieut.
B.T.O. Mhow Cav: Bde:
1st Ind: Cav: Div:

1916. Place	Date	Hour	Summary of Events and Information	Remarks and references to Appendices
	Aug			
Roëllecourt	1/9		Ordinary routine. All wagons being camouflaged.	
"	10	9.a.m	Brigade moved from Roëllecourt to Cambligneul. Transports moved with units.	
Cambligneul	"	12.10 p.m	B.H.Q & Mobile Vet: Sec: moved under my command leaving at 9 a.m. & arriving in new billets at 12.10 p.m. all well. Distance travelled about 12 miles.	
"	11/13.		Ordinary routine. Camouflaging completed.	
"	14/		Transports commenced to draw their own rations & supplies from Tincques Station (railhead).	
"	15/30		Ordinary routine. All vehicles requiring repairs ordered to SAVY.	
"	31	11 p.m	Received orders to stop Transports drawing their supplies & rations	

J. A. Haig Lieut.
B.T.O.
Mhow Cav: Bde
1st Sept. 1916

2449 Wt. W14957/M90 750,000 1/16 J.B.C. & A. Forms/C.2118/12.

SERIAL NO. 269

Confidential

War Diary

of

TRANSPORT OFFICER, MHOW CAVALRY BRIGADE.

FROM 1st SEPTEMBER 1916 TO 30th SEPTEMBER 1916

B230.

Instructions regarding War Diaries and Intelligence Summaries are contained in F. S. Regs., Part II. and the Staff Manual respectively. Title Pages will be prepared in manuscript.

1916

WAR DIARY ~~or~~ ~~INTELLIGENCE~~ SUMMARY

(Erase heading not required.)

Army Form C. 2118.

J. A. Haig, Lieut. A.S.C.
B.T.O. Mhow Cav: Bde:
1st Ind: Cav: Div:

43

Place	Date	Hour	Summary of Events and Information	Remarks and references to Appendices
	Sept.			
Camblignuel –	1.		Ordinary routine – preparing to move in the morning.	
"	2	9.15 a.m.	A & B. Echelons of C.I.H. M.G.C. M.V.S. marched at 9.15 under my command to new billets at St. Michel arriving 1 p.m. H.Q. at Grand Camp.	Fit all well
Grand Camp	3.	9.30 a.m.	Same units as above marched via Hertin-le-Vieil. Errins – Flers to Canchy-sur-Canche arriving about 1 p.m.	Fit all well
Canchy-s-Canche	4	9.15 a.m.	Same units as above marched via Buire-au-Bois – Auxi-le-Chateau. Hiermont to Noyelle-en-Chaussee, arr. about 1.30	Fit all well
Noyelle-en-Chaussee	4/10		Ordinary routine.	
"	11	6.30 a.m.	B. Echelon marched via Hiermont to Auxi-le-Chateau to billets at Rumaisnil arriving all well about 10.30 a.m.	
Rumaisnil	12	7.45	B. Echelon marched via Doullens to Billets at Autheule arriving about 10.30 a.m. all well.	
Autheule	13	12.30 p.m.	B. Echelon marched via Hulimer Beauval, Divisionalized under Lt. Col. Young A.S.C. to camp at Querrieu arr. about 10 p.m. H.Q. at Allonville. 14th ordinary routine.	
Allonville	15	5 a.m.	Bde. H.Q. marched at 5 a.m. leaving me with B. Echelon – I moved to Querrieu at noon & joined remainder of B. Echelon – now under my command – Capt. Barnett A.S.C. O.C. ~~[illegible]~~ B. Echelon 1st Ind: Cav. Div:	
Querrieu	16/26		Ordinary Camp Routine. Lt's: Freer-Smith – 8th Dgs: – V. Smith 2nd Lancers – Lt. Mangin C.I.H. are T.O.'s of their respective units.	
"	27	1.20 p.m.	Recd: orders verbally from Col. Young to move B. Echelon immediately to camp at Bussy-les-Daours. Soon after T.O.'s Bde. marched at 2.40 p.m. and: Bussy at 3. p.m. B. Echelon wagons rejoined their units, with T.O.'s	
Bussy-les-Daours	28	9 a.m.	B. Echelon Brigades marched with Sialkot B. Echelon Brigades under my command via Amiens to Billets near la Chaussee arriving there all well about 2.30 p.m. A long column over 1 Kilom:. H.Q. at Belloy.	
Belloy.	29	9 a.m.	Above also Bde: with B. Echelon, Sialkot Bde: marched via Flixecourt to Billets round Mouflers H.Q. at Chateau at Vauchelles-les-Domart. all well –	
Mouflers	30	9 a.m.	B. Echelon marched Bde: via Ailly-le-Haut-Clocher, St. Riquier to fresh billets at Drucat, arrd. about 5 p.m. all well – about 21 miles.	

J. A. Haig Lieut. A.S.C.
B.T.O.

2449 Wt. W14957/M90 750,000 1/16 J.B.C. & A. Forms/C.2118/12.

www.ingramcontent.com/pod-product-compliance
Lightning Source LLC
Chambersburg PA
CBHW080857230426
43663CB00013B/2567

* 9 7 8 1 4 7 4 5 0 1 6 0 6 *